JORDI ROCA

IGNACIO MEDINA

CASA CACAO

This English language edition published in 2019 by
Grub Street
4 Rainham Close
London
SW11 6SS

Email: food@grubstreet.co.uk

Web: www.grubstreet.co.uk
Twitter: @grub_street
Facebook: Grub Street Publishing

First published in Spanish by Editorial Planeta, S. A., 2018
Text copyright © Jordi Roca and Ignacio Medina, 2018
Photographs ©
Sergio Recabarren, pp. 9, 10, 14, 16, 64–71, 137–149, 155, 156, 160–176, 180–201, 205–209, 218, 227, 228, 229, 230, 231, 232, 235, 277, 278, 280, 281, 283, 284, 285 and 344
Joan Pujol-Creus, pp. 21, 26, 34, 40, 42, 44, 46, 49, 62, 74, 75, 80, 84–117, 119, 120, 123, 125, 128, 129, 131, 135, 137, 153, 159, 179, 203, 211, 213, 217, 222, 223, 242, 243, 244, 245, 246, 247, 248, 250, 251, 253, 255, 257, 259, 260, 261, 262, 264, 265, 266, 267, 269, 270, 271, 272, 273, 274, 287–343
Francesc Guillamet, pp. 30, 31.
Quim Turon, p. 37
Herinz Plenge Pardo, p. 73
Marina García Burgos, p. 221
RUN, p. 236
Casa Cacao Project © Virtual recreation produced by Render4tomorrow studio, pp. 239, 240, 241

A CIP catalogue record for this book is available from the British Library.

ISBN 978-1-911621-39-3

JORDI ROCA

IGNACIO MEDINA

CASA CACAO

THE JOURNEY BACK

TO THE SOURCE OF CHOCOLATE

GRUB STREET • LONDON

CONTENTS

To the cacao growers,
the forgotten side of chocolate.

WE ARE THE ORIGINAL OWNERS OF CACAO

WE HAVE BEEN HERE SINCE THE CREATION and the beginning of everything. This is our land; we do not come from other places or from other worlds. We are here because we were created at the beginning with all the elements and Mother Nature. Cacao, *múnzuwa*, was bequeathed to us by our father, Terunna, to guide us in all the activities inherent to our culture and to enable us to focus on them. Although everything that was created must be preserved and not abandoned, there was a time when we had distanced ourselves from it, owing to the invasion and colonisation that robbed us of our territory. Through our struggle and insistence on regaining our ancestral rights, the government has recognised the sacred words of our culture and supported our successful efforts to recover a part of the land, and there we continue to grow cacao. We never had many seeds, but we are tending them, fulfilling our obligations at each stage of the plants' development. We are the original owners of cacao, *múnzuwa*, which is of vital importance in caring for our spirituality. It is the essential pillar through which we preserve and strengthen the development of our thoughts. For this reason, we advise our younger siblings, *bunachu*, when they obtain our product, that before tasting it, they should take a moment to appreciate this thousand-year-old tradition and the ancestral message that advocates peace and harmony among all that exists, seeking the balance of Mother Nature.

Mamo Camilo Izquierdo
Catanzama, August 2018

MÚNZUWA ZUPÁW KÚCHU NÚNKURA NANÍ

Níwiri ka'gᵻmᵻsin i'ba abonᵻn núnkura nanunó, emari niwinhúmᵻke naní, aɟwᵻnka pari, ᵻɟwa ka'gᵻmᵻse' pari ana'na na'naní, kᵻtᵻkᵻnᵻn inᵻ abori uye pari i'ba kwákura nᵻname' emi ákwᵻya ní. Kakaw *Múnzᵻwari Terunnase'* niwi kᵻchᵻsana ní. ᵻyari biga ɟuna nikamᵻ níwizey kunsamᵻsí awi uzweykwey niga'ba, niwikᵻnari nanᵻngwasi awiri duna nárigᵻn arunhey niwigwasi niwi kᵻchusana naní. Inᵻ niwi kᵻchukumey nᵻneykari, du chwᵻn niwingwasi, re'tisa au'nanᵻngwasi nᵻneki, mᵻná nánᵻkin peykᵻ kᵻnika awkwa nᵻnari. Ayéy niwikᵻre'bori, ɟugaɟina niwikᵻpari, ka'gᵻmᵻ niwinhagusi zoyana'ba ni'na ní. Ey uyeki, zapᵻnnari, ayéy niwi ka'bona uneykari niwikᵻɟwakumeyza nanunᵻnno yanari, gobiernu ga'kᵻnamᵻ azᵻna, kunsámᵻsin nᵻ'na niwi kinokwa ᵻwame', ta nanunó a'zᵻname', ingiti ka'gᵻmᵻ niwipᵻnhakumey zoya'bari, *múnzᵻwa* zarisi azwein nuga ní; zaɟuna awᵻn niwikᵻnanu' nᵻneki, kunsámᵻse' anikuyáy ayéy kinki chwi, tikᵻrigᵻn izasari azwein nuga ní. *múnzᵻwa* zᵻpáw kúchu núnkura naní, awiri ari niwinhánugwe duna niwi kᵻchwᵻn nuga, arusí arunhᵻn niwigwásᵻya, kᵻchona awᵻndi niwi wanu' nari, ey ᵻwame' ɟuga ɟinari ga'kᵻnamᵻ kuwanᵻndi nazᵻneykari, niwizey *múnzᵻwa* ipana ukumanige'ri, mᵻnᵻ nánᵻkin dú azarunha ukumeyzanᵻndi, kᵻtᵻkᵻnᵻn niwikuchukumanáy kingwi a'chwi zwein nuga, i'ngwi ka'gᵻmᵻse' kwey ᵻweykari niwikᵻchukumanáy i'ngweti paperi enanᵻyáy zoyᵻn, i'ngwi ka'gᵻmᵻse' tanᵻ zanamᵻ kwákumey zweynᵻnno.

BEFORE CHOCOLATE, AFTER CACAO

THE AMAZON RAINFOREST IS CACAO ANARCHY. There, the search for varieties is an adventure; chance is a compass; and luck is a destination. Cacao plantations. Words now connected with recollection and imagery. The fragrance, feel, thermal sensation and flavour of a bitter essence that is transformed into a sweet smile after a metamorphic, almost alchemic journey. And above all that can be grasped by the external senses is the exceptional magic of cacao, venerated since ancient times and even to the present by the indigenous communities that saw in it a gift that the gods left on their lands; one that had the power to invigorate their warriors like a magic potion brewed by Getafix.

My brother Josep has always asserted that there are as many wines as there are people. And it is by travelling, becoming acquainted with producers, even interviewing them together with a psychologist, that he has been able to form a connection with those wines that surpasses intellectual knowledge, capturing their essence, their intrapersonal and interpersonal substance. There is something behind a natural product, when it is lovingly tended and honoured by human hands, that transcends all understanding. Likewise, my contact with the cacao people – in the way that Josep speaks of his 'wine people' – has allowed me not only to open my perception to a new and rich spectrum of creative possibilities, but to a reconnection with the intangible dimension of what we eat.

Before this journey to cacao, my relationship with chocolate went from a fixation to the proclamation of its infinity. From my obsession with chocolate and the great chocolate bonbon – a debt owed to an insatiable childhood when I wanted to try every single chocolate in the box of Caja Roja at Christmas, before demolishing them – to the intuitive need to rebel, to break down the stifling barriers of the conventional and to deconstruct it anarchically in the form of my Chocolate Anarkia. There are more than forty different creations on a single plate, in random order. They say that there is no such thing as chance. In my forties, and with barely any voice left, I was gifted with another bridge from which to take a quantum leap, to expand my possibilities for expression together with those of cacao. Cacao is richly expressed in the course of silent communication. Its slimy pulp produces 'sounds' like lychee, soursop and custard apple, even dairy. Its astringent, bitter and invigorating seeds range in colour from purple to white. And when fermented,

they give off notes of almost every variety of fruit: cherry, passion fruit, banana, of wild, brined and pickled fruit, and of fresh and candied fruit. Once dried, the emerging notes are of black tea, tobacco and wood, like a veil of mature complexity waiting to be revealed.

You have to be brave to enter into the jungle. *Atzumisare*, welcome. Entering into chaos to bring order to an expression of beauty. The leader of the Arhuaco community in the Sierra Nevada de Santa Marta mountain range of Colombia received us with these words: 'This is a sacred place. Cacao was born with us. Our spiritual father, Terunna, left us this crop. We have preserved its knowledge and wish to share it with you, in exchange for what you bring us.' Here in the cradle of magic realism, hearing this sentence made you wonder if it was all a dream. A possible exchange. A necessary connection. A full circle. When I returned to Girona, news continued to reach me from the other side of the Pond. The Awajúns, one of the communities we visited, were looking for land with a group of entrepreneurs, which would allow them to process all the highly dispersed wild cacao at their own facility. And I began to dream. To realise the sense that our Casa Cacao project was taking on something that went beyond mere production. Yes, we want this to be one of its pillars. We want those communities to prosper, to create opportunities. And I begin to dream of announcing to the world that there is a new chocolate in Peru called Awajún … and that is something the world is going to see. From the tree to life.

Jordi Roca
Girona, July 2018

A GREAT OPPORTUNITY

AFTER FIVE HUNDRED YEARS, CHOCOLATE is reaching for new horizons. The most popular sweet in history enters into a new era nearly five hundred years after the first encounter between cacao and sugar. According to historians, this took place in 1534, in the kitchens of Monasterio de Piedra, a Cistercian monastery located a little over a hundred kilometres away from the Spanish city of Zaragoza. The doors were opened to a new world that had little to do with the *txocolatl* of the Mayans, except for the role played in both cases by cacao. It seemed that there was nothing left to learn after the rise of the Swiss chocolate makers in the nineteenth century, until a significant part of what we took for granted came into question. I see the trigger for this change in the new interests that have shaped the culinary world since the end of the twentieth century. The introduction of science and technological development into the work performed in kitchens, the necessary deepening of knowledge of products and, finally, the social perspective that accompanies the advancement of new trends broke new ground and brought about significant changes in the food industry.

What is known of the world of chocolate has gradually undergone a transformation with the amalgamation of the small details on which it was built, bringing into view new horizons that are often striking, at times surprising, and almost always exciting. The new age of chocolate making is exemplified by the installation of a large number of companies, the most advanced artisan production facilities and the laboratories that still assist the creative work done in the kitchens of certain restaurants. I am particularly interested in the consequences of the work carried out by a number of small chocolate-making businesses and artisan chocolatiers who have turned the cacao bean into the starting point for a new vision for chocolate. The seed or bean of the cacao plant, whichever it is referred to in the course of the journey that makes up this book, has always been at the core of chocolate making, from day one. It has always been this way, and it cannot be any other way, despite the existence of substitutes. In order to gauge the real scope of the change, you have to look behind the labels. It is not so much the seed as it is the search for identity that makes it special, and the consequences this implies. Cacao beans today bear labels comprising names, surnames and family backgrounds that turn our attention to the spaces in which they were born. The characteristics of the environment in which cacao is grown and the conditions of the people who make it possible are as important as the source and attributes of the seed.

The cacao bean has definitely made a name for itself. Thirty years ago, we learnt to speak of origin in generic terms – Madagascar or Venezuela, to mention two of the most prestigious ones at the time – later adding precision with certain specific sources and varieties of cacao, such as Río Arriba in Ecuador, and Chuao and Porcelana in Venezuela. In the course of the last 12 years, we have raised the discourse to include the species of tree, the name of the farmer who tended it, and the estate where it was harvested. These three details are meant to draw the attention of a market that is set on seeking out differentiating labels. New users want identity, content and meaning, and are seeking responsibility and, above all, consequences. We want to know who produces what, the place they work and under what conditions. Chocolate has stopped being a product with a greater or lesser degree of purity, higher or lower proportion of sugar, with or without milk, or modified with the addition of certain fruits, nuts or aromatics, in order to acquire the identity it had always been denied. Today, more than ever, chocolate has its beginnings in the tree.

There has been a change in direction, and attention is now focused on the variety, the farmer and the environmental conditions. The world of chocolate is undergoing a revolution that begins with the cacao. The entry into the market of small-scale buyers who are more interested in quality than any other circumstance has transformed a large part of the discourse. On Latin American plantations, there is increasing talk of responsibility and value added, while terms such as 'genetics' and 'hybridisation' are starting to become common in conversations within the industry.

In the course of the work that has led to this book, I asked many professionals about the events that helped to change their way of understanding chocolate. Most of them coincided in pointing out the small town of Tain l'Hermitage, in the Rhone valley of southern France, from where the Valrhona company launched its first dark couverture chocolate containing 70 per cent cacao for professional use. It was called Guanaja, and it came out in 1986, a time when no manufacturers had been using more than 55 per cent cacao in the formulation of any of their products. That was four years before the launch of Manjari, the first single-origin chocolate to come to market, also by Valrhona. Other important names would subsequently emerge, such as Los Ancones, the first single-estate chocolate, produced in the kitchen of the Norman chocolatier Michel Cluizel, and the work with single-origin chocolates by Amadei, a company founded by Cecilia Tesseri, the world's first female master chocolatier, in the Tuscan town of Pontedera.

In addition to these and the Mast Brothers, New York-based exponents of the booming bean-to-bar movement, there are a number of others who are showing that there is still much to explore and even more to discover in the world of chocolate. There are, for instance, the ideas outlined by Santiago Peralta in Quito – a pioneer in a number of fields, such as that of *raw* chocolate, which is just that, and untoasted – through the Pacari company, and the work by Art Pollard at Amano Chocolate and the perspective brought to the relationship with chocolate by a person from a world totally unrelated to it. Just to show part of what lies ahead, there is the work by Damian Allsop with his water ganache, first, and now in association with Jordi Roca, chocolates with vegetables and what has been christened 'kraft chocolate' or 'two-ingredient chocolate'.

The change will have consequences throughout the industry. It will be absolute, and whatever happens, it will break certain dynamics, such as the servitude of growers to the buying companies and large-scale manufacturers. The entry of new buyers is triggering a series of changes. This is happening in Colombia, where the sector had stagnated and there was little future, until a number of small processing companies began to break the monopoly held for decades by two large local companies. The resulting removal of this stranglehold that was stifling the cacao plantations paved the way to far-reaching changes. The competition emerging in the quest for quality is driving the transformation of cacao plantations, bringing demands for public policies for the medium and long term to the forefront, giving weight to the need for genetic research programmes to underpin the plantation system, and giving growers the leading role that they had never had.

We started out by wanting to find the maximum expression of the cacao, removing part of the sugar that concealed its features, before seeking a way of making the most of the personality of a certain variety or region. To do this, we needed to bring the growers on side and to have them in the centre of the field of play. This was explained as simply as possible by the Japanese woman Mayumi Ogata, an essential figure who guided us, one tree at a time, through the cacao plantations of the Sierra Nevada de Santa Marta mountains, in the north of Colombia: 'When the farmer is happy, everybody is happy; the cacao, the chocolate and the consumers are happy, and I, too, am happy'. She was right: we are all happy.

And together with the farmer, the beans. The chocolate revolution has its beginnings in the tree, although the actual starting point lies under it, in the soil that nourishes it, and in its surroundings, in the climate that accompanies its growth. The bean is the result and manifests all of these factors: the effects of the climate, the consequences of good or bad growing practices, the way fermentation and drying are carried out, and more particularly, the essence of the variety. The interest to be found in the new forms of chocolate making is based on enhancing the personality of the seed. Chocolate is evidenced by the seed and its personality unfolds from what it transmits. It can be the fruity and aromatic notes, floral profile and freshness of the quality white beans of Piura cacao, or the restraint, elegance and presence of Río Arriba cacao from the Vinces region.

We are giving life to a new way of understanding chocolate that is able to disrupt many of the principles that were until very recently considered unchangeable and which covered the entire production process, including fermentation processes. These are now manipulated to enhance and showcase certain characteristics of the cacao, or to achieve others that we had never imagined could be found. Double fermentations are one of the second last steps in this sense, although there are many more yet to come.

Bitterness is no longer a virtue or a defining feature and neither is colour. There may be chocolates that are more or less dark, just as there are chocolates with reddish tints or in rich, bold browns. It depends more on the origin of the cacao and the production process than anything else. Bitterness is no longer a synonym of purity and character, nor is it an inseparable feature of chocolate; it is only an attribute which, more often than it should, shows poor quality roasting, which is designed more to standardise production or to conceal flaws in low-grade cacaos than to extol the virtues of a good bean.

The success of the bean-to-bar philosophy is the driver for and confirmation of the tree-to-bar model, which takes it a step further. Directly from the cacao plantation to the chocolate, non-stop, which is the same as saying directly to the end consumer. None of these models can exist without taking the farmer into consideration.

A book for chocolate

Everyone has their own idea of chocolate. It may be that we are born with it attached to one of the genes that control pleasure, fantasy and nostalgia, because our relationship with chocolate is always linked to the innermost of our emotions which, one way or another, always take us back to our childhood. With every portion of chocolate, we see the world with the eyes of the child we carry within ourselves. It is a matter of details: the oily feel on the fingertips; the pungent, profound and familiar aroma that draws us to its presence; the warm and smooth sensation in the mouth; and the taste buds dancing to the rhythm of symphonies that can

never be forgotten. Chocolate is always changing, but it always takes us back to the same place.

We are the reflection of what we eat, and at those times when we eat as we are, the neurons responsible for the most joyful feelings are triggered and the nervous system activates half plus one of our pleasure systems. The same thing happens with sugar, the flavour linked to the most primary of emotions of those that define our nature, and it is repeated almost to the same extent as it is with chocolate. There is a lot of magic in chocolate.

This book begins with chocolate before going on to deal with cacao, with the path returning again to the starting point, but this time seen from the perspective of the dynamics and tastes that constitute its new relationship with the market. It is also a round trip that goes back in time. It starts in the factory that materialises the

THE INTEREST TO BE FOUND IN THE NEW FORMS OF CHOCOLATE MAKING IS BASED ON ENHANCING THE PERSONALITY OF THE SEED.

work and ideas of Damian Allsop and Jordi Roca, one of the most advanced artisan chocolatiers of the moment and a leading *postrero* ('dessert maker') – pardon the use of the term, but 'confectioner' sounds like something from a different time, while the more standard Spanish term *repostero* (pastry chef) actually denotes a very different profession. It also refers to the person who is in charge of preparing sweets, biscuits and cold meats, in addition to the care of wines. Seen in this light, in order to have a *repostero,* we would need to combine the three Roca Brothers into a single body – before looking at the challenges faced by the next Roca venture. It is called Casa Cacao, and it will very shortly become a chocolate factory that is part of a complex containing a small boutique hotel that is soon to open in the old town of Girona.

From practically the very first day, Damian Allsop and Jordi Roca's work in the chocolate factory has never ceased to pose questions. The questions began to grow in significance and frequency when they began to work directly with the fermented and dried beans, resulting in a twist to the concept of bean-to-bar, turning it into bean-to-plate, and without being restricted to sweet creations, because cacao has also had, and still does have, an important role to play in savoury cuisine. It is usual for more advanced professionals to work with large companies, such as Valrhona and Cacao Barry, which are dedicated to providing practically everything a restaurant or pastry chef requires: flavour profiles, single-origin cacaos, blends, and any type of specific product designed to cater for each need arising in the kitchen, or to go one step ahead, in order to break new ground. From time to time, other companies operating on a smaller scale manage to join the suppliers of ready-made chocolates for professional use.

Our encounter with the cacao bean led to quite a number of surprises and, more particularly, raised a large number of doubts. When dealing with cacao beans, there are huge differences found between one single-origin cacao and another, between one supplier and another, and between one batch and another. The questions only multiplied. There were those about possible flavour profiles based on varieties, soils, climate, and processing after harvesting in fermentation boxes and dryers; regarding the result of the grower's work on the estate; about the possibility of influencing the final flavour by modifying the fermentation process; related to the consequences that dealing directly with growers would have, on their living conditions, on the environment and on the quality of the cacao they produce; and on the thousands of opportunities that a change in the model would create for small-scale chocolatiers and restaurants on their final product, for customers, and above all, for the growers and the areas in which they live.

The questions raised by the work of new professionals led us to journey back in time in the history of chocolate to cacao and its origins. In order to know the ways of chocolate, we first have to know those of cacao. The new chocolates are, more than ever, the children of cacao, or at least they are from a different perspective. They can only continue to change and progress to the degree that their relationship with cacao does.

The signature chocolate of the future will feature the name of the farmer on the wrapper more than that of the actual chocolatier. This journey was our response to the need for knowledge and the obligation to break with the paradox surrounding so many professionals dedicated to working with a product that so few know directly. Like many of them, Jordi Roca had never set foot in a cacao plantation; he had never seen a locally run collection, fermenting and drying plant in operation, nor had he plunged his hands deep into a fermenting box, leaving his arms covered with the pungent and sour smell of the beans as they are being transformed. He had never looked inside a cacao pod cut from the tree seconds before being split open, just as he had never experienced the extreme sweetness and intense acidity of the mucilage before it starts to oxidise, within the first seconds of its exposure. He had never seen the face of the farmer who harvested the beans that arrived at the factory in Girona, nor did he have any idea of the tiny fraction that the farmer would finally receive out of the total amount he paid to the intermediary who supplied the product.

We have seen a different world, one filled with hope. Cacao is awakening awareness in every corner of Peru's Amazonas region, where today the discourse of the pioneers, the new entrepreneurs, is being put into practice. People have come to understand the magnitude of the treasure they handle; they are no longer settling for the pittance paid to them by buyers and middlemen; they have their dignity and have decided to make cacao and their work into the driving force for change. We have seen it in the Arhuaco communities in the Sierra Nevada de Santa Marta mountains of Colombia, in the communal meetings of the Awajún, who defend the integrity of the rainforest in the Alto Marañón region of Peru, and far from there, in the determination of many of the children and grandchildren of settlers who share the hopes and sufferings of the former.

I became familiar with cacao through my relationship with growers before I did through chocolate. I accompanied Astrid Gustche, the pioneer and standard bearer for Peruvian chocolate, on some of the trips she had arranged to allow her to write her book (*Los guardianes del cacao* [The Guardians of Cacao], Planeta). During the trip, I began to see the story from the other side of the barrier that is often raised by the brands between the source and the consumer. The journey through some of the cacao production areas of Junín, San Martín and Amazonas showed me that everything always revolves around the growers. Although each of them has a different face, they are humble folk who have turned cacao into the banner for their struggle for survival, and in many cases for their way out of the dark pit of drug trafficking, slavery and even extermination caused by terrorism. I began to collaborate on development projects linked to cacao even before furthering my knowledge into chocolate, and I always understood that it was there – so far away from the places where the fashions, practices and trends of the industry are decided and defined – that the fate of chocolate would be resolved. At some point, I came to dream that, in a just future, it should be there, in the place where cacao originated, that tomorrow's chocolate trends come to life.

Casa Cacao is the story of a journey to the source, and aims to show a world that we discovered to be inhabited by entrepreneurs. It is the result of an agreement between the Roca Brothers and the BBVA banking group since they began their world tours in 2014 and began to travel with their restaurant – kitchen and staff included – around the world, especially throughout the Americas. Houston, Dallas, Monterrey, Bogotá, Mexico City, Lima, Miami, San Francisco, Phoenix, Santiago and Buenos Aires witnessed the arrival of the first travelling pop-up ever created in the world of fine dining. There have been other international destinations, such as London, Istanbul and Hong Kong, and they have visited different Spanish cities over the last two years with the same approach: to gain in-depth knowledge of local foods and traditions in order to turn them into a menu designed with the philosophy of the house – solid, appealing and surprising.

I attended one of the dinners held in Lima in August 2014, and I collaborated on part of the schedule they had put together for the city. These included meetings with culinary students, lectures and seminars. The highlight was a demonstration offered by Jordi Roca at the chocolate factory at the Virgen de Fátima women's prison in Chorrillos, which was a highly emotional experience. I also assisted with the preparatory trip made by Josep a few months before. He was in search of producers who could show him the most outstanding and emblematic Peruvian food products and projects that were deserving of support. I was surprised by this candid vision of fine dining promoting the creation of opportunities, and I arranged a number of meetings for them and a few rather exhausting itineraries to source products. There was something else I found striking. In every city visited by El Celler de Can Roca, the staff was supplemented with students from a local cooking school. When in Lima, they turned their attention to the Pachacútec outreach project and asked for collaboration from students in its cooking and hospitality schools. As had occurred in the earlier stops along the tour, two cookery students received grants for three months' work experience at El Celler de Can Roca. In Lima, this was expanded to include a student from the waiter training school. The same thing happened at all the places visited in this and subsequent tours, and grants were given to front-of-house students in Buenos Aires and Santiago, and in different Spanish cities in these last two years. For three years, the Pachacútec Waiter Training School enjoyed an extension of the programme by being opened to the same number of graduates. The three made careers for themselves at some of the best restaurants in Lima, and are still employed by them.

The relationship between El Celler de Can Roca and BBVA has led to the making of four documentaries – *Cooking up a Tribute*, *El heladero del Himalaya* (The Ice Cream Maker of the Himalayas), *Turkish Way* and *Casa Cacao*, which is still being edited – and two books, *Cocinando un tributo* (Cooking Up a Tribute) and *Homenaje a Chile* (Tribute to Chile). The book you are holding, *Casa Cacao*, is the third book of the series. I suggested it, with the subheading *The Journey Back to the Origins of Chocolate*, because I felt it condensed everything we were searching for with this project: reducing the world of cacao to the intimacy of a small kitchen, the serenity of a leading restaurant and the modesty of a small farm and the work and home of a small-scale grower. Chocolate is shown as a means with which to try and shake up a world that has no choice but to change. This book, this journey and those chocolates which, at times seem about to leap out of these pages, are justified by their determination to create opportunities. Also by the need to clarify some of the many dark clouds that blight the industry. I shall finish with the words from Mayumi Ogata that made me reflect: 'Cacao is a material asset, but behind cacao are stories that are somewhat dark, political stories that are also a bit dark, economic stories that are also a little dark, and other stories that I could never have imagined before. Now I can imagine and I can see the truth: whenever I see cacao, I find the social, political and economic truth of the country.' Since that time, this is what I think whenever I hold chocolate in my hands, and when I eat it, I see many things that I never used to see: faces, lots of faces, and also landscapes, but I mostly see hope.

Ignacio Medina
Lima, July 2018

1
A BEGINNING
TO EVERYTHING

ANARKIA AND THE NEW FORMS
OF CHOCOLATE

THE FIRST ANARKIA COMPRISED eight creams, four jellies, nine sauces, three ice creams, five crunches, three fresh components and six dry components. The fresh ones were apple, cherry tomato and carrot, and to understand the concept of 'dry', you need only read the list: puff pastry, shortbread, macaron, meringue, spiced bread and pistachio financier. The number and the components served no particular purpose. They came to the dish in an organic fashion, for no specific reason, as if by chance. It was simply because the basic ingredients were there. There were bits from everywhere: from the cool room, from the chocolate factory, from the preparations made for the savoury dishes for that day, and from the creative workshop. They were to hand, ready to bring other dishes to life, and although nobody had planned it, they brought new creations to life and ended up playing a part in the construction of the pillars on which chaos would be born. There could have been many more, but as fate or chance would have it that day, these were the chosen ones. Anarkia was created with what was in Jordi Roca's head and the ingredients available at El Celler de Can Roca on the day he decided that the time had come to break it all apart.

It is easy to work out a maze when you are holding the plans: the entrance is here; the exit is there; and this is the route. The unexpected ceases to exist and takes on meaning when you see the recipe, which includes the incoherent disorder that prevails over the landscape defined by Anarkia. I asked to see the first recipe to be written down, and everything became clear on paper. Each component is shown separately and explained in detail, step by step. This is how the mint water jelly is made; this formula is for the tonka bean cream; that one is for the pistachio crisp; the melon ice cream is made by following these instructions ... not to mention the pistachio financier, the jellies and the meringue, each with reference to their own recipes. When we finally come to assembling the dish, disorder reigns in the kitchen. Put things wherever you like; leave a little space between them so they look appealing or group them where you prefer; combine colours, shapes and textures if you feel like it; or if you prefer, divide it up into squares which can tell you the approximate positions of each component. Group them into families; or – why not? – separate the families and send each member to one end of the plate. Do we really need to use a plate? Shall we follow the fashion for canvas? Do we spread it out over a platform or look for a board? It makes no difference; you can do what you like. This is Anarkia, chaos made dessert. The institutionalisation of disorder in this universe governed by the laws of absolute precision that is pastry-making and, by extension, the fine dining of our time.

The transformation of cooking driven by the cutting-edge cuisine of the nineties is largely the result of a generation of chefs trained in the techniques and practices in use in pastry kitchens. I found a close relationship between their work and that made standard by the second wave of freestyle chefs coming in the wake of the break with the mandates of classic cuisine. It was not so much the removal of the barriers between sweet and savoury proposed by Ferran Adrià at elBulli, which would come later, but the shift in culinary techniques towards an exercise in precision based on the millimetric control of times, temperatures and measures, which has always been the case in fine pastry-making.

Anarkia represented a paradigm shift as it questioned the foundations on which the fine dining of the twenty-first century were built, claiming a space for spontaneity and uncertainty within the culinary framework. The formula opened the door to confusion, incoherence and the lack of reasoning. It was a declaration of freedom. The proclamation of rebellion against the obsession for explaining the dish as the core of rigid culinary order in which everything must follow a sequence that is able to construe or to be construed. The justification for its existence, the nature and arrangement of the ingredients that comprise it, the culinary techniques applied or the way in which it is presented, narrated and accompanied.

I was unable to understand that part the first time Anarkia was brought to my table. If my notes do not deceive me, this happened between the end of 2008 and halfway through 2009. The date is not very clear, and I noted it down as a fantasy. A fantastic explosion of flavours and possibilities that places the fate of the dish in the diner's hands, making them the sole administrator of the emotions contained in it. This was clear, and it was absolutely new. The chef took a back seat. The diner alone was left to decide the contents of each bite and the order in which they were to take place, depending on the components brought together each time on the spoon and the reaction with which they were met. For a moment, the line drawn by the spoon over the plate would transcend the dictates of the chef to take on primary importance. The dish could become one thing or another depending on what you decided to eat and the order in which you did so. The climax would come as the result of an almost infinite succession of opportunities. An unpredictable and always different dish born out of the fragmentation of pastry-making,

ANARKIA IS AN UNPREDICTABLE AND
EVER-CHANGING DISH THAT AROSE FROM
THE FRAGMENTATION OF PASTRY-MAKING
INTO AN ALMOST INFINITE SUCCESSION OF
POSSIBILITIES.

able to open the doors to a world whose limits were impossible to guess.

I keep notes on two versions of Anarkia compiled on two separate occasions. I stopped taking notes when, finally, I became aware that the brilliance and the tremendous risk embodied by the discourse unfolding in the dish – there is no one way to this, given that the combination of components and the order in which they are eaten can also lead to doubt or rejection – demonstrated something much deeper. This puzzle in the form of a dish led to something that I had never even sensed before: the vindication of the chef's freedom and the return to creations that were self-justified. Without the need for a story or a past that explains the whole, without being part of a sequence, without regard to the dish preceding it or to the one following it in the order of the menu. Just one dish, created for its own sake. Nothing more.

No Anarkia was ever the same as the one that came after it. The last one to come to my table comprised 14 creams, four ice creams, five crisps, eight jellies and the same number of sponges, and three spheres. There were other versions, but there is no point in listing them. However you look at it, there is no defined pattern aside from a calculated and unsettling disorder.

Jordi's explanation corroborates the story.

'It happened ten or twelve years ago, after an argument with my brothers about the meaning of a dish, a St George's mushroom consommé, and all the justification and reasoning involved. It was a time when we would give much thought and discussion to the discourse of a dish, and I was determined to show that the only reason is the one you yourself give, that when you try a dish and you like it, no explanation is necessary. So I experimented with this dish, which I made using a little of everything I had to hand. We served it without any explanation, and every customer gave me a different evaluation. Some were thrilled with the combination of violet and coffee; others told me that the rum and orange flower reminded them of something or other, good or bad, or something completely different. The result was a dish that people might like more sometimes and less at other times, but which left nobody indifferent. It was an absurdity, but at the same time, it had all the meaning in the world. I found it to be a revelation and a way of understanding that everything was possible, and that there was no one line, one philosophy or one way of reasoning that needs to be embraced in order to be creative. That was one of my breakthroughs, and it's why Anarkia became so important to me, in a process where I somehow needed to get past that moment we all go through when we have to 'kill the father', which in my case was to overcome the reasoning given by Joan and Pitu (Josep) in order to free myself from those things. Anarkia was a resource that would bring about adventure, free up every dish, every bite, and every person.

'Every time we had to assemble it in the kitchen, it was different, and it required a huge crew involved in a major operation to arrange a lot of components on a plate. Assembling the dish, setting up for it beforehand, preparing it before the desserts and finishing it off on the spot. It was a challenge to serve it to every diner at every service, because there's no point in creating a spectacular or highly detailed dish for ten people if it can't be realistically served to everybody.'

Jordi's rebellion was illustrated by a demanding and painstaking dish. It started with the ingredients available at the restaurant, but it required as many different preparations as there were components, and ended up appearing on and disappearing from the menu for a couple of seasons, always in a different form, until it disappeared for good one day.

'Such a complicated and complex dish like that one needs a good reason to stay on the menu. It was there for my sake at the time, because I was looking for conceptual freedom. But when I felt free, there was no longer any sense to putting so much work into that dish.

'Honestly? I got tired. I stopped making it because it was such a pain. That's all there is to it.'

Chocolate Anarkia

The culinary forms that came into existence with the emergence of nouvelle cuisine and new Basque cuisine changed the way we thought about cooking. Nothing in the world of flavours would ever be the same after that; cooking threw off its restraints and a succession of changes came at unimaginable speed. Against the strict rules, convention and distance that governed classic haute cuisine, there was freedom to create market cuisine and to draw from the dishes enjoyed by the masses. The revolution also affected the nature of dishes, which ceased to have an eternal life. Until then, established chefs would repeat practically the same dishes and the same sauces throughout their careers. After then, dishes were brought to life. They were born, grew, became transformed, and died. The only exception to the rule were those dishes Adrià labelled '10/10 dishes', which were destined to survive in time and to bring forth sequel after sequel, the equivalent of culinary immortality.

In one way or another, dishes are consigned to oblivion or die outright when they lose their reason to continue to exist. Anarkia was more than a challenge; it was a goal and at the same time the tool that would make it possible to achieve.

Once it was achieved, all justification for it remaining on the menu was gone. And besides, as Jordi says, it was a 'pain' that required a huge operation.

But Anarkia was not gone completely. It was resurrected in 2014, after three years of being parked away in the archives that contain the dishes retired from El Celler de Can Roca. The reason for this was the new relationship Jordi Roca developed with it. It came as a response to the change experienced in the pastry kitchen at El Celler de Can Roca, where chocolate had long ceased to be identified by different preparations or the use given to them, but was now identified by where it came from. The place from which cacao is sourced creates quite striking differences between one chocolate and another. Madagascar, Ghana, Mexico, Guatemala, Ecuador, Peru and Colombia became much more than simple names of countries and began to define the differences between aroma and flavour profiles. Chocolate Anarkia was then seen as the beginning of a quest for the identity and nature of chocolate based on the source of the cacao. This time it came with the restoration of order to the world of pastry-making chaos. Disorder was abandoned, or regulated at any rate, without losing the multifaceted view that was now given to the world of chocolate, as a response to the desire to achieve new goals.

The name was the same, although as Jordi explained to me four years later, it was no longer a sequence.

'I brought Anarkia back for the chocolate, because I saw a lot of sense in the application of every possible technique to a product that I was starting to see in a different light. I realised that it was possible to rescue it and that it was coherent to apply it to chocolate, and the variety of chocolates I was working with at the time, with very different techniques that were built on very powerful aromatic points, born from combinations with all sorts of spices, chillies and fruits … meant that not only did it make sense, but it also allowed chocolate to be seen from a different perspective.'

I came across it again eight months later, in Lima, during the first tour that El Celler de Can Roca undertook together with BBVA through the Americas, which would take it to the United States, Mexico, Colombia and Peru. The most interesting part of the story is that it had to be served away from its home, in the midst of a gruelling back and forth between one city and another, and with more limited means. The tour involved the entire restaurant staff, supplemented by students from local hospitality schools, but it is never the same to work at home as it is to work away from home. Even so, the journey gave life to two new versions of Chocolate Anarkia. The first contained chocolates made from Mexican cacaos, and the second with chocolates made using Peruvian cacaos. Each stop on the tour had its

CHOCOLATE ANARKIA CAN BE SEEN AS THE BEGINNING OF A QUEST FOR THE IDENTITY AND NATURE OF CHOCOLATE BASED ON THE SOURCE OF THE CACAO.

own different version. There was also one in Colombia, although with new twists that I would later see recreated, at the beginning of 2018, among the latest sweet offerings at El Celler de Can Roca. Back in early September 2014, I saw an Anarkia being produced with Peruvian chocolate in the least likely place. It was the day before the first of the dinners that the Roca Brothers and BBVA were holding in Lima was to take place and I accompanied Jordi Roca to the Virgen de Fátima women's prison in Chorrillos. Vanadis Pompiu had just opened a chocolate factory there where a dozen inmates worked, and we asked Jordi to come and chat with them, to give them encouragement. He took with him all the components of the dish that he would be revealing the following night, and he assembled it in front of the inmates and a few of the prison staff who did not want to miss out, while explaining the story, process and finer details of his formula. It was a joyful morning, and so different from everything experienced in their kitchens and surroundings that it left an indelible mark on everybody. The surprise, nostalgia, joy, hope and sadness that could also be seen in those dozen pairs of eyes gave the dish an aura of life that I cannot imagine it ever having again. Four years have passed, and some of those inmates have left behind their life in jail. Two of them continue to work with chocolate together with Vanadis. I would like to think that the session they took part in helped them to move on, firmly linking their new lives and dreams to chocolate.

A long time has passed and Chocolate Anarkia also came off the El Celler de Can Roca menus. If it were to come back, it would be so different as to be unrecognisable. In fact, it has come back. It goes by the name of Marabillao (a play on the Spanish world *maravillado*, 'amazed') and is absolutely nothing like it, but it is without a doubt the legitimate heir to Chocolate Anarkia, although that is another story which will have to wait to be told. Many more things have happened along the way.

The most significant was the creation of the chocolate factory. It started out as a small ground floor premises four or five blocks away from the restaurant. There the research work by British chocolatier Damian Allsop was combined with the creative madness he shared with Jordi Roca. The factory has grown, and the presence of Damian – who years before played an important part in the pastry kitchen at El Celler de Can Roca, even becoming Jordi's immediate superior prior to consolidating his relationship with pastry-making – has helped to develop the work with chocolate, opening doors to worlds that neither of the two had ever dared to enter into before. The first of these, and also the one that would have the greatest consequence, was seen in the change in the model of their relationship with cacao, the day they received the first samples of fermented and dried cacao beans. They came from Piura, from the Amazonas region of Peru, and with their arrival, the factory's conventional dynamic of working with processed cacao was broken.

The factory began to produce its own chocolates from the fermented and dried beans, in a process that marked a definitive change, providing the opportunity for playful experimentation and testing, and striking results. They embarked on their first adventure with the use of fruit juices and pulps to bring about a second fermentation – more precisely, the maceration of the beans – stimulating the fruity character of the beans and bringing it out in the chocolate. Along the way, new products began to appear that would break with the concept of chocolate held at this and at many other establishments until that time. Among them were chocolates with vegetables, made by combining the cacao paste with freeze-dried vegetables. The formula still needs work and requires certain details to be fine-tuned and a number of important issues to be resolved. However, they moved on from peas to lemon verbena (*Lippia citrodora*), and a little later they turned their attention to carrots and then corn nuts (fried, toasted and salted corn kernels). It cannot take much shaping at the moment, so it is limited to being spread out into sheets with a thickness of just under five millimetres. It was served to me as part of a dessert, and it made me start thinking. I found it to be quite exciting.

'I SAW A LOT OF SENSE IN THE APPLICATION OF EVERY POSSIBLE TECHNIQUE TO A PRODUCT THAT I WAS STARTING TO SEE IN A DIFFERENT LIGHT.'

I returned to the factory in January 2018 to finish compiling documentation for the book, taking part while I was there in the final days of filming for the documentary being made by BBVA simultaneously with the process of preparing this book. I still had to record three long conversations on the process of creating a dish with Jordi, Damian and the people heading the El Celler de Can Roca creative workshop, Bernat Vivancos and Nacho Baucells, the latter also the head chef of the restaurant. The first of these was with Damian, who turned up with another novelty. It was presented to me as a 'two-ingredient chocolate: kraft chocolate', made exclusively with cacao paste and sugar, with no added cocoa butter. It was intense, evocative and intriguing, but the lack of fat caused problems for handling. Jordi appeared halfway through the conversation, seeming less interested in changing the formula than in investigating modifications to the machinery used in the production process. I was left with the feeling that we would soon see it on the market.

Things were happening at breakneck speed after the first cacao beans arrived at the chocolate factory. So fast in fact that the early work would soon become obsolete. A few months after the last time we had spoken about Chocolate Anarkia, I brought up the subject again in a new attempt to fill in a few gaps. 'Why did you do Chocolate Anarkia that way?' I asked Jordi. His reply was clear, direct and concise. 'Because I didn't know then what I know now about cacao processing.' In less than a year and a half, Chocolate Anarkia had run its course.

It was a whole new ball game. New ideas arose, giving life to preparations, techniques and products. Each cacao variety and each new single-origin cacao provided a different perspective and opened doors that neither Damian nor Jordi had ever ventured through. This new, much wider and more open view of the world of chocolate making would never cease to create new paths, each leading to new doubts. The questions began to build up. What can be found in other production areas? Will this be the best possible cacao? How was it fermented? What results would I have if it had been fermented differently? Which cacao trees did it come from? Is it the variety I need? Who grew them? Where do they live and in what conditions? Can my work improve their living conditions? Where does all the money I pay for each kilo of cacao go? What part do they get? Can I buy directly from them? What is a cacao plantation like? Do all the trees produce the same variety? What makes each cacao different? In the end, two things were certain. The first was a starting point: we know everything, or almost everything, about chocolate; to the same extent, we are ignorant of what really goes into the cacao bean, the pod it comes from and, finally, the tree that gave life to it. The second was the announcement of a different future: everything would change if you could gain control over the fruit.

Jordi Roca and Damian Allsop had barely even opened a crack in the door to a world about which chocolatiers tend to have little knowledge. They were beginning to understand that on the other side of the door was a fascinating world, and the idea began to take shape in them that would end up becoming a certainty: they needed to discover it. Each question would shed light on new doubts, bringing us closer to the journey to the source of cacao that we relate in this book.

Damian Allsop, El Celler de Can Roca's chocolatier

I find Damian Allsop at the El Celler de Can Roca chocolate factory. He looks at me and holds out a piece of chocolate. 'Try this,' he says. It is a thick and compact bar, quite matt and dark. I find it expressive and profound, although the texture is more consistent and dense than I am accustomed to trying, and I note a lightly caramelised flavour profile. I ask him what it is. 'Two-ingredient chocolate,' he replies. I raise my brows, a gesture that I need further explanation, and he responds to my action. 'I'd call it kraft chocolate.' It is often difficult to communicate with Damian. Although born in Britain, he casually mixes Catalan with Spanish, peppered with a few technical terms in English. It forces me to think about each of his replies and to rearrange the words, but it all makes sense in the end. A great deal of sense.

The two-ingredient chocolate is the latest chimera created at Damian Allsop's chocolate factory, which today belongs to El Celler de Can Roca, and will soon be a part of Casa Cacao. He had previously come up with the idea of water ganache, and he has been working for some time to develop the technique, which is one of the great advances of contemporary confectionery. By taking apart the original concept for this coating used for bonbons and biscuits and replacing the cream with water, he removed the dairy notes in order to showcase the chocolate instead of concealing it. He has been working with water ganache for 15 years, to the extent that he has a line of chocolates made with this technique that he supplies to high-class restaurants throughout much of Europe. As far as Damian is aware, five other specialists are working with the same technique today. Its development is among his greatest obsessions, and defines a career that seems to flourish with every challenge. 'I used to say that I want to work without problems. And if it meant I had to add fat, then I did, like everybody else. Now, I couldn't care less about difficulty. I'm sure of what I have to do and I look for the way to do it, and the road is usually more difficult.'

Chocolate has monopolised the last 15 years of a career built up alongside

some of the leading figures of pastry-making and cooking in recent times: Robert May; John Huber, known as The King of Pastry; Patrick Woodside, head pastry chef under Raymond Blanc and Marco Pierre White, in succession; Joël Robuchon; Gordon Ramsey; and Giorgio Locatelli. That was before he opened his own restaurant, La Magraña, in Girona. It was not successful, and his next stop was El Celler de Can Roca. There he was made head of the pastry kitchen, which made him the boss and mentor of Jordi Roca, who at the time was not very keen on being told what to do.

They were different times in the life of El Celler de Can Roca. It was still in the old premises, next door to his parents' business – today it is an extension of the bar and eatery where Montse and Josep serve their daily set menu – and it had not yet made its name. 'There were seven of us in the kitchen back then, when it was full. Joan was the boss and cooked at every service. It was very small, very dynamic. Josep managed the front of house, Joan, me … It was completely different in a way, but it was also very similar, because each person did their own thing. Pitu with the wines, Joan in the kitchen...' And Jordi? 'Complicated; he didn't know what he wanted.'

An accident interrupted his career and his life for close to two years and took him back to London, first as the manager of a chocolate shop in Notting Hill, and a little later at his own chocolate business using the water ganache technique. His work was focused on fine dining and his customers were some of the best restaurants at the time. A chocolate-making concept aimed at the luxury market can either be big business or a source of problems; it all depends on the state of the market. So when the crisis came, it was no longer a good idea. It was the beginning of the road back to El Celler de Can Roca.

Damian Allsop is about to complete his third year as the head of chocolate and bonbon production at the restaurant, in the factory set up for this purpose. He plays no part in the preparation or design of desserts, given that his work and life are confined to chocolate, which is at the centre of a never-ending quest. He continues to improve his water ganache in order to achieve greater purity of the chocolate flavour and new variations in texture. He is beginning to define the way in which to adjust the elasticity of his chocolates with vegetables, in which the freeze-dried vegetables take the place once occupied by powdered milk, and is on the verge of shaking up the industry with what he has christened 'two-ingredient chocolate'. He has done more things than many can boast, but the challenges continue to accumulate. Working directly with cacao beans is shedding light on a certainty that leaves all of the previous things in the shade: the incredible network

JORDI ROCA AND DAMIAN ALLSOP HAVE ONLY OPENED A CRACK IN THE DOOR TO A WORLD ABOUT WHICH CHOCOLATIERS TEND TO HAVE LITTLE KNOWLEDGE.

of roads that are opened by each cacao variety or each single-origin cacao when you have control over the process for transforming it into chocolate. Later comes the total concept, the dream of any chocolatier, the possibility of starting their work even before that, with the selection of the fruit, fermentation and drying. And together with this is the essential challenge that is also a necessity: 'enabling your chocolate to change the life of cacao growers'.

Seen from this angle, a great deal still needs to be done in the world of chocolate. Damian has no doubts about this. 'I'm learning to get to know chocolate and I see a future for it that we'd never imagined. Two weeks ago I saw things differently from the way I see it now, and in time we'll find other possibilities and other roads. There's still a lot to do.'

THE FORMULATION OF THE CREATIVE EFFORT IS DECISIVE FOR UNDERSTANDING THE DIFFERENT ROADS THAT WILL LEAD TO THE CONSTRUCTION OF TOMORROW'S CUISINE.

THE CREATIVE EFFORT

WHAT IS THE PROCESS FOR CREATING A DISH? This question has been in my head since I came into contact with the new forms of cooking. It is still there 35 years later. I repeat it every time I set foot into a restaurant, and with emphasis: what is the creative process here? Nobody is ever put off by my curiosity any more, just as the answers increasingly offer fewer surprises. This was not a trivial question in the early eighties, and it often turned out to be as startling as some of the dishes led to its asking. However, the answers were essential to being able to understand and later explain what we were beginning to discover. Today I ask it even more frequently and much more intentionally, although we now have to focus more on the nuances, and more particularly, to broaden horizons. The formulation of the creative effort seems to me a determining factor for understanding the different roads that will lead to the construction of tomorrow's cuisine.

It was a timely question, although quite uncommon in the context of the culinary boom that came with the phenomenon of nouvelle cuisine, first, and everything that the emergence of new Basque cuisine, immediately afterwards, meant and involved. There were many visions – often, in the literal sense of the word – and a lot of joking in the tiny circle that was fine dining at the time. One

French food critic – pardon my imprecision, but the name escapes me – came to describe Parisian nouvelle cuisine as the result of a crash between two fruit trucks at the entrance to the old Les Halles market at first light. One of them was carrying raspberries, and the other kiwi fruit, and a crowd of chefs pounced on the cargo, taking the fruit back to their restaurants free of charge. He was right. There were lots of raspberries, masses of strawberries, tons of blueberries and loads of kiwi fruit indiscriminately distributed over the new dishes of the time, although behind this exercise was a legion of chefs who were more interested in taking paths that would allow them to be different, rather than in creating. Creating is something entirely different. At the time, the creative process was more about devising techniques and defining trends than it was about following trends. Many years have passed since Ferran Adrià made famous Jacques Maximin's words at the height of the culinary upheaval of the nineties, 'creativity means not copying'. These words are more valid than ever 30 years later. Creativity means not copying. I would even go so far as to say that creativity is not about breaking the canvas of the dish in order to construct it differently; it is about managing to give it soul, regardless of its form. I agree with what Jordi Roca told me in one of our conversations held in the last year: 'it has to mean something'.

Creativity can be born with an idea, a memory or a chimera. It can grow, driven by the demands imposed by the change in season for a product, by a specific request coming from the kitchen, or by working directly with a product or a combination of products. It is the more habitual route taken at El Celler de Can Roca and can be marked by a flavour recovered from traditional cuisine, by one's own initiative or an idea communicated by Joan, or by the need arising from changes in the menu. A few years ago, I asked Joan about the number of different tasting menus he had designed in the restaurant during the previous year. He raised his eyes and replied, 'more than twenty'. Products come and go, even within a season, at the same rate as ideas come and go. The trigger also comes with the search for a new technique or the need to transform an old one. And then there is the difference between creation, variation and evolution, which is best left for another time. The pathways multiply at each turn in the creative action, but all are subject to the basic principle pointed out by Nacho Baucells, one of the leaders of the creative work carried out at El Celler de Can Roca. 'The first thing we need to consider is that the dish that goes out can't just be good; it has to be very good.' The dish is above all else.

El Celler de Can Roca's creative workshop has a name for the moment when the Roca Brothers decide whether a dish is worthy or unworthy of the cut, if it must wait for a place in the kitchen at a future date, or if it is to feature on the next tasting menu. It is 'the verdict of the Holy Inquisition', and it defines the moment when each new creation is subjected to triple examination by Joan, Josep and Jordi. There are dishes that pass with the endorsement of two, but the norm is that total consensus is needed. There have been times when none at all are passed, but this does not happen often. There is also a moment where a bit of madness is called for. When it arrives, Jordi Roca is summoned. 'Jordi still has madness left in him,' says Nacho. 'Whenever I'm working on a dish and I get stuck, I get him to help me break with the dynamic and think of something strange. I show him what I'm working on and he suggests things to me that are impossible at times, but when you try them, they're really interesting. That's how we've come up with many fun dishes, like when he suggested turning the asparagus ice cream with black truffle we made in 2012 into a *Comtessa* (a popular brand of ice-cream cake with layers of crunchy chocolate, now marketed as Vienneta) or when he gave us the idea for the béarnaise sauce *Phoskito* (another industrial product in the form of a slice of Swiss roll).'

'YOU HAVE TO BE CONVINCED; YOU HAVE TO BE TRUE TO YOURSELF; YOU NEED TO HAVE SOMETHING ASSOCIATED WITH YOURSELF, ESTABLISH A VERY CLOSE RELATIONSHIP WITH YOUR WAY OF LOOKING AT LIFE.'

Creative madness

The first work of madness by Jordi that I experienced was Messi's Goal, served right at the end of a lunch in 2009. Anarkia was before that, but that was something completely different. More than a dessert, Messi's Goal was a slap in the face, but it showed that subversive side that I sometimes like to find in cuisine. Or perhaps it was the solution to a challenge, or who knows, a show of disrespect. I would not know how to classify the impulse to turn one of the historic goals by the Argentine player at Barcelona into something edible, but it was so much fun. It seemed refreshing, irreverent and rejuvenating. I remember being the only person in the dining room to be served it that day, and when it arrived at the table, announced over the loudspeaker, half of the room turned to look at me. The dessert came in a bowl shaped like half a football and filled with grass on which to replicate the player's moves. You had to eat the rival defenders – made from certain sweet preparations – one at a time, before crashing the ball through a sugar net into what was the actual dish, while the radio presenter's shout when the goal was scored was repeated over and over through an integrated speaker. I burst out laughing and I was unable to contain myself for quite some time. I don't remember the rest. What remains is not the recipe, but the way of breathing life into a challenge.

Jordi Roca gives more weight to the warmth of experience over the apparent coldness of work in a laboratory. Without looking down on the latter, he prefers the personal view and individual legacy. 'There's no system or formula for creativity. It's related to everything, and it can be set off by anything, but there must always be a driving force which begins with life itself and which increasingly separates creativity from life.' 'The idea of making lists of flavours – fruits, spices and the like – on a slate and combining them with each other can work. We tried it with Damian and we came up with 50 different recipes in an instant. We mapped out products arranged from the highest to the lowest intensity. Then we combined them and came up with a great many flavours, which we could use to build up a tasting menu. It was good groundwork, but you ultimately have to be convinced; you have to be true to yourself; you need to have something associated with yourself, establish a very close relationship with your way of looking at life, with your personal experiences. Without that, there's no point, because there will be nothing of yourself in what you do. It has to come from you. We've learnt to master techniques, but they have to mean something.'

In order to explain it, he turns to two of the most famous desserts of his career, Journey to Havana and The Pine Grove, two ideas seventeen years apart, which nonetheless show very similar pathways. Journey to Havana was created in 2000, and was one of first glimmers of brilliance that would draw attention to Jordi Roca. A chocolate cylinder was made to resemble a cigar, which was filled with whipped cream impregnated with Havana cigar smoke and set with gelatine. The end was dipped in a little grated sugar charcoal and more was placed on the plate, resembling ash. It was served with a mojito reconstituted using lime jelly, mint granita and rum sweets.

The formula highlighted some of the finer details that come after a creative discourse and which would continue to grow afterwards. 'I made it after doing an ice-cream making course, during which I learnt that air is a part of making an ice cream and can alter its flavour. At first I used it on a technical level, but behind that – the idea itself and motivation for the dessert – there was something much deeper that I only came to understand some time later. Journey to Havana coincided with the time I left home. Until then, I was living with my parents, in a room above the bar. I was 20 or 21, and I moved nearby, but I became independent, and that's a significant moment. It was a time when you could smoke everywhere, and I felt a yearning for home and the smell of cigars and cigarettes in the bar. In the end I found that behind that technical motivation, behind that event, there was a more essential reason which had something to do with life. Now, whenever I think about the dish, I think about our old parties, the memory comes to me of the times we were living in, and it all makes sense.'

The Pine Grove appeared on the menu of El Celler de Can Roca in the summer of 2017, a very difficult time in Jordi's life. 'It came at a time when the problems I had with my voice were driving me to desperation. I tried lots of things and all sorts of therapies; I even sought help through a course in breathing based on meditation. Every morning we would go for a walk through a pine grove and woods where you could feel a sense of peace and tranquillity that revitalised me. That's how The Pine Grove came about. It was another dessert associated with a very important time in my life.'

Some have compared The Pine Grove to a landscape, but I prefer to see it as a personal and nostalgic recreation of this walk in edible form, a dessert that stands for the innermost emotions. It is very likely that its success actually lies in its ability to convey those sensations and the fact that they are all shown to be shared emotions. The dish condenses the scents of the Mediterranean forest, dominated by the Aleppo pine (*Pinus halepensis*). At its base is pine honey ice cream covered with a crumbled thyme, oregano and rosemary biscuit and rounded off with a few fresh pine nuts and a few stick-like pine honey tuiles, reminiscent of pine needles.

Jordi Roca sees creativity as an endeavour that is more emotional than anything

else. It can come by itself or be triggered, but it must never become an obsession. 'When it's an obsession, it doesn't work; you end up forcing combinations; you mix ideas and concepts, and you end up losing your way. The result doesn't work in the end. It may even be good, but it will have lost all meaning.'

'And what about chocolate?' I ask. 'Chocolate can go as far as we want it to. I've always thought that anything that hasn't been done is what remains to be done. Translated into the world of chocolate, this means that anything that hasn't been done is an unfathomable mystery waiting to be unlocked. And we're seeing this a little at a time, as we scrape away at the bubble of known reality in order to enter into what we don't know, which has just happened to us. This is the first time we've made a chocolate using only cacao paste and sugar, and the result is a thing of interest that has taken us to the threshold of an adventure. From here on, everything changes. We're seeing that the type of chocolate is going to affect the way we work with it, and this includes the suitability

'THE TYPE OF CHOCOLATE IS GOING TO AFFECT THE WAY WE WORK WITH IT. WE'RE CREATING A NEW WORLD, AND THAT'S FASCINATING.'

of adapting the machinery in order to work with it... We're creating a new world, and that's fascinating.'

This is the way to make chocolate

I had approached this book with the preconception that the world of chocolate was static. I had been hearing it for years from practically all the chocolatiers I know: everything has been invented. This belief ruled out any creative effort because, in their opinion, there was no longer any room for new techniques – at most, there was only room for flavours created from the presence of spices and fruits in the composition of the end product or, in any case, depending on the possibilities offered by nature and the source of the bean. I continued to hold this misconception until Jordi Roca and Damian Allsop crossed my path, even until a little later. It was the time I needed to delve more deeply into the nature of the work being carried out at the El Celler de Can Roca chocolate factory and to begin to learn about the water ganache thought up and developed by Damian. Later came the chocolates with vegetables – freeze-dried to replace the conventional use of powdered milk – to underpin what I was sensing and to fuel my doubts, and two-ingredient chocolate – only sugar and cacao paste, with no added cocoa butter – for definitive confirmation. There *is* a lot of room for creativity when it comes to technique.

You only have to learn to think differently. Seeing the way in which he approaches his relationship with chocolate, it is clear that Damian does, at least since he first tried Amadei chocolate in the nineties. 'It was a Chuao with notes of fresh plums that I've never again encountered since then,' he recalls. The same thing happened years later with a chocolate produced by Art Pollard for Amano. 'It was amazing, made from Madagascar beans; you get back that "this is the best I've ever tried", and you find out it was made by a computer programmer who's also devoted himself to chocolate and doesn't think like a pastry chef, and that he's all about other ways of reasoning and reaches different conclusions and results.'

Damian's outlook changed when he went to work for Giorgio Locatelli, after a visit to the Amedei chocolate factory. He had an epiphany moment with some of their chocolates, and on his return decided to use them in his work. They had an incredible chocolate, different from anything he had ever worked with, and with 30 chefs at his disposal, nothing could go wrong. 'I'm going to make a mousse to blow your mind,' he thought. He made one. 'Egg yolk, cream... I followed the classic recipe, and when I tried it, it didn't work. Everything that had been explained to me, everything I'd learnt about this structure and about this chocolate was no good. I tasted the mousse and the flavour of the chocolate was different, dairy, all cream, and the chocolate was relegated, half concealed, almost nothing special. I set about looking for a way of working with a flavourless liquid, and I began with water. It was the late nineties and I hadn't yet seen anybody working with it. I began to thicken the water with the process for making sorbet, because I'd seen that ice creams are thickened in the fridge, and started with that. First I made a mousse, later an ice cream ... I tried all the possible textures, and in the end I settled on chocolate bonbons because I saw that as the way to showcase purity and identity; the only ingredient with flavour in the recipe is chocolate. This logic enabled us to respect the identity of the chocolate; we could distinguish the most subtle differences between each chocolate, which would be hidden when covered with cream. The chocolate began to show greater complexity and interest when we left out the cream.'

He had followed trends until that moment. 'I worked the chocolate as a normal pastry chef would in restaurants, hotels... You take it, you temper it... sometimes you think you know, but you don't know. Until I came across Amedei. That was when I realised that the mousse was no good, nor was anything leading up to it, and I began to work with water. I set everything I'd been taught to one side and I had to think differently. Until then my recipe box would always come with me, and everything I did would come out of it; but since that time, the recipe box has been set aside and I've been doing things in a different way. I've changed my way of working, and I look for a freer way of operating and creating.'

The chocolates with vegetables came about while he was looking for an ingredient that allowed him to replace the powdered milk used in making chocolates. 'I wanted to work with a bread made with freeze-dried tomato, but there was a queue for the freeze-dryer and nobody would turn it on for me, so as I looked for a solution, I remembered the Sosa freeze-dried peas. The first thing I found was a strange texture; it turned out very pasty, so I start adding cocoa butter, and little by little that sensation was reduced, but not completely.' It is another open road, much like the one facing two-ingredient chocolate, which he approaches with a close-up perspective that allows him to subsequently uncover a long list of technical challenges to overcome. 'This is the purest chocolate you can make. As I was making it,

I had the feeling of being an artisan, a deep connection with what I do and what I want to do, and I thought: "this is the way to make chocolate". I felt a change by making it; it was a different experience. It's truer that what I've made up to now.'

The new perspective of working from the bean brings up alternatives that have barely been explored. The connection with growers is starting to become a reality at the chocolate factory and will bear fruit very soon. It is no longer about working directly with beans of different single origins, in bean-to-bar mode; rather, it is the possibility of transforming the characteristics of the bean by acting at the source, as Mikkel Friis Holm of Copenhagen does with Nicaraguan cacaos. 'They develop very interesting products because the beans undergo different fermentations, which can be long, medium or short, which broadens the possibilities for each bean. The changes in the type of fermentation and the ways of drying open up very different pathways.'

Research is also an exercise in paring back. This is why, when Damian works to incorporate specific flavours, he prefers chocolates with less personality. 'I realise that when there is a battle between egos and you have to decide in the end, you can't have everything, and this has to be made very clear. Sometimes when you add something that is very good to something else that is very good and you eat it, you realise that you've lost. It doesn't pick you up. What matters most is balance.'

Damian Allsop works chocolate with a very close-up perspective. 'I want emotion. I want to capture your attention when you see the chocolate and then when you eat it. I basically work for myself. If I try it and get tingles all over my body and they do things to me, I show it to Jordi first and, when I can, to the other brothers. What I've learnt working at El Celler is that they want me to do what I like, to dare to think and to invest all my energy into it, to dare to think and then to dare to do... Nobody has ever said this to me, but I have the feeling that I know what they want, which is why I do what I do.'

ANARKIA

Creams

Pepper, cinnamon, aniseed, juniper berry, cocoa, ginger, vanilla, tonka bean.

Jellies

Orange flower, Campari, passion fruit, coffee.

Sauces

Yoghurt, liquorice, mint, basil, tarragon, fennel, saffron, eucalyptus, green tea.

Ice creams

Lychee, watermelon, melon.

Crisps

Raspberry, pistachio, caramel, white chocolate, strawberry.

Dry components

Puff pastry, shortbread, macaron, meringue, spiced bread, pistachio financier.

Fresh components

Apple, cherry tomato, carrot.

MEXICAN CHOCOLATE ANARKIA

Chocolate water jellies

66% cacao chocolate and liquorice jelly

45% cacao milk chocolate and porcini mushroom jelly

42% cacao chocolate and yuzu jelly

70% cacao chocolate and tonka bean jelly

85% cacao dark chocolate and balsamic vinegar jelly

65% cacao chocolate and peanut jelly

69% cacao chocolate and cardamom jelly

Spiced chocolate creams

45% cacao milk chocolate and coffee cream

65% cacao chocolate and chilli cream

85% cacao chocolate and ginger cream

69% cacao chocolate and cardamom cream

70% cacao chocolate and tonka bean cream

42% cacao chocolate and saffron cream

66% cacao chocolate and Java pepper cream

Pralines

Pine nut praline

Pistachio praline

Peanut praline

Hazelnut praline

Almond praline

Walnut praline

Sachertorte
Chocolate foam
Microwave chocolate sponge cake
Chocolate caramel
Chocolate sauce
Chocolate ice cream
Chocolate sorbet
Chocolate granita
Sugar-coated cacao nibs

Rosemary oil

Chilli oil

Ginger oil

Peta zetas (popping candy)

Cacao nibs

For the chocolate water (7 varieties)

For each type of chocolate, use the following amounts:

500 g chocolate

1.5 kg water

Heat the water to 85ºC and pour over the chocolate. Use a hand-held blender to blend until smooth. Transfer to a Superbag placed inside a deep container to collect the water from the mixture. Leave to filter in the refrigerator for 12 hours.

For the flavoured chocolate waters (7 varieties)

Chocolate and liquorice water:

250 g 66% cacao chocolate water

10 g liquorice paste

Chocolate and porcini mushroom water:

250 g 45% cacao milk chocolate water

1.5 g porcini mushroom powder

Chocolate and yuzu water:

250 g chocolate water

Grated zest of 1 yuzu

Chocolate and tonka bean water:

250 g chocolate water

1 grated tonka bean

Chocolate and balsamic vinegar water:

250 g 85% cacao dark chocolate water

5 g cream of balsamic vinegar

Chocolate and peanut water:

250 g 65% cacao chocolate water

40 g natural peanut butter

Chocolate and cardamom water:

250 g 69% cacao chocolate water

2.5 g ground cardamom

    Use a hand-held blender to mix each type of chocolate water with its corresponding flavouring and set aside in the refrigerator for 12 hours.

For the textured chocolate water (7 varieties)

For each flavoured chocolate water, use the following amounts:

200 g flavoured chocolate water (previously prepared)

100 g simple sugar syrup

3 g agar-agar

0.3 g xanthan gum

    Combine the ingredients in a saucepan and bring to the boil. Blend the mixture until smooth with a hand-held blender, press through a sieve and fill a piping bag. Refrigerate.

For the water chocolate jellies (7 varieties)

For each textured chocolate water (previously prepared):

500 g chocolate water

2.5 g agar-agar

50 g sugar

    Combine the ingredients in a saucepan and bring to the boil. Pour into two 20 x 12.5-cm moulds to a depth of 1 cm. Leave to set in the refrigerator.

    Unmould, cut into 4-mm cubes and set aside.

For the chocolate creams

For the cream base

2.5 kg milk

2.5 kg cream

500 g sugar

25 g ice-cream stabiliser

    Combine the milk, cream and 300 g sugar in a stockpot and heat to 40°C. Add the rest of the sugar mixed with the stabiliser and heat to 85°C.

    (Use the hot cream base immediately to make the chocolate creams.)

For the plain chocolate creams (7 varieties)

Plain 85% cacao dark chocolate cream

1 kg cream base (previously prepared)

600 g 85% cacao dark chocolate

Plain 65% cacao dark chocolate cream

1 kg cream base (previously prepared)

400 g 65% cacao chocolate

Plain 45 % cacao milk chocolate cream

1 kg cream base (previously prepared)

400 g 45% cacao milk chocolate

Plain 69% cacao chocolate cream

1 kg cream base (previously prepared)

600 g 69% cacao chocolate

Plain 70% cacao chocolate cream

1 kg cream base (previously prepared)

380 g 70% cacao chocolate

Plain 42% cacao chocolate cream

1 kg cream base (previously prepared)

620 g 42% cacao chocolate

Plain 66% cacao chocolate cream

1 kg cream base (previously prepared)

400 g 66% cacao chocolate

Pour the hot cream base over the corresponding amount of chocolate and use a hand-held blender to combine. Refrigerate.

45% cacao milk chocolate and coffee cream

750 g plain 45% cacao chocolate cream

18 g coffee

Combine the ingredients and blend until smooth with a hand-held blender. Refrigerate.

65% cacao chocolate and chilli cream

700 g plain 65% cacao chocolate cream

1.5 g chilli pepper

Combine the ingredients and blend until smooth with a hand-held blender. Refrigerate.

85% cacao chocolate and ginger cream

700 g plain 85% cacao chocolate cream

2.1 g ground ginger

Combine the ingredients and blend until smooth with a hand-held blender. Refrigerate.

69% cacao chocolate and cardamom cream

750 g plain 69 % cacao chocolate cream

7.5 g cardamom

Combine the ingredients and blend until smooth with a hand-held blender. Refrigerate.

70% cacao chocolate and tonka bean cream

690 g plain 70 % cacao chocolate cream

1.5 g tonka bean

Combine the ingredients and blend until smooth with a hand-held blender. Refrigerate.

42% cacao chocolate and saffron cream

760 g plain 42% cacao chocolate cream

0.6 g saffron

Combine the ingredients and blend until smooth with a hand-held blender. Refrigerate.

66% cacao chocolate and Java pepper cream

700 g plain 66% cacao chocolate cream

4–5 Java peppercorns

Combine the ingredients and blend until smooth with a hand-held blender. Refrigerate.

For the pralines (6 varieties)

Pine nut:

150 g pine nut butter

150 g milk chocolate

Pistachio:

150 g pistachio butter

150 g milk chocolate

Peanut:

150 g natural peanut butter

150 g milk chocolate

Hazelnut:

150 g hazelnut butter

150 g milk chocolate

Almond:

150 g almond butter

150 g milk chocolate

Walnut:

150 g walnut butter

150 g milk chocolate

Combine the nut butter with the milk chocolate in the bowl of a Thermomix. Set the temperature to 37°C and blend the ingredients together for several minutes. Set aside.

For the chocolate brownie

170 g unsalted butter

3 eggs

270 g sugar

75 g plain flour

60 g cocoa powder

270 g 40 % cacao Ghana chocolate

Lightly heat the butter in a saucepan until it melts. Set aside.

Beat the eggs with the sugar at a temperature of 30°C. Whisk in the melted butter until fluffy.

Mix the flour with the cocoa powder, sift and fold into the previous mixture. Incorporate the chopped chocolate. Bake for 25–30 minutes in the oven pre-heated to 170°C. Cut into 1-cm cubes and set aside in an airtight container at room temperature.

For the Sachertorte

210 g egg yolks

150 g cacao paste

430 g almond butter

150 g eggs

130 g icing sugar

100 g plain flour

100 g cocoa powder

100 g softened unsalted butter

250 g egg whites

150 g sugar

Mix the egg yolks with the cacao paste, almond butter, whole eggs and icing sugar, and then beat with a hand-held blender until fluffy.

Combine the flour and cocoa powder and sift together. Lightly heat the butter in a saucepan until it melts, then incorporate into the previous mixture.

Combine the sugar and egg whites in a bowl and heat in a bain-marie until the sugar dissolves. Then beat to a meringue. When stiff peaks have formed, fold in the almond butter mixture, followed by the sifted flour and cocoa powder. Bake for 20 minutes at 200°C. Cut into 1-cm cubes and set aside in an airtight container.

For the chocolate foam

1.2 kg 66% cacao chocolate

1.2 kg 35% cacao chocolate

300 g 84% cacao chocolate

300 g hazelnut praline

960 g milk

3.6 kg cream

720 g egg yolks

600 g sugar

6 g xanthan gum

720 g egg whites

Mix the milk with the cream in a saucepan and bring to the boil. Beat the egg yolks with the sugar and xanthan gum, add to the cream and milk and heat the mixture to 85°C. Pour the hot mixture over the chocolates and praline in a bowl and mix with a whisk. Cool quickly by placing the bowl in an ice bath.

When cold, add the egg whites and beat with a hand-held blender. Fill a siphon with 650 g of mixture, insert three gas cartridges and set aside.

For the microwave chocolate sponge cake

600 g 70% cacao chocolate

625 g egg whites

400 g egg yolks

5 g salt

100 g plain flour

3 g cocoa powder

400 g sugar

10 g baking powder

Melt the chocolate and keep at 45°C. Use a hand-held blender to incorporate the egg whites and yolks, then add the salt, flour, cocoa powder, sugar and baking powder. Mix until smooth. Strain, fill a 1-litre capacity siphon with the 650 g of the mixture and insert three gas cartridges.

Pipe the mixture into 33-ml capacity plastic cups, filling halfway. Cook in a microwave on high power for 45 seconds.

Place the cups upside down on a rack and leave to cool. When cool, unmould the sponge cakes and cut into 1.5-cm cubes. Set aside in an airtight container at room temperature.

For the chocolate caramel

1 kg fondant

500 g glucose

500 g isomalt

200 g 64% cacao chocolate

Combine the fondant, isomalt and glucose in a saucepan and heat to 135°C. Add 22 drops of citric acid and heat the mixture to 160°C. Incorporate the chocolate when the temperature of the mixture falls to 145°C, mixing well.

Turn out the chocolate caramel and roll out as thinly as possible between two sheets of silicone paper. Cut into 2-cm squares and set aside.

For the chocolate sauce

320 g cream

560 g water

800 g sugar

320 g cocoa powder

Mix the cream, water and sugar together in a saucepan and bring to the boil. Remove from the heat, add the cocoa powder and mix with a hand-held blender. Strain and set aside in the refrigerator.

For the chocolate ice cream

392 g water

682 g whole milk

78 g cream

80 g cocoa powder

360 g dextrose

60 g sugar

14 g ice-cream stabiliser

74 g skimmed milk powder

60 g inverted sugar

200 g 70% cacao chocolate couverture

Mix the water, milk, cream, cocoa powder, sugar and dextrose together in a saucepan and heat to 40°C. Add the stabiliser, milk powder and inverted sugar, mix and heat to 85°C.

Pour over the chocolate couverture and mix with a hand-held blender. Strain and leave to rest for at least 12 hours in the refrigerator. Churn in an ice-cream maker.

For the chocolate sorbet

2.740 kg water

900 g sugar

159 g inverted sugar

100 g dextrose

600 g 66% cacao chocolate couverture

600 g cocoa powder

200 g liquid glycerine

400 g vodka

Mix the water with the sugar, inverted sugar and dextrose together in a saucepan and bring to the boil. Pour the hot mixture over the chocolate couverture and cocoa powder. Cool in the refrigerator. Mix the glycerine with the vodka, then incorporate the cold chocolate mixture. Strain and leave to rest for at least 12 hours in the refrigerator. Churn in an ice-cream maker.

For the chocolate granita

400 g water

2 gelatine leaves

50 g 66% cacao chocolate couverture

10 g cocoa powder

20 g mandarin liqueur

Bring the water to the boil and add the softened gelatine leaves. Pour the hot mixture over the chocolate couverture and cocoa powder, mixing with a hand-held blender. Incorporate the mandarin liqueur. Strain the mixture and pour to a depth of 1 cm into 5 x 2.5-cm moulds. Freeze.

For the sugar-coated cacao nibs

20 g water
50 g sugar
100 g cacao nibs

Combine the water and sugar in a pan and bring to the boil. Remove from the heat and add the cocoa nibs while stirring with a wooden spoon until the sugar sticks to the nibs. Remove the sugar-coated nibs from the pan and drain. Then spread over silicone paper and leave to cool. Set aside.

For the rosemary oil

100 g sunflower oil
20 g rosemary

Combine the oil with the rosemary in a bag and vacuum seal at 100%. Heat in a Roner water bath at 60ºC for 3 hours. Strain, leave to cool and set aside.

For the chilli oil

100 g sunflower oil
12 g chilli pepper

Combine the oil with the chilli in a bag and vacuum seal at 100%. Heat in a Roner water bath at 60ºC for 3 hours. Strain, leave to cool and set aside.

For the ginger oil

100 g sunflower oil
30 g ginger

Combine the oil with the ginger in a bag and vacuum seal at 100%. Heat in a Roner water bath at 60ºC for 3 hours. Strain, leave to cool and set aside.

Assembly and finishing

Peta zetas (popping candy)
Cacao nibs

Arrange the components on a plate anarchically.

2
CACAO'S JOURNEY HOME

THE AMAZON RAINFOREST AND THE THREE CIRCLES OF CACAO

THE BIRTHPLACE OF CACAO IS TO BE FOUND in the Amazon rainforest for anybody who seeks it. It is the only possible destination for a journey that seeks to find its roots. We need to know the reality that is not evident in a pastry kitchen, or even in a chocolate production facility, where it tends to be drowned out by the clamour of the conching machine. In order to find it, we have to follow the trail that leads to the Amazon.

Somewhere within the largest tropical rainforest on the planet is the original home of cacao. It is said to lie in the north-western part of the Amazon region, but it is impossible to locate it accurately in an area covering seven million square kilometres and traversing the borders of nine countries; and although the region shrinks a little more every day – more than 800,000 km² of forest has been lost since 1970 – there are still large areas that remain unexplored. This is the birthplace of cacao, and from here it spread north to conquer the different Mesoamerican peoples, who raised it to great heights and paved the way to its international recognition.

The Arhuacos, Awajúns, Wampis and other native peoples are the guardians of the first of the three circles that describe the journey made by the Amazonian cacao. This is the central circle, which includes the heart of the rainforest and areas which, for one reason or another, have remained on the sidelines of so-called civilisation. In some cases, drug trafficking was the reason behind the barriers existing between established society and these communities, or with the rainforest itself. In other cases, the reason was the existence of paramilitary groups or terrorism, while in others it was distance and obscurity. As these barriers began to fall, the rainforest began to reveal part of the incredible treasure that it still harbours, in the form of Criollo cacaos, which are destined to set the tone for the new directions taken by the chocolate industry. It is the inner circle of Amazonian cacao, the point that defines a major part of the future of chocolate.

The second circle actually encompasses the areas where the great barriers were once raised, regions formally devoted to the growing of coca leaves or those previously oppressed by war and the drug trade. These lands have been earmarked for coffee and cacao cultivation by international cooperation programmes. They

THIS IS THE BIRTHPLACE OF CACAO, AND FROM HERE IT SPREAD NORTH TO CONQUER DIFFERENT CULTURES, WHO RAISED IT TO GREAT HEIGHTS.

THE ARHUACO, AWAJÚN, WAMPI AND OTHER NATIVE PEOPLES
ARE THE GUARDIANS OF THE FIRST OF THE THREE CIRCLES
THAT DESCRIBE THE JOURNEY MADE BY CACAO.

FINDINGS WERE MADE OF
CEREMONIAL POTS WITH THE
REMAINS OF PREPARATIONS
MADE USING CACAO BEANS.

are the site of the cacao plantations that have expanded in the last 15 to 20 years in association with the programmes put in place by international organisations and development agencies, such as the United States Agency for International Development (USAID). This second circle is dominated by clones, led by the plague of CCN-51, the preferred cultivar of agencies and governments. It is fast-growing and brings in revenue in the short term; it is more resistant to pests and it produces high yields. However, it is at a disadvantage in terms of quality and market price, subjecting growers to the dictates of buyers and the large chocolate manufacturing companies. These varieties are increasingly being replaced in Peru and Colombia.

The third circle of Amazonian cacao extends far beyond its birthplace in the rainforest, encompassing the places to which it has spread over the last 300 to 350 years, driven by the success of chocolate in the courts of Europe and subsequent popular demand, elevated in the nineteenth century by the consequences of the booming Swiss chocolate industry. The introduction of cacao to these areas was decided by their proximity to the sea and to ports that made the processing of the cacao and shipping to Europe easier and cheaper. Piura and Tumbes, with their white cacaos, are the most notable example, with their cacao plantations coinciding in time with the boom in rubber, later abandoned after the rise of African cacao plantations, and revived in the course of the last decade by market demand for quality cacao.

Cacao's first great journey

It is not clear when cacao began its journey through the jungle that covers today's Central America until it definitively made a home for itself in Guatemala and southern Mexico. It has been there ever since, which is the same as saying that it has practically always been there, associated with the lives of the native peoples who still inhabit a part of their ancient lands. We can see this in Bocas del Toro, Panama, with increasing importance in the life of the Ngobe people, and a little to the north, in the Talamanca Valley of Costa Rica, where it has been a part of the culture of the Bribri people for thousands of years. The connection between these ancient growers and cacao remains alive and has been saved after long years of hardship, which in some cases brought it to the verge of extinction. The Mayangna people who inhabit the Bosawas Biosphere Reserve in northern Nicaragua retain their links to cacao, as is the case across the present-day border with Honduras with the indigenous Pech communities who live in the southern regions, and nearby, with the Q'eqchi people who tend their cacao crops around Lake Lachua in Guatemala. Beyond, in the Mexican states of Oaxaca, Tabasco, Veracruz and

Chiapas, are the Chinantecs, Mochos, Zapotecs and Chontals, people who preserve their traditional beverages – *popo, chorote, puzunque, tejatre* and *bupu*, among others – made from cacao.

There is no evidence of the first migratory journey taken by cacao towards the rainforests of North America, but it must have been much earlier than the earliest dates recorded. In these lands they correspond to those of the ceramic pots found at the excavations carried out in Macaval, in the municipality of Hidalgotitlán, in the state of Veracruz. These excavations brought forth ceremonial objects, jewels and carvings, and among them a number of ceramic pots used to store liquids and beverages. Radiocarbon dating determined that they were from about 1750 BC, while subsequent ultra-violet radiation analysis of the contents of one of the pots showed the remains of a component of cacao known as theobromine. It was a fantastic discovery proving that beverages had been made from cacao by people of the Olmec culture of the time, allowing them to be dated back some 3,800 years. Other findings were made of ceremonial pots with the remains of preparations made using cacao beans, such as those from the Cerro Manatí and Puerto Escondido sites of Honduras, but they were from a later date. The archaeological evidence, corresponding to different historical periods prior to the arrival of the first Spaniards, is repeated in Belize, Guatemala, Honduras and in different parts of Mexico.

The Mesoamerican cultures transformed cacao beans into a mystical beverage

THE SECOND CIRCLE ENCOMPASSES AREAS PREVIOUSLY DEVOTED TO THE GROWING OF COCA LEAVES OR OPPRESSED BY WAR.

that was able to connect different worlds and dimensions. The Olmecs taught the cultivation and use of cacao to the Mayans, who took it to other areas of Mesoamerica, and they worshipped a god of cacao, Ek Chuah, whose rule was also extended to war and merchants. Bravery, pain and prosperity combined in a single fruit. Testimony of all these certainties is spread over time and through the different discoveries, including the first written representation of the word 'cacao'. It was part of a label found on a Mayan drinking vessel, used by their leaders, and contained the three signs corresponding to the phonetic particles *ka-ka-wa*. Researchers consider it to be the synthesis of two phonemes of the Mayan tongue spoken in the Yucatán Peninsula *kaj* ('bitter') and *kab* ('juice'), associated with the pots found in the Tikal region, part of the Guatemalan region of Petén.

Described as the origin of a number of ritual beverages reserved for nobles and priests, cacao would reach the height of its importance when the Aztecs made the cacao bean their currency and expanded its use throughout all the kingdoms of Central America. According to Gonzalo Fernández de Oviedo, a seventeenth century writer and historian, this was the case among the Nicarao people: 'One rabbit is worth ten beans; four beans will obtain eight pieces of the fruit called *munoncapot*; ten will buy the company of a lady; and a slave is worth more or less one hundred beans'. The Aztecs must have experienced a high rate of inflation, because the account by another historian, the missionary friar Toribio de Benavente, puts the value of a rabbit at 30 cacao beans and the favours of a woman at a figure that could vary between 20 and 50 beans, while a slave able to read and write was valued at 2,500 beans, and could even go as high as 4,000 cacao beans.

The quest for gold by the Spanish conquistadors would, more often than not, end in disappointment, as the closely guarded treasure houses of the indigenous peoples tended to be filled only with piles of sacks filled with cacao beans. They quickly understood the significance of this, and they spread the cultivation of cacao throughout the Chiapas region of Mexico as the basis for speculation. Cacao was in fact a treasure that affected almost every aspect of Aztec life. It was the core of ritual ceremonies, legal tender for trade and a source of food and medicine. The Aztecs divided cacao beans into four categories, basing their value on their size and condition. The three largest categories were used for trading and the payment of contracts, while the smallest, oldest and most deteriorated were used for the preparation of beverages.

There are written references to a beverage called 'precious water', which

THE MESOAMERICAN CULTURES TRANSFORMED CACAO BEANS INTO A
MYSTICAL BEVERAGE THAT WAS ABLE TO CONNECT DIFFERENT WORLDS
AND DIMENSIONS.

combined roasted and ground cacao with honey, chilli water and different herbs. While the Mayans drank it cold, the Aztecs served it hot or warm. Simpler versions are also mentioned that combined vanilla, cacao and annatto (achiote), turning it a bright red colour. The Mayans found a way of growing these ingredients together, and would later add new ingredients, including chilli peppers.

A temple to change the course of history

Most researchers insist that cacao's first journey between the Amazon rainforest and the jungles of Mesoamerica was in the form of a wild plant or fruit, and that it was only when it reached its destination that it was domesticated and transformed. Contradicting this belief, however, are the commercial links between modern-day Guatemala and Mexico achieved through the mastery of seafaring by the Machalilla culture that developed on the coast of present-day Ecuador between 1800 and 1000 BC, to which some attribute part of the responsibility of the spread of cacao towards the north. The signs and references were so overwhelming that few could question what was still considered a hypothesis until the discovery of a strange temple in the canton of Palanda, in the Ecuadorian province of Zamora Chinchipe, located in the valley of the River Chinchipe, whose waters twist and turn along the border between Peru and Ecuador before flowing into the River Marañón. The temple was excavated by the archaeologist Francisco Valdez, who in 2014 completed twelve years of campaigns to reveal a strange structure topped by an ascending spiral ending in a tomb where, among other artefacts, a ceremonial vessel was kept. Traces inside the container were identified by laboratory analysis to be the remains of a beverage that contained cacao. Another receptacle was also found to contain a granule of cacao starch, which suggests a process of cooking or toasting. The information provided by radiocarbon dating has changed everything known until now, as it dates this starch particle back some 5,300 years to between 3500 and 3350 BC. The analysis was performed by Dr Sonia Zarrillo of the University of Calgary, Canada, between 2010 and 2011. In subsequent sampling, Dr Claire Lanaud was able to recover and sequence the DNA of the cacao found, dating the specimens to between 2265 and 1885 BC.

The temple, attributed to what is known as the Mayo-Chinchipe culture, reveals that cacao was domesticated and grown in the Amazon region long before beginning its journey north. Moreover, cacao was given a ceremonial use by this culture some 1,500 years before the first evidence was found of this taking place in Mesoamerica. Later representations of cacao have appeared among other cultures that inhabited the territory of modern-day Ecuador and coincide in history with

THE TEMPLE DISCOVERED IN MONTEGRANDE, NEAR THE TOWN OF JAÉN IN PERU, IS THE TWIN OF THE ONE EXCAVATED IN PALANDA, ECUADOR. IT DATES BACK MORE THAN 5,000 YEARS.

the Olmecs, such as the Chorrera people (1500–500 BC).

This is story written on both sides of the border between Ecuador and Peru, in an area bound by the valleys of the rivers Chinchipe, Marañón and Utcubamba. Six thousand years ago, it was dominated by a highly advanced culture of which there was barely any visible trace until the unearthing of the Palanda temple. The discovery in Ecuador was followed a few years later with a finding on an unusual hill overlooking the town of Jaén in Peru. The place in question is called Montegrande.

In 2009, the Peruvian archaeologist Quirino Olivera began to excavate this site and found the remains of monumental public architecture incredibly similar to those found in Palanda a few years earlier. The dig was prolonged until 2012 to expose a twin temple, although much larger in size. As had happened with the temple discovered in Ecuador, the building had been sealed and covered over by the same culture that had built it, and the summit of the temple contained an intact tomb, which was that of the figure occupying the apex of the local religious

hierarchy. Owing to lack of sufficient funding that would allow the tomb to be opened or a roof built to protect it, the temple was again covered over. In 2013, the Montegrande temple was distinguished at the Shanghai Archaeology Forum as one of the ten major archaeological field-discoveries in the world that year. Completion of the excavation is on hold until funding can be arranged.

Through chance and history, cacao has preserved the aura of magic with which is was held by ancient peoples. Remarkably, it is both elusive and reliable, laid bare while concealing part of its identity. I often think that its life is parallel to that of the Amazon rainforest, and in the same way, we will never fully come to know it.

Cacao became chocolate

It is highly unlikely that Christopher Columbus or his crew became acquainted with the existence of cacao, at least on their first three voyages to the New World. Until the third, Columbus had never set foot on the mainland, and when he did it was on the coast of modern-day Venezuela, quite a distance from the areas under

CACAO WAS TRANSFORMED INTO CHOCOLATE DURING THE FIRST HALF OF THE SIXTEENTH CENTURY, WHEN IT WAS COMBINED WITH SUGAR.

the influence of cacao and *xocolatl*. There is recorded testimony of an encounter made on his fourth voyage – the first that led him to reach Central America, on 17 July 1502 – although it would appear that it did not take place on dry land, but upon inspecting a canoe that had set off from the Yucatán Peninsula, on which cacao beans were found, used as currency.

The first documentary evidence connected with the arrival of cacao at the Spanish court dates from 1544, where it is included as part of the offering presented to Prince Philip during the visit by the delegation of Q'eqches, a Mayan people from what is now the inland Alto Verapaz region of Guatemala, who had been pacified by the preaching and certain complementary measures taken by the Dominican friar Bartolomé de las Casas. Featured in the list of gifts brought by the delegation were 2,000 quetzal feathers, decorated pots and certain food products, including chilli peppers, beans, maize and copal. They also served the prince a frothy beverage called *xocolatl*, which Spanish chroniclers began to transcribe from the Nahuatl language into Spanish, turning it into *chocolate*. It was both bitter and spicy, resulting in the lack of interest shown to it by the court.

The date of the official visit by the Q'eqches has caused some discrepancies with the history of the other chocolate, the one that was born in Europe from the meeting of cacao and sugar. Conflicting accounts place this event at an earlier time, either in the kitchen of a religious institution in Oaxaca, Mexico (1529), which would in time become the convent of Santa Catalina de Siena, or in the kitchen of the Cistercian monastery of Monasterio de Piedra, in Aragon (1534). According to historical records, the first cacao beans were sent by the friar Jerónimo de Aguilar. They were sent, together with the recipe for *xocolatl*, to the abbot of Monasterio de Piedra, Antonio de Álvaro. The fusion between those beans and the interpretation of the recipe would give rise to the first chocolate of the modern age. The vanilla was retained; cinnamon was added as a flavouring; and, most importantly of all, sugar was added to neutralise the bitterness. The popularity of the recipe led this beverage to spread to other monasteries of the order, and it soon reached the different royal courts of Europe.

Chocolate became an established part of life at the Spanish court at the end of the sixteenth century, from where it was taken to Italy in 1606 by the merchant Francesco Carletti. This new fashion was soon adopted by European royalty. It is said to have reached France in 1615. The first accounts to place it at the English court date from 1657, where it was enthusiastically received. Through the networks of a growing empire, chocolate reached the British colonies in North America, creating in the course of the eighteenth century a new leg for this almost endless journeying back and forth by cacao since its birth.

Chocolate became fashionable, and cacao had lost none of the mystical sense that was attributed to it in the New World. The botanist Linnaeus presented it as 'food of the gods', translated into Greek as *Theobroma*, in his work *Species Plantarum* (1753), and the reputation of the plant was definitively established. It became a part of life for the European upper classes, to the point where it was mentioned in a number of works by Calderón de la Barca, including *'Tis Well It's No Worse*; it was referenced by Alexandre Dumas; and it was allocated a place among the ingredients for the banquet ordered by the Marquis de Sade in *The 120 Days of Sodom*.

Chocolate becomes Swiss

The first factory producing solid chocolate opened in Turin in 1800. Historical accounts speak of a city steeped in chocolate, and it drew the attention of professionals and enthusiasts from all over Europe. Chocolate factories mushroomed and they became centres for the dissemination of the new, more refined and increasingly popular methods. One of the factories trained a young Swiss man named François Louis Callier, who returned to the canton of Vaud and opened the first chocolate factory in Switzerland. It was located in Corsier, near the town of Vevey, and it played a major role in the development of automated production processes, which allowed costs to be reduced and laid the foundations for the consumption of chocolate by the masses.

The Callier factory was the starting point of the race that would lead to the opening of a large number of factories that have left their mark on the history of chocolate. Philippe Suchard opened his factory in Neuchâtel in 1825; the German-born industrialist Henri Nestlé would open his own in Vevey in 1866; and a year later, in 1867, a Paris-trained confectioner named Jean Tobler would set up in Bern, giving the world the legendary Toblerone forty years later. Rodolphe Lindt would be the last great name from this list to enter the chocolate industry. He did so in 1879, choosing Bern as the location for his business.

These men were responsible for some of the events that would define the development of the industry. Production processes were automated; cocoa butter was separated from the cacao liquor and added to the chocolate; conching was developed to smooth out the texture; and a way was found that would revolutionise the chocolate market: the addition of milk. The idea belonged to the Swiss Daniel Peter, a collaborator of Henri Nestlé's who began with another of his own inventions, which he called 'condensed milk'. The use of milk made production cheaper and expanded the market, making it a smooth, easy-to-eat and familiar product.

A RECENT TIMELINE FOR CHOCOLATE

1780

The first chocolate-making machine is built in Barcelona.

1800

The first solid chocolate is made in Turin.

1806

Gianduja, chocolate combined with hazelnut butter, is invented in Italy.

1819

François Louis Cailler founds the first Swiss chocolate factory in Vevey.

1820

The first bar of chocolate as we know it today is made in England.

1825

Philippe Suchard opens his chocolate factory in Neuchâtel and invents the *melangeur* for mixing chocolate.

1868

Cadbury launches the first box of chocolates.

1875

The Swiss Daniel Peter adds milk to the chocolate mixture.

1879

Rodolphe Lindt develops the conching process with the invention of the conche, a machine that aerates and smooths out the mixture.

1882

Hermann Emil Fisher synthesises theobromine.

1895

Louis Dufour invents the chocolate truffle in Chambéry, France.

1908

Toblerone is born.

1828

Casparus van Houten patents a hydraulic press, allowing cacao nibs to be ground down. The result is cocoa powder.

1828

Cocoa butter is separated from the cacao liquor.

1830

Charles Amédée Kohler invents the first solid chocolate with hazelnuts.

1832

Franz Sacher creates the *Sachertorte*.

1841

Theobromine, an alkaloid contained in the cacao bean, is isolated in a laboratory.

1847

Fry & Sons produces the first dark chocolate bar in England.

1912

Jean Neuhaus invents the praline (ganache-filled chocolate bonbon) in Brussels.

1921

Christian Nelson makes the first chocolate-covered ice-cream bar in Onawa, Iowa.

1930

First white chocolate.

1986

Valrhona presents Guanaja 70%, the first chocolate to have a cacao content greater than 55%.

1990

Valrhona creates Manjari, the first commercially produced single-origin chocolate.

1996

Manufacture Cluizel launches Los Ancones, the first single-estate chocolate.

CACAO'S SECOND GREAT JOURNEY

CACAO HAS NEVER CEASED to travel. Cacao took its first leap to the neighbouring Caribbean islands in the sixteenth century. Trinidad and Tobago and Cuba were its first destinations, followed soon afterwards by plantations being set up in the Portuguese territory of Brazil. It was then that an interesting process began whereby cacao made the journey back to the places where it originated. The Spanish colonies in the New World created their first cacao plantations stocked with varieties from the former Aztec and Mayan lands. This occurred in Colombia, where the plantations flourished in regions such as Cauca, leading to the intense commercial activity that would drive development in the port city of Cartagena, and in the coastal valleys of Venezuela, from where Mexican markets were served via the port of Veracruz. In 1650 alone, 250 tonnes of cacao were exported from Venezuela to what was then known as New Spain.

During the seventeenth century, the French expanded cacao cultivation around the Caribbean, to the island of Hispaniola and Grenada, while the Spanish sent the first plants to the Philippines and Indonesia, both in Asia. This migratory movement multiplied in the eighteenth century. The British and the Dutch concentrated their efforts in Asia (India, Ceylon, Indonesia and Malaysia), whereas the French concentrated on their Caribbean colonies (Martinique and Saint Lucia). The first cacao plantations appeared in Africa during the nineteenth century, following the course taken in other colonies established by the great European powers. The French took it to Ivory Coast and Madagascar, the British to Ghana, the Germans to Cameroon, and the Portuguese to São Tomé and Príncipe, and Bioko. The French rounded off the presence of cacao in Asia by introducing it in Vietnam. Cacao had needed thousands of years to journey through the jungles of the Americas, but it took barely three centuries for it to circle the globe.

Some of these countries have become leading cacao producers, although most of them are not known for the quality of their products. They specialise in high yields and low prices in order to supply less selective markets. Ghana, Indonesia and Ivory Coast are the giants of the sector. Together, the three countries account for 72 per cent of world production, according to the UN Food and Agriculture Organization (FAO) statistics for 2016. Nonetheless, they are at the bottom of the list in the production of fine cacao. Indonesia scarcely produces one per cent

THE SPANISH COLONIES IN THE NEW WORLD CREATED THEIR FIRST CACAO PLANTATIONS WITH VARIETIES FROM THE AZTEC AND MAYAN LANDS.

IVORY COAST	34%
GHANA	21%
INDONESIA	17%
BRAZIL	7%
CAMEROON	6%
NIGERIA	6%
ECUADOR	4%
PERU	2%
OTHERS	9%

in this field, while Ghana and Ivory Coast do not even make it into the statistics.

World cacao production skyrocketed to 4.733 billion tonnes in 2017, an increase of about 600,000 tonnes on the previous year, leading to a reduction in price at origin of about 41 per cent. Like coffee and sugar, the benchmark prices for most cacao production are set on the futures market. The drought that affected several African regions in 2014 and 2015 led to a drop in production, which caused prices to rise and new plantations to be created. The excellent forecasts for 2016 harvests, the entry into production of new plantations and speculation by hedge funds caused prices to weaken, but not the market.

The world of cacao is a giant with feet of clay, accustomed to mistreating the people who keep it going, in other words, the millions of small and medium growers. The truth is that the price of a kilogram of fine cacao, for which a price of between one and two dollars is paid to most Latin American plantations, can be multiplied by ten by the time it reaches a buyer in Spain. The price at destination can reach 12.5 dollars per kilogram. The large buyers, who negotiate directly at origin and handle large volumes, save themselves having to pay these extra charges and increase their profits without passing anything on to the growers.

The statistics provided by the Latin American Cocoa Initiative (ILAC), developed by the Development Bank of Latin America (CAF), are significant. Ninety per cent of the cacao produced in Latin America comes from small-scale family holdings of less than five hectares. If we apply this to the ILAC analysis framework (Ecuador, Peru, Bolivia, Brazil, Mexico, Puerto Rico, Trinidad and Tobago, Panama and the Dominican Republic), it means that for a surface area of 1.865 billion hectares, 329,607 growers harvested, processed and sold 723,380 tonnes of dried beans. It is estimated that activity in this sector affects the lives of three million Latin Americans.

The world is changing and the demand for cacao continues to rise. The incorporation of the major Asian markets to the consumption of chocolate and the social development taking place in Latin America and certain regions of Africa, together with the growing demand for cocoa butter from the cosmetic and pharmaceutical industries, is driving the constant growth in demand. The International Cocoa Organization (ICCO) estimates that this upward trend will be sustained in the coming years, far outgrowing the possibilities of the market, with a resulting increase in international prices. Their forecast for the 2022–2023 period is that a tonne of cacao will reach the price of 3,700 dollars (on 18 June 2018, the futures market set a price for cacao at 2,446 dollars), which does not actually mean much. This affects the commodities market, which is built on speculation. The reality is to be found with the cacao plantations, and what they tell us is that there is life beyond the futures market. The key is the value added that comes with quality. Latin America is the world's leading producer of fine cacaos.

On one side of the world of cacao, the large companies decide on the lives of the growers, and they set prices and conditions. On the other side, the injustice is committed on a small scale, starting with the most remote cacao growers, who are always the most vulnerable. Its instrument is the buyer, an often shadowy figure who operates on a small scale, one grower at a time, and whose business has little concern for quality. Buyers always set a low price for the baba – the freshly harvested cacao beans with the external fruit flesh – and a slightly higher price for the dried beans, regardless of the fermentation process or drying conditions. The state of the beans is of least concern to them. The greater the distance and remoteness of the grower, the less money that is paid.

CHOCOLATE
CLASSICS

Serves 20

173 g eggs
227 g sugar
216 g softened
  unsalted butter
135 g 70% cacao
  chocolate
142 g roasted walnuts
108 g plain flour
1.3 g salt

CHOCOLATE BROWNIE

Beat the eggs with the sugar until thick and pale.

Mix the butter with the chocolate in a saucepan over a low heat. The mixture should not turn to liquid. Chop the walnuts and set aside.

Gently mix the beaten eggs, half at a time, with the butter and chocolate mixture. Incorporate the sifted flour and the salt. Add the walnuts. Pour the mixture into a 20 x 30-cm cake tin and bake at 180ºC for 15 minutes.

Cut and serve.

113 g unsalted butter
100 g sugar
100 g cane sugar
60 g pasteurised egg
160 g plain flour
3 g bicarbonate of soda
150 g roasted
  hazelnuts
3 g salt
15 g cornflour
225 g 44% cacao
  chocolate chips

CHOCOLATE CHIP COOKIES

Mix all the ingredients together, except the chocolate chips, to a smooth dough. Finally, add the chocolate chips. Chill the dough a little in the refrigerator, then roll into 35-g balls. Rest in the refrigerator for 10 minutes. Arrange on a baking tray and bake at 170ºC for 15–18 minutes.

Chocolate core
275 g couverture
  chocolate
310 g water
86 g inverted sugar
0.3 g xanthan gum

Chocolate fondant
201 g 70% cacao
  couverture
  chocolate
13 g sunflower oil
54 g chestnut flour
54 g ground almonds
121 g sugar
80 g egg yolks
107 g egg whites
Chocolate cores
  (previously prepared)

CHOCOLATE FONDANT

For the chocolate core

Combine the water and inverted sugar in a saucepan and heat to 70ºC. Pour the mixture over the chocolate and whisk with a hand-held blender. Add the xanthan gum and whisk until smooth. Fill the cavities of a Flexipan cylinder mould with the mixture and freeze.

For the chocolate fondant

Melt the chocolate, together with the sunflower oil, in a saucepan at 50ºC. Mix the chestnut flour and ground almonds together in a bowl. In the bowl of a mixer fitted with a flat beater, mix together the sugar, egg yolks and egg whites. Gradually add the chocolate and flour mixture, alternating with the sunflower oil, until fully incorporated. Mix until smooth.

Fill 6-cm-diameter and 5-cm-deep cylinder moulds halfway with the fondant batter, insert a frozen chocolate core, and finish filling with batter. Bake at 180ºC for 8 minutes.

Assembly and finishing

Serve on a plate topped with a scoop of ice cream.

This recipe is a version of the original by Michel Bras. We have removed both dairy and gluten, making it suitable for most food intolerances.

70% cacao chocolate pastry cream
50 g pasteurised egg
  yolks
22 g cornflour
253 g cold milk
63 g cream (35% fat)
63 g sugar
95 g 70% cacao
  chocolate

Chocolate croissants
301 g medium-strength
  flour
68 g sugar
17 g salt
36 g fresh yeast
365 g organic milk
274 g strong flour
27 g cocoa powder
365 g unsalted butter
1 egg for glazing

Assembly and finishing
Neutral glaze
Cacao nibs

CHOCOLATE CROISSANT

For the 70% cacao chocolate pastry cream

Mix the egg yolks with the cornflour and a little cold milk. Strain and set aside.

Combine the remaining milk with the cream and sugar in a saucepan and bring to the boil. Remove from the heat, cover with a lid and leave to stand for 20 minutes. Strain and mix in the egg and cornflour mixture. Return to the heat and bring back to the boil. Remove from the heat and add the chopped chocolate. Mix until the chocolate melts. Pour the pastry cream into a tray, cover with cling film in direct contact and set aside in the refrigerator.

For the chocolate croissants

Combine all the ingredients, except the butter, in the bowl of a mixer fitted with a flat beater and mix on medium speed for 5 minutes. The dough should be even but a little rough. Wrap the dough in cling film and freeze for 24 hours. Thaw out the dough in the refrigerator for a few hours. In the meantime cut the butter into a rectangle and leave to soften until pliable.

Roll out the dough into a rectangle, place the rectangle of butter over the dough and fold over the two longer sides to encase. Give the dough one double turn (book fold), followed by one single turn (letter fold) without resting in between.

Wrap the dough in cling film and rest in the refrigerator for 90 minutes. Roll into the desired size and cut out and roll into croissants.

Freeze for 1 hour, wrap in cling film and freeze again. They can be stored frozen for up to 1 month.

Assembly and finishing

Thaw out the croissants for a few hours in the refrigerator. Arrange on a baking tray and prove for 1 hour 45 minutes at 28°C.

Brush with egg and bake at 180°C for 18 minutes. Leave to cool for a few minutes, brush with the neutral glaze and decorate with cacao nibs.

Put back into the oven for 1 minute at 180°C until the glaze melts. When at room temperature, fill with the chocolate pastry cream and serve.

Makes 10

150 g 70% cacao
  chocolate couverture
200 g unsalted butter
500 g pasteurised egg
  whites
500 g sugar
200 g ground almonds
200 g plain flour
24 g baking powder
0.5 g salt
Cacao nibs

CHOCOLATE FINANCIER

Melt the chocolate in a saucepan with the butter, heating to 40ºC. Whisk the egg whites with the sugar in a bowl. Sift the ground almonds with the flour and baking powder into another bowl. Add the melted chocolate and butter to the dry ingredients and mix well. Add the salt and fold in the beaten egg whites. Fill piping bags and set aside.

Pipe the batter into moulds. Sprinkle the top with cacao nibs and bake for 5 minutes at 195ºC with 0% humidity and medium fan speed. Allow to cool and arrange on a plate.

6 egg yolks
2 eggs
150 g sugar
800 g milk
200 g cream
200 g 75 % cacao
  chocolate couverture

CHOCOLATE POTS

Mix the egg yolks with the whole eggs and sugar in a bowl. Combine the milk with cream in a saucepan and bring to the boil. Remove from the heat and mix with the egg and sugar mixture. Add the chocolate and mix until melted. Filter the mixture through a fine-mesh sieve and fill ramekins; in our case, we use small glass jars. Bake for 45 minutes at 95°C and set aside in the refrigerator.

78 g eggs
155 g sugar
124 g plain flour
8 g baking powder
185 g milk
92 g 65% cacao
    chocolate
108 g olive oil

CHOCOLATE MAGDALENAS (SPANISH MUFFINS)

Beat the eggs with the sugar.

Mix the flour with the baking powder.

Bring the milk to the boil in a saucepan and pour over the chocolate in a bowl. Whisk, add the oil, and whisk again to the consistency of mayonnaise. Set aside.

Add the flour and baking powder mixture a third at a time to the beaten eggs, alternating each addition with the chocolate mixture, and mix until very smooth. Rest in the refrigerator for 24 hours.

Fill a piping bag with the batter and pipe into the desired moulds. Bake at 200°C for 18–20 minutes.

SPONGE FINGERS

Makes 25

392 g pasteurised egg
   whites
215 g sugar
2 g salt
94 g pasteurised egg
   yolks
196 g plain flour
59 g ground almonds
39 g cocoa powder
3 g baking powder
2 g grated lemon zest

*Assembly and
finishing*
Icing sugar

Beat the egg whites with the sugar and salt. Fold the yolks into the beaten egg whites. Sift the flour, ground almonds, cocoa powder and baking powder, and fold in together with the lemon zest. Fill a piping bag and pipe biscuits of the desired size over a baking tray lined with a silicone mat.

Bake at 200°C for 4–5 minutes until they begin to turn golden. Leave to cool and set aside.

Finish by dusting with icing sugar.

Makes 25

Chocolate pastry cream
346 g milk
30 g cornflour
69 g egg yolks
86 g cream (35% fat)
86 g sugar
0.4 g lemon zest
0.4 g cinnamon stick
129 g 65% cacao chocolate

Chocolate puff pastry
272 g plain flour
49 g strong flour
18 g unsalted butter
198 g still mineral water
9 g salt
49 g cocoa powder
31 g roasted hazelnut butter
371 g unsalted butter for folding

Assembly and finishing
Cocoa powder

CHOCOLATE MILLEFEUILLE

For the chocolate pastry cream

Mix a little cold milk with cornflour, dissolve well and add the egg yolks.

Combine the remaining milk with the cream, sugar, lemon zest and cinnamon in a saucepan and bring to the boil. Remove from the heat and leave to stand for 20 minutes.

Strain, heat again and add the milk, egg yolk and cornflour mixture. Bring to a gentle boil. Remove from the heat and add the chopped chocolate. Mix until the chocolate melts. Set aside in the refrigerator until time to use.

For the chocolate millefeuille

Mix the flours with the 18 g butter, water and salt in a mixing bowl. Add the cocoa powder and hazelnut butter. Knead for 4 minutes on very low speed to an even but rough dough.

Rest for 2 hours in the refrigerator before beginning the turning process. Roll out the dough into an even 30 x 20-cm rectangle. Roll out the butter into a 15 x 20-cm rectangle and chill in the refrigerator to a temperature of 10–12°C (the ideal temperature for incorporating into the very cold dough).

Lay the butter over the dough and encase. Give the dough five single turns: e.g. roll out the dough to a 60 x 20-cm rectangle and fold in three like a letter to obtain a 20 x 20-cm square with several alternating layers of dough and butter. Repeat the operation another 5 more times. Rest the dough for 1 hour in the refrigerator between each turn.

Then refrigerate for 24 hours. Roll out the dough to a 3–4-mm thickness. Cut into 10 x 4-cm rectangles and bake at 160°C for 40 minutes.

Assembly and finishing

After baking the puff pastry and chilling the pastry cream, assemble the millefeuille comprising 3 layers of pastry and 2 layers of pastry cream. Finish by dusting with a little cocoa powder.

Liquid jelly
300 g water
3 g agar-agar
50 g glucose

Chocolate²

Meringue
175 g egg whites
75 g glucose
A pinch of salt

CHOCOLATE MOUSSE

For the liquid jelly
Mix all the cold ingredients together in a saucepan and bring to the boil. Leave to cool at room temperature.

Once the jelly sets, blend in a Thermomix to a runny consistency.

For the chocolate²
Prepare 350 g using the proportions given on page 252.

For the meringue
Bring the egg whites to room temperature (20–25ºC). Whisk, adding the glucose and salt.

Assembly and finishing
Heat the liquid jelly to 40ºC.

Melt the chocolate at 40ºC.

Whisk the jelly with the chocolate. Gently fold in the meringue without deflating. Rest in the refrigerator for at least 2 hours.

Use a hot spoon to shape into a quenelle.

PAIN AU CHOCOLAT

*Yeast-leavened
laminated dough*
3 kg plain flour
3 kg strong flour
180 g salt
180 g sugar
4 kg milk
120 g fresh yeast
1 kg dry butter

*Water base for the
dark chocolate
ganache*
200 g still mineral
  water
180 g atomised
  glucose
2 g salt
1 g citric acid
11 g glycerine

*Dark chocolate
ganache*
260 g water base
240 g 72% cacao
  Madagascar
  chocolate
120 g sunflower oil

*Assembly and
finishing*
Extra virgin olive oil
Maldon salt flakes

For the yeast-leavened laminated dough
Put all the dry ingredients in the bowl of a kneader. Mix together thoroughly on low speed for 2 minutes. Heat 1 litre of milk to 35°C and dissolve the yeast. Add all the milk to the dough while still on low speed. When all the milk is absorbed, knead on medium-high speed.

Continue kneading until the gluten develops and the dough becomes elastic.

Divide the dough into four 2.6-kg portions. Knead each to make smooth, shape into balls, and place on trays and cover with cling film. Rest in the refrigerator for 5–6 hours.

Bring the dry butter to room temperature.

Cut the block of butter into four 260-g portions.

Roll out the dough into a square a little larger than a portion of butter. Place the butter on the dough and fold in each of the four corners to cover the butter. Give one double turn (book fold). Leave to rest, and then give one simple turn (letter fold).

For the water base
Mix all the ingredients together in a saucepan and bring to the boil.

For the dark chocolate ganache
Melt the chocolate at 40°C and heat the water base to 40°C.

Mix and then whisk.

Add the sunflower oil to the mixture and mix until smooth.

Assembly and finishing
Spread chocolate ganache over the rolled out dough sheets.

Roll up the dough sheets and cut into lengths weighing 40–45 g each.

Refrigerate overnight. The next day, prove the dough at 33°C in a combi oven for 1 hour with 10% moisture on combination steam and convection mode.

Bake at 180°C with 10% moisture on combination steam and convection mode for 12–15 minutes.

Drizzle with a little olive oil and season with a few salt flakes.

Sourdough
First stage
158 g strong flour
158 g water
Second stage
474 g strong flour
For the glaze
103 g ground almonds
267 g sugar
21 g cornflour
103 g pasteurised egg
  whites
7 g cocoa powder

Panettone
316 g sourdough
  (previously prepared)
1.11 kg strong flour
316 g sugar
555 g water
277 g egg yolks
333 g unsalted butter
316 g strong flour
24 g salt
166 g egg yolks
316 g sugar
111 g multiflower
  honey
8 g Bourbon vanilla
  extract
4 g ground vanilla
  powder
333 g unsalted butter
583 g candied orange
  peel, diced
277 g 36% cacao
  chocolate
277 g roasted hazelnut
  butter
40 g flaked almonds
50 g pearl sugar

GIANDUJA AND CHOCOLATE PANETTONE

For the sourdough

For the first stage work the flour with the water for about 5 minutes to a smooth dough. Leave it at room temperature for 10-15 days until it ferments.

In the second stage, make a dough with half the fermented dough and the 474 g of flour and leave for 24 hours at room temperature.

After this time, each time, knead in the same weight of flour as the weight of the fermented dough and also a weight of water equal to half the weight of the fermented dough and leave to stand for 4 hours. Repeat this process a few times until it ferments and triples in volume every 4 hours.

For the glaze

Mix all the ingredients together and whisk with a hand-held blender. Set aside in the refrigerator.

For the panettone

Set the kneader speed to medium and add the flour, sugar and water. When the mixture is even, add the sourdough and knead for 7 minutes. Over the next 3 minutes, gradually add the cold egg yolks. Once incorporated, continue to knead for 3 more minutes until very smooth. Next, gradually add the cold softened butter, and lower the kneader speed in the last 5 minutes. The ideal temperature of the dough should be 23°C.

Rest the dough at 28–30°C for 10–12 hours until it triples in volume.

Then transfer the dough to the kneader bowl, add the flour and salt, and knead for 8 minutes on speed setting 2. Gradually incorporate the egg yolks, sugar, honey and vanilla into the dough in 4 or 5 additions, kneading until the dough comes away from the sides of the bowl and is smooth, about 4 minutes.

Finally, add the cold but softened butter during the last 3 minutes.

When fully incorporated, add the candied orange peel, chocolate and hazelnut butter, and rest on the table for 20 minutes.

Weigh out 550 g of the resulting dough, shape into a ball and put into moulds. Prove for 7–10 hours at 28–30°C, until it rises to the top of the moulds.

Use a piping bag to cover each panettone with 50 g of glaze and decorate the surface with flaked almonds and pearl sugar.

For 550 g of dough, bake at 155°C for 35 minutes, 30 minutes with the vent closed and 5 minutes with the vent open. The panettone must go into the oven preheated to 190°C, because the temperature will fall as it is put inside.

When they come out of the oven, pierce stainless steel needles horizontally halfway down through the panettone, turn upside down and hang for 12 hours before serving.

Neutral glaze
1.333 kg water
933 g sugar
667 g glucose
53 g pectin NH
13 g lemon juice

Sponge cake
237 g unsalted butter
63 g icing sugar
237 g 70% cacao dark
 chocolate
114 g egg yolks
170 g egg whites
158 g sugar
119 g plain flour

Cherry gel
713 g wild cherry
 purée
16 g pectin
71 g sugar

*Tahitian vanilla
mousse*
3.750 kg cream (35%
 fat)
19 g Tahitian vanilla
 pods
376 g sugar
34 g gelatine leaves

*Assembly and
finishing*
Amarena cherries
Sponge cake
 (previously prepared)
12 cm x 4 cm x 5 cm
 moulds

BLACK FOREST GÂTEAU

For the neutral glaze
Mix all the ingredients together in a saucepan and bring to the boil.

For the sponge cake
Mix the still slightly cold butter with the icing sugar until fluffy. Gradually add the melted chocolate while continuing to mix, and add the yolks half or a third at a time. Beat the egg whites with the sugar, and then fold into the previous mixture. Sprinkle in the flour and sugar and incorporate. Pour 1.1 kg of batter into each mould and bake at 200ºC for 9 minutes.

For the cherry gel
Mix the sugar with the pectin and add to the hot purée in a pan. Bring to the boil, then transfer to a container and cool. Whisk the set jelly and pipe over the previously cut sponge cake (See Assembly, below).

For the Tahitian vanilla mousse
Bring 750 g of cream to the boil in a saucepan with the sugar and vanilla, and leave to infuse for a few hours. Heat the mixture to 60°C and dissolve the softened gelatine. Strain the pods and cool to 35°C. Whip the remaining cream to soft peaks. Mix a little into the infused cream, then add the rest. Use immediately.

Assembly and finishing
Cut the sponge cake to the desired size and pipe cherry gel to cover. Arrange pieces of Amarena cherries on top and freeze. Fill three-quarters of the moulds with the mousse and add the frozen sponge and gel insert. Freeze. Brush with the neutral glaze and decorate as you like.

265 ml water
5 g agar-agar
20 g cornflour
300 g 70% cacao
  chocolate
60 g egg yolks
200 g egg whites
85 g sugar

For the moulds
Butter
Grated chocolate

CHOCOLATE FONDANT SOUFFLÉ

For the moulds

Grease selected moulds in which the soufflé is to be cooked with melted butter and cover the sides with grated chocolate. Set aside in the refrigerator.

Mix the cold water and agar-agar powder in a saucepan. Bring to the boil while stirring constantly. Dissolve the cornflour in a little cold water in a container. Add the boiling water with agar-agar while whisking with a hand-held blender to a smooth cream. Add the chopped chocolate to the hot mixture and continue to whisk until the chocolate melts. Finally, incorporate the egg yolks.

Beat the egg whites with the sugar to a meringue. Gently fold the meringue into the previous mixture without deflating. Fill a piping bag with the mixture and fill the soufflé moulds to the top.

Preheat the oven to 190ºC and bake for 7–9 minutes, depending on the mould size, immediately before serving.

Water base
205 g water
151 g atomised
  glucose
31 g dextrose powder
2 g salt
1 g citric acid
13 g glycerine

*70% cacao water
ganache*
403 g water base
  (previously prepared)
410 g 70% cacao
  chocolate
45 g cocoa butter
142 g sunflower oil

Cocoa shortbread
199 g unsalted butter
358 g plain flour
99 g icing sugar
4 g salt
40 g cocoa powder
50 g egg

*Assembly and
finishing*
750 g cocoa shortbread
  (previously prepared)
1 kg 70% cacao water
  ganache (previously
  prepared)

CHOCOLATE TARTLETS

Water base

Mix all the ingredients together in a saucepan and bring to the boil. Cool in the refrigerator for a few hours.

For the 70% cacao water ganache

Heat the water base to 30ºC. Melt the chocolate with the cocoa butter, add the warm water base and finish with the oil. Whisk the mixture and fill a piping bag.

For the cocoa shortbread

Soften the butter and add all the solid ingredients. Finish with the egg, mix and leave to cool in the refrigerator. Roll out to a 2-mm thickness and line the desired moulds. Rest in the refrigerator for a few hours before baking. Bake at 160ºC for 12 minutes.

Assembly and finishing

Brush the inside of the baked tartlet shells with a very thin layer of the same chocolate to preserve their crunchy texture longer. Fill the tartlets with the ganache at 32ºC and rest for a few hours at 16ºC. Serve at room temperature.

Dark chocolate glaze
500 g 70% cacao
  chocolate
500 g cocoa butter

*Cocoa, Baileys and
coffee syrup*
280 g water
140 g sugar
17 g cocoa powder
56 g Baileys
6 g instant coffee

Coffee pastry cream
201 g egg yolks
80 g potato starch
806 g milk
100 g sugar
10 g instant coffee

Pâte à bombe
109 g egg yolks
55 g egg
93 g sugar
44 g water

Mascarpone mousse
200 g cream (35% fat)
180 g sugar
16 g gelatine leaves
1.002 kg mascarpone
300 g pâte à bombe
  (previously prepared)
801 g cream (35% fat)

*Pain de Gênes
(almond cake)*
590 g Provence almond
  paste (50% almonds)
580 g eggs
184 g unsalted butter
110 g plain flour
Anise-flavoured liqueur
  (optional)

TIRAMISU

For the dark chocolate paint
Melt the chocolate and cocoa butter separately at 42ºC. Mix the two ingredients and keep hot until use.

For the cocoa, Baileys and coffee syrup
Mix all the ingredients together.

For the coffee pastry cream
Mix the egg yolks with the potato starch and a little cold milk. Strain. Mix the remaining milk with the sugar in a saucepan and bring to the boil. Remove from the heat, cover with a lid and leave to stand for 20 minutes. Strain and mix with the egg yolk and starch mixture in a saucepan. Bring to the boil. Add the instant coffee and mix to dissolve. Pour the pastry cream into a tray, cover with cling film in direct contact and set aside in the refrigerator.

For the pâte à bombe
Mix all the ingredients together in a mixing bowl and heat in a bain-marie to 85ºC. Whisk until fluffy.

For the mascarpone mousse
Mix the smaller quantity of cream with the sugar in a saucepan and bring to the boil. Add the softened gelatine leaves and pour the mixture over the mascarpone. Mix well. When the temperature falls to 30ºC, mix with the warm pâte à bombe and the remainder of the cream whipped to soft peaks.

For the pain de Gênes
Heat the almond paste in the microwave. Incorporate the eggs one at a time and whisk until the mixture cools. In the meantime, melt the butter and sift the flour. When the almond and egg mixture is at the ribbon stage, take a small amount and mix with the melted butter. Optionally, a little anise-flavoured liqueur may be added. When the butter and anise mixture is light, incorporate into the almond and egg mixture, and then fold in the flour.

Pour the batter into 6-cm-diameter ungreased ring moulds and bake at 160–180ºC in a convection oven, or at 200ºC in a deck oven with the vent closed, for 15–20 minutes.

Assembly and finishing
Remove the pain de Gênes from the ring moulds. Trim the cakes to the desired size. Soak with the syrup, cover with the coffee pastry cream and freeze. Fill dome moulds with the mascarpone mousse and cover with the cream-coated cake inserts. Freeze. When frozen remove the dome mould and brush the frozen pastries with the chocolate paint and serve.

CHOCOLATE IN SAVOURY CUISINE
JOAN ROCA AND THE OTHER CUISINE OF EL CELLER DE CAN ROCA

IN OUR MOTHERS AND
GRANDMOTHERS' KITCHENS, A
BLOCK OF UNCONCHED, STONE-
GROUND CHOCOLATE WAS JUST
AS NECESSARY AS IT WAS SALT, PEPPER,
TOMATOES AND ONIONS.

IN THE COURSE OF ITS TRAVELS, CHOCOLATE FOUND ITS WAY into the traditional cuisine of Catalonia. In our mothers and grandmothers' kitchens, having a block of unconched, stone-ground chocolate to hand was just as necessary as it was to have salt, pepper, tomatoes and onions. Chocolate was amassed and treasured in the post-war years. It had been greatly missed during the years of famine left by the Spanish Civil War, when the 'chocolate of the poor', made from carob, was unable to elicit the same smiles as that made from cacao. It was typically used in the kitchen to finish sauces. We continue to use it today, by itself or in the picada. What is the picada? It is the final touch added to a stew. It is a trick, a secret, inspiration taken from recipes that often go unwritten. Picada, meaning 'chopped', is made by crushing different ingredients in a mortar, such as almonds, pine nuts, hazelnuts, a biscuit, toasted bread, chocolate, garlic, parsley, saffron, chicken livers, rabbit livers or fish livers, among others. No recipe exists for picada, because it is an infinite concept that no longer depends on the family, but on the personality of the person in charge of the kitchen. I imagine one day, somewhere, someone threw chocolate into the picada, making it part of the tradition and a pantry essential. I have always thought that the idea of picada is much like that of an instant mole. Chocolate is a vital ingredient of the dark mole negro sauces.

Many of the great stewed seafood and meat dishes in Catalan cuisine contain dark chocolate in the picada. Describing the philosophy of picada in writing would be a vast undertaking, and the use of chocolate would form an essential chapter. In any case, the important thing is to know that the chocolate is always added after the stew has finished cooking, over a low heat. It would lose its qualities if it were to be excessively heated. In traditional cookery, we use stone-ground chocolates with a high proportion of cacao. The result is dark brown, juicy, sweetish and spicy sauces.

Chocolate is indispensable in game stews. A number of academics I have consulted, such as Salvador Gracia-Arbós, suggest that it would have initially been used as a substitute for blood, or to complement it in order to keep its flavour and thick consistency. Jugged or *civet* dishes made with wild boar or hare are a perfect

match for chocolate. Many of my friends would consider such a dish unfinished if it did not contain chocolate. In addition to hare, a number of rabbit stews are finished off with a picada containing chocolate and the animal's liver in the sauce, a delight for people who love to mop up the remainder with bread. The *Hare with Mole* made at our restaurant actually came about through the search for inspiration from traditional Catalan cooking and my love of Mexican food, becoming a combined tribute to both culinary cultures. Mention should also be made of the dish *Quails with Roses, Strawberries and Mole*, inspired by the powerful and moving novel by Laura Esquivel, *Like Water for Chocolate*.

It has always been my belief that the dishes that express the heights of our passion for chocolate appear the closer we are to the sea – lobsters, langoustines, squid, octopus, cuttlefish... – or when we interpret *mar i muntanya* ('surf and turf') dishes such as rabbit with langoustines and chicken with lobster, or Catalan-style lobster, which is famous for being made with a chocolate sauce. Throughout the history of El Celler de Can Roca, in addition to game dishes, we have created dishes inspired by that tradition, based on our memory of flavours in which cacao has always been present, as in *Baby Octopus with Cocoa and Onion*. We would also cover the langoustine in a very thin and crunchy layer of cocoa caramel. We have recently reinterpreted it, now using fresh cacao pulp, which arrived in our kitchen thanks to Jordi's travels through cacao-producing lands.

While the traditional dishes we refer to were handed down to us via our mother, there is one very special recipe that comes from my father Josep Roca Pont, *The Boss*. He prepares few dishes at Can Roca. Instead, he is in charge of the barbecue – he has extraordinary control over times and temperatures – and of his only dish, snails with spider crab. This emblematic surf and turf dish with its final addition of grated chocolate, which melts into the sauce, is so fascinating, that I took it with me to El Celler to use it on parmentier dishes with rabbit loins and kidneys or with sea and land snails.

The borrowings from chocolate made by savoury cuisine have been generously matched. In recent years, we have been witnessing a reverse phenomenon, whereby ingredients from savoury cuisine, such as salt, chilli and corn nuts, have been incorporated into chocolate bonbons and bars. Cacao has no borders. Every so often, a customer overcome with nostalgia will remind us of one of the iconic dishes from the early days of El Celler de Can Roca, the *Foie Gras Nougat*. It was invented one December in our old premises. Inspired by the large amounts of nougat consumed at that time of the year, it occurred to us that we could revisit this Christmas treat but replacing the fat in the recipe with foie gras, and we could coat it in a very thin layer of chocolate applied with an airbrush. It is one of those dishes that could easily come at the beginning of a tasting menu as it could at the end, as a transition to the desserts, or in place of them.

SNAILS WITH SPIDER CRAB AND CACAO

Spider crab
1 (1-kg) female spider
  crab
2 kg water
10 g salt

**Spider crab
coral sauce**
40 g crab coral
  (roe) and innards
  (previously prepared)
10 g extra virgin olive
  oil
Salt

Mirepoix
1.300 kg onions
200 g carrots
900 g leeks
100 g extra virgin olive
  oil

Spider crab sauce
600 g spider crab
  carcasses
30 g extra virgin olive
  oil
50 g mirepoix
  (previously prepared)
500 g water
A pinch of salt

Snail sauce
750 g snails
1 female spider crab
80 g extra virgin olive
  oil
3 cloves garlic
150 g onions
150 g tomatoes
1 bay leaf
1 sprig thyme
100 g white wine
1 sprig parsley
Water
Xanthan gum
A pinch of salt

For the spider crab
Prepare an ice bath.

Bring salted water to the boil in a large stock pot and cook the crab for 10 minutes. Remove the crab from the pot and refresh in the iced water. Drain the crab and open. Remove the meat from the legs and head. Make sure there are no pieces of shell. Set aside the coral and the innards from the head separately.

For the spider crab coral sauce
Brown the coral and innards in a frying pan with extra virgin olive oil. Blend, season with salt and set aside.

For the mirepoix
Cut the vegetables into mirepoix and sauté in a pan over a low heat until they turn a deep golden colour. Set aside.

For the spider crab sauce
Sauté the crab carcasses in a pan with the extra virgin olive oil and add the mirepoix. Fry gently and then deglaze the pan with the water. Bring to the boil and then simmer for 30 minutes. Strain, reduce by one-third and season with salt. Set aside.

For the snail sauce
Wash the snails in a large container with plenty of water and a pinch of salt. Clean well, removing any empty shells and dead snails. Sauté the snails in a pan with extra virgin olive oil until the slime disappears.

Cut up the spider crab and sauté in a frying pan with extra virgin olive oil. Remove from the pan.

In the same oil, gently brown two peeled and chopped garlic cloves, then add the chopped onions and brown. Add the grated tomatoes, bay leaf and thyme, and cook for 30 minutes. Return the sautéed crab pieces to the pan, then add the wine and reduce completely. Finally, add the snails. Cover with water and cook for 30 more minutes.

Crush the remaining garlic clove with the parsley in a mortar and add to the pan. Mix and leave to steep for a few minutes. Strain the liquid and weigh it. Set aside the snails. Add 0.2 g of xanthan gum for every 100 g of liquid and whisk with a hand-held blender until completely dissolved and the sauce has thickened. Set aside.

For the snail stew
Remove the snails from their shells. Blend the snail sauce with the cocoa powder in a pan over a low heat. Add the snails and set aside

For the La Vera hot paprika oil
Lightly toast the paprika in a frying pan over a very low heat and then add the oil. Heat to 60°C and then remove the pan from the heat. Leave to infuse for 10 minutes, cool and set aside.

Assembly and finishing
Put a serving of snail stew in the middle of a plate and arrange the clean crab meat around it. Drizzle around the stew with the spider crab sauce, and arrange a few dots of La Vera hot paprika oil over the sauce. Finally, put a little spider crab coral sauce on top of the stew and finish with two small mounds of ground cacao nibs around it.

Snail stew
100 g snails (previously prepared)
50 g snail sauce (previously prepared)
10 g cocoa powder
Salt

La Vera hot paprika oil
10 g La Vera hot paprika
100 g extra virgin olive oil

Assembly and finishing
Ground cacao nibs

Brine
1 kg water
100 g salt

Langoustines
10 langoustines
Brine

Toasted langoustine shells and oil
300 g langoustine shells (previously prepared)
200 g extra virgin olive oil

Mantis shrimp sauce base
700 g mantis shrimp
100 g extra virgin olive oil
1.2 kg water
300 g toasted langoustine shells (previously prepared)

Mantis shrimp and coconut sauce
800 g mantis shrimp sauce base
1 g soya lecithin
1 g xanthan gum
133 g Thai coconut milk powder
2 g salt

Cacao pulp emulsion
400 g cacao pulp
1 g xanthan gum
2 g salt
10 g Chardonnay vinegar
60 g extra virgin olive oil

CACAO PULP AND SPICED CHOCOLATE SAUCE WITH LANGOUSTINES

For the brine

Combine the water and salt in a saucepan and bring to the boil. Leave to cool, strain and set aside in a closed container in the refrigerator.

For the langoustines

Clean the langoustines by removing the innards from the head and peeling the tails. Set aside the tails, innards and shells separately. Soak the tails in the brine for 4 minutes. Take out, dry and set aside.

For the toasted langoustine shells and oil

Clean the shells well, removing any trace of roe or innards. Gently toast in a frying pan with the olive oil. Then remove and crush. Strain and set aside both the oil and shells.

For the mantis shrimp sauce base

Lightly sauté the shrimp in a frying pan with olive oil. Combine with the water and toasted langoustine shells and blend. Bring to the boil, making sure nothing sticks to the pan. Lower the heat and cook for 30 minutes. Strain, pressing as firmly as possible on the shells, and set aside. Skim the fat off the stock, and set aside stock and fat separately.

For the mantis shrimp and coconut sauce

Heat the mantis shrimp broth base in a saucepan. Add the lecithin and blend, and then incorporate the xanthan gum until the broth thickens. Mix the coconut milk powder into the hot broth and season with salt. Set aside.

For the cacao pulp emulsion

Use a hand-held blender to whisk the cacao pulp with the xanthan gum. When thick, add the salt and Chardonnay vinegar. Whisk with the olive oil. Set aside.

For the mole negro

Blanch the chillies by covering with boiling water in a container and leaving to soak for 15 minutes. Transfer to a Thermomix together with the blanching water, sesame seeds, garlic, cloves, peppercorns, pumpkin seeds, almonds, tortilla and chilli seeds. Blend to a paste. Strain and set aside.

Heat the corn oil in a pan, preferably cast iron, add the paste and bring to the boil, mixing constantly until smooth. Cook for 30 minutes. Add the chocolate and allow to melt completely, then whisk the mole. Remove from the heat and rest for a few minutes before mixing again. Set aside.

Mole negro

10 pasilla chillies, roasted
2 mulato chillies, roasted
2 ancho chillies, roasted
16 g toasted sesame seeds
1 clove garlic, toasted
2 cloves, toasted
3 black peppercorns, toasted
8 g pumpkin seeds, toasted
5 unpeeled almonds, toasted
1 corn tortilla, toasted
6 g chilli seeds, toasted
20 g corn oil
30 g 80% cacao dark chocolate

Spiced chocolate sauce

15 g 70% cacao chocolate
40 g mole negro (previously prepared)
40 g water
1 g salt

Lychees

4 tinned lychees

For the spiced chocolate sauce

Use a Microplane grater to grate the chocolate, then incorporate the remaining ingredients. Blend thoroughly and set aside in a squeeze bottle.

For the lychees

Pit the lychees and cut into 3-mm x 1-cm segments. Set aside.

Assembly and finishing

Cut the langoustine tails into 1-5-cm-thick slices.

Make 5 cacao bean-shaped dots of spiced chocolate sauce on the plate.

In a saucepan, cook the langoustine tails in the cacao pulp emulsion. Arrange a slice of langoustine over the dots of spiced chocolate sauce and cover lightly with the emulsion in which they were cooked. Lay a lychee segment on each langoustine slice and season each one with a drop of langoustine oil.

Serve the mantis shrimp and coconut sauce separately in a jug.

Candied rose petals
1 rose
100 g water
100 g sugar

Seared strawberries
5 strawberries

Rose water dew
100 g rose water
1.1 g agar-agar

Rose jam
100 g water
20 g fresh roses
100 g sugar
10 g pectin

Strawberry coulis
250 g strawberries
Burning embers

Kuzu thickener
150 g kuzu (kudzu)
   root starch
250 g cold water

Mirepoix
1.5 kg onions
250 g carrots
150 g leeks
15 g extra virgin olive
   oil

Quail jus
1 kg quail bones with
   meat
160 g mirepoix
   (previously prepared)
1.5 kg water
Extra virgin olive oil
Salt
Kuzu thickener
   (previously prepared)

QUAIL WITH MOLE, ROSES AND STRAWBERRIES

For the candied rose petals

Mix the water and the sugar in a saucepan and bring to the boil. Separate the petals from the rose and cook for 5 seconds in the syrup. Remove, drain off the excess syrup and lay flat over a silicone mat. Dry out in a dehydrator at 45ºC for 48 hours. Set aside in a container with silica gel.

For the seared strawberries

Wash the strawberries and hull with a knife. Cut into 3-mm-thick slices and lightly sear over oak or charcoal embers.

   Store in a container until ready to use.

For the rose water dew

Mix the rose water with the agar-agar in a saucepan. Bring to the boil and remove from the heat. Skim if necessary.

   Place a gastronorm tray over another filled with ice to keep chilled. Fill a syringe with the rose water jelly solution and pipe droplets that will set on the chilled tray. Set aside the rose water jelly droplets in a closed container in the refrigerator.

For the rose jam

Combine the water, roses and 75 g of sugar in a saucepan and bring to the boil.

   Mix the remaining sugar with the pectin in a bowl and gradually add the mixture to the pan while stirring continuously. Reduce to the consistency of jam, bearing in mind that the mixture will thicken as it cools. Set aside.

For the strawberry coulis

Wash and hull the strawberries. Put the strawberries with the embers into a smoker box and leave for 5 minutes. Take out the strawberries and purée with a hand-held blender. Strain and set aside.

For the kuzu thickener

Mix both ingredients together and set aside. Stir the preparation every time it is used.

For the mirepoix

Dice the vegetables roughly into a mirepoix and sauté in a pan with the oil over a low heat until they turn a deep golden colour. If necessary, deglaze the pan from time to time with hot water, leave to reduce, and continue to brown. Set aside.

For the quail jus

Put the quail bones into a roasting tin and brown in the oven at 200ºC. Then drain off the excess fat and combine with the mirepoix in a stock pot. Deglaze the roasting tin with water to dissolve the caramelised juices and add to the pot. Cover the contents of the pot with cold water and cook for 2 hours over a low heat.

Then strain and reduce the liquid to 200 g of jus. Adjust the seasoning with salt, thicken with the kuzu thickener and set aside.

For the recado negro

Heat a frying pan and add the chillies. Apply a blow torch to the chillies until completely charred.

Transfer to a container with the water and salt and soak for 24 hours. Next, strain the chillies and blend with the remaining ingredients to a smooth paste.

For the quail mole

Combine the cream, recado negro, quail jus and chocolate in a pan and bring to the boil. Adjust the seasoning with salt and thicken with the kuzu thickener, stirring constantly. Set aside.

For the brine

Combine the ingredients in a container and mix until the salt dissolves. Set aside in the refrigerator.

For the sous-vide quail legs

Clean the quail legs. Remove the bone from the thigh and scrape clean the exposed part of the leg bone for presentation. Soak in the brine for 20 minutes. Remove, pat dry with kitchen paper and season with pepper. Vacuum seal in a bag with the oil. Cook sous-vide in a Roner water bath at 63ºC for 3 hours and cool in an ice bath. Set aside.

For the quail breasts

Clean the breasts and soak in the brine for 20 minutes. Remove from the water and pat dry with kitchen paper. Set aside.

Assembly and finishing

Reheat the quail legs in the Roner at 63ºC. Sear the breasts on both sides in a non-stick pan, starting on the skin side. Rest for 1–2 minutes. Arrange 3 seared strawberry slices in the middle of a plate. Place a quail breast over the slices and season with a few salt flakes. Surround with a few dots of strawberry coulis, rose jam, candied rose petals, rose water dew and quail mole. Finally, lightly sear the skin of the quail legs in a frying pan. Arrange one leg on the plate over a tablespoon of quail jus. Decorate with 2 wild strawberries.

Recado negro
50 dried yucateco or cha'wa chillies
1 litre still mineral water
3 g salt
4 allspice berries
4 black peppercorns
4 cloves
1 g cumin seeds
3 cloves garlic, roasted
½ onion, roasted
50 g orange juice

Quail mole
20 g cream
60 g recado negro (previously prepared)
120 g quail jus
20 g 80% cacao chocolate
Kuzu thickener (previously prepared)

Brine
1 kg still mineral water
100 g salt

Sous-vide quail legs
12 quail legs
500 g brine (previously prepared)
30 g extra virgin olive oil
Black pepper

Quail breasts
12 quail breasts
500 g brine (previously prepared)

Assembly and finishing
Wild strawberries

HARE À LA ROYALE WITH MOLE AND CHOCOLATE

Duxelles
120 g white
  mushrooms
120 g porcini
  mushrooms
120 g shallots
30 g extra virgin olive
  oil

Hare à la royale
375 g hare meat
185 g pork dewlap
  (fatty cut from under
  the neck)
10 g black truffle
100 g hare liver
100 g milk
75 g hare blood
20 g Armagnac
50 g pasteurised egg
  white
65 g white bread, crust
  removed
85 g duxelles
  (previously prepared)
12 g salt

Mirepoix
1.3 kg onions
200 g carrots
900 g leeks
100 g extra virgin olive
  oil

Hare jus
850 g hare bones
200 g mirepoix
  (previously prepared)
75 g red wine
1.5 kg water

Kuzu thickener
150 g kuzu (kudzu)
  root starch
250 g cold water

For the duxelles

Clean the mushrooms, cut into small dice and set aside. Peel and cut the shallots into small dice and sauté in a frying pan with the oil until soft and lightly coloured. Add the mushrooms, allow the water they contain to evaporate, and cook over a very low heat for 20 minutes. Set aside.

For the hare à la royale

Mince the hare and pork, and finely chop the truffle and liver. Mix together and set aside.

Mix the milk with the blood, Armagnac and egg white. Add the bread and soak for 15 minutes. Blend, add to the minced meat mixture with the duxelles and season with salt.

Use cling film to firmly roll the mixture into 6-cm-diameter cylinders and seal both ends. Take care not to trap the cling film inside the mixture. Prick the cylinders to remove any trapped air and squeeze firmly while wrapping with more cling film.

Put the cylinders into a bag and vacuum seal at 100%. Cook sous-vide in a Roner water bath at 65ºC for 4 hours. Take the cylinders out of the bag, cool quickly in a blast chiller and set aside.

For the mirepoix

Dice the vegetables roughly into a mirepoix and sauté in a pan with the oil over a low heat until they turn a deep golden colour. Set aside.

For the hare jus

Put the bones into a roasting tin and brown in the oven at 180ºC. Then drain off the excess fat and transfer to a stock pot. Deglaze the roasting tin with water to dissolve the caramelised juices and add to the pot. Add the mirepoix and wine and bring to the boil. Cover the contents of the pot with cold water and bring back to the boil. Skim and simmer over a very low heat for 3 hours. Strain the stock and reduce to 200 g of hare jus. Leave to cool and set aside.

For the kuzu thickener

Mix both ingredients together in a container and set aside. Stir the preparation every time it is used as the starch may sink to the bottom.

For the hare sauce

Bring the hare jus to the boil in a saucepan. Add the kuzu thickener while stirring constantly with a whisk. Incorporate the chopped chocolate and butter, and whisk the sauce to an emulsion. Strain. Immediately before serving, stir in the hare blood, strain

Hare sauce
200 g hare jus
  (previously prepared)
20 g kuzu thickener
  (previously prepared)
35 g 80% cacao
  chocolate
30 g unsalted butter
40 g hare blood
Salt (as needed)
Black peppercorns (as
  needed)

Hare liver parfait with cacao
110 g hare liver
10 g extra virgin olive
  oil
110 g unsalted butter
18 g cocoa powder
Pinch of salt

Brioche
36 g sugar
30 g milk
14.4 g yeast
150 g eggs
300 g flour
150 g butter, softened
3.6 g salt

Mole negro
250 g chilhuacle negro
  chillies
250 g chilhuacle rojo
  chillies
250 g mulato chillies
250 g pasilla chillies
The seeds from the
  chillies
2 large onions, sliced
1 kg lard
1 head garlic
2 plantains, peeled
300 g brioche
100 g sesame seeds,
  toasted
100 g peanuts, toasted
100 g walnuts
150 g almonds

again and season with salt and freshly ground pepper.

For the hare liver parfait with cacao

Put the hare liver in a container with water and ice for at least 12 hours to remove the blood. After this time, remove the livers and pat dry with a kitchen paper. Heat the extra virgin olive oil in a frying pan and sauté the livers until cooked. Blend the livers with the butter and cocoa powder and add a pinch of salt. Pass through a fine sieve, and set aside.

For the brioche

Put the sugar, milk, yeast into a bowl and mix until combined. Add the eggs. Sift the flour and fold into the mixture half at a time. Then add the softened butter and salt. Knead the dough until it is smooth, elastic and comes away from the side of the bowl. Place in a bowl, cover and rest in the refrigerator for 12 hours.

Shape into a ball, place in a loaf tin and ferment for 40 minutes at 40°C with 45% humidity. Preheat the oven to 180ºC without humidity on fan setting 4. Bake the brioche for 25 minutes or until golden brown. Remove from the tin and place upside down on a rack. Let cool and set aside.

For the mole negro

Roast the chillies, take out the seeds and set aside. Put the roasted chillies into a container and cover with hot water for a few minutes. Drain, cover with cold water and soak for 30 minutes. Drain the chillies and set aside.

Toast the chilli seeds in a pan until they burn. Soak in water to remove the bitterness, then drain and set aside.

Sauté the onions in a frying pan with half the lard. Add the chopped garlic, peeled and sliced plantain, sliced brioche, toasted sesame seeds, toasted peanuts, walnuts, almonds, pumpkin seeds and raisins.

Put the tomatoes and tomatillos in a pan, cover with water, season with salt, and bring to the boil for 5 minutes. Remove, purée and strain. Set aside the cooking water. Blend the chillies together with their seeds and the toasted corn tortillas. Strain, add the spices and mix well. Add to the mixture in the frying pan.

Put the rest of the lard in a large pan, add the contents of the frying pan and sauté. Add the puréed tomatoes and tomatillos, together with 1 litre of cooking water and leave to cook for 20 minutes. Incorporate the chocolate, sugar and avocado leaves, and simmer for at least 1 hour 30 minutes, stirring frequently to stop from sticking. Set aside.

Assembly and finishing

Put a tablespoon of hare liver parfait with cacao in the middle of the plate. Arrange the hare à la royale over it and cover with the hare sauce. Pipe a circle of mole negro around the cylinder of hare à la royale and finish by arranging cacao nibs over the mole.

100 g pumpkin seeds
100 g raisins
2 kg ripe tomatoes
1 kg tomatillos
2 corn tortillas, toasted
3 g nutmeg
1 stick cinnamon
0.6 g oregano
0.8 g thyme
0.5 g marjoram
1 g aniseed
2 g cumin seeds
5 cloves
5 allspice berries
250 g Mexican stone-
  ground chocolate
100 g sugar
6 avocado leaves,
  toasted
Salt (as needed)

Assembly and finishing
Cacao nibs

Serves 8

Marinade
2 kg water
150 g salt
100 g sugar
2 g ground black
  pepper

Marinated chicken
1 (2-kg) chicken
2 kg marinade
  (previously prepared)

*Chocolate and spice
lacquering sauce*
100 g soy sauce
50 g honey
30 g sugar
35 g red wine vinegar
15 g cocoa powder
5 g salt
2 g black pepper
1 g pink pepper
0.5 g cumin seeds
0.5 g dried rosemary
0.3 g ground cloves
The grated zest of 1
  lime

Lacquered chicken
1 marinated chicken
  (previously prepared)
50 g extra virgin olive
  oil
200 g chocolate and
  spice lacquering
  sauce (previously
  prepared)
Kitchen twine

*Assembly and
finishing*
Fresh bay leaf
Fresh rosemary
Fresh thyme

CHOCOLATE AND SPICE-LACQUERED CHICKEN

For the marinade
Mix all the ingredients together in a container and set aside.

For the marinated chicken
Soak the chicken in the marinade for 24 hours. Remove, pat dry with kitchen paper and set aside.

For the chocolate and spice lacquering sauce
Mix all the ingredients together in a container and set aside.

For the lacquered chicken
Truss the chicken, tying the wings and legs snugly to the body. Precook the chicken for 1 hour 30 minutes in a steam oven at 65ºC. Take out and pre-heat the oven to 200ºC. Brush the chicken with the oil and put into the dry oven at 200ºC for 5 minutes. Open the oven and brush the chicken with the chocolate and spice lacquering sauce, and repeat the process every 2 minutes for 15 minutes. Take the chicken out of the oven and rest for 20 minutes.

Assembly and finishing
Untie the chicken. Tie the fresh bay leaf, rosemary and laurel into a bundle and put into the cavity of the chicken. Serve hot.

FOIE GRAS NOUGAT

PX reduction
200 g Pedro Ximénez
  wine

Foie gras nougat
200 g duck foie gras
50 g hazelnut praline
50 g hazelnut butter
15 g unsalted butter
30 g cocoa butter
10 g white truffle oil
10 g PX reduction
  (previously prepared)
Salt

Nougat paint
100 g 70% cacao
  couverture chocolate
100 g cocoa butter

*Assembly and
finishing*
Bean sprouts
Soy sauce
Salad burnet leaves
Rosemary flowers
Edible gold leaf

For the PX reduction

Heat the wine in a saucepan and reduce to 85 g.

For the foie gras nougat

Sauté the foie gras, searing on both sides. Transfer to a Thermomix together with the praline, hazelnut butter, butter, melted cocoa butter, truffle oil, PX reduction and salt. Blend thoroughly and press through a fine conical sieve.

Transfer the mixture to a metal bowl set inside an ice bath and whisk with a hand-held blender until it turns a lighter colour and its consistency changes. Fill 2.5 x 5 x 1-cm ingot moulds and freeze. Each mould should contain 10 g of the mixture.

For the nougat paint

Melt the couverture with the cocoa butter and mix. When the temperature of the mixture reaches 40°C, strain and fill a paint sprayer.

Unmould the nougat from the ingot moulds. Turn on the air compressor and coat the nougat ingots with a very thin layer of the paint. Set aside in the freezer.

Assembly and finishing

Cut the bean sprouts to the size of grains of rice and soak for 30 seconds in the soy sauce. Drain off the excess sauce and arrange over the nougat. Decorate with a salad burnet leaf and rosemary flowers, and make a dot of PX reduction on one corner, topped with a piece of gold leaf.

3

JOURNEY TO THE SOURCES OF CACAO

PIURA, THE GATEWAY TO CACAO

ALFONSO GARCÍA'S ESTATE was started by his father some eighty years ago and christened María Vicenta, after his mother. It covers six hectares equally divided into cacao and banana trees. It lies in the Olguín district on the outskirts of the Peruvian town of Buenos Aires, one of the thousand eponymous localities scattered throughout Latin America. This is one to the east of Piura, a little below Morropón, in the area that runs along the upper and middle sections of the valley of the River Piura as it flows down from the Andes. When his father bought the farm, a few cacao trees had already been planted. Most of the cacao trees are thought to be about 80 years old, with a good few closer to a century. Almost all were planted from seed, and they have never received grafts. At the entrance to the holding is a modest house with a few animals roaming freely, and around it all is vegetation and shade, and an unbearably stifling heat. In this land at the mercy of the sun and drought, cacao needs shade more than anything else, and Alfonso's trees require additional attention to replace the humidity of the rainforest. During the first three years of their lives, until the cacao trees begin to produce, banana trees offer a protective mantle. After this, they need to change partner, because the banana tree makes a bad travelling companion. It starts to compete with the cacao tree for nourishment and the same air. Change is inevitable. There are alternatives, which on Alfonso's land are citrus, avocado and tamarind trees. It is an old

CACAO NEEDS SHADE. DURING THEIR FIRST THREE YEARS, UNTIL THE CACAO TREES BEGIN TO PRODUCE, THE BANANA LEAVES OFFER PROTECTION.

plantation laid out like a maze, nothing like the new, ordered and almost rectilinear plantings seen in other areas.

Alfonso García's plantation is the first one we visit on our journey to Peruvian cacao. Alfonso has shifted his crops towards organic farming, like practically all the cacao growers in the area. Peru is the second largest producer of organic cacao in Latin America, behind the Dominican Republic. There is a lot of tamarind, and banana trees remain a constant feature, now clearly separated from the cacao. One and the other provide shade and fruits, which supplement the grower's income. The price of cacao is rising, but the price of banana is variable, indifferent to the generosity of a plant that provides a harvest every week and a half to two weeks. The current national market rate is a little over 200 soles (about 60 US dollars) per thousand fruit; in other words, six US cents for each banana. If the destination lies beyond the border, the fruit is packed into 18-kilogram batches at a price of six dollars per box.

According to the maps, there is no river here, but actually there it is, defining the life of the Buenos Aires farmers with its floods. Most of the plantations are found on the left bank, and are occasionally cut off dur-

ALFONSO HAS SHIFTED HIS CROPS TOWARDS ORGANIC FARMING, LIKE PRACTICALLY ALL THE CACAO GROWERS IN THE AREA.

ing the rainy season, complicating the transport of the cacao to the fermentation plant. Last year, with the strength of the El Niño phenomenon, Alfonso's farm was flooded for several days. Had it been a normal year, the cacao harvest would have reached seven tonnes, but it was only three.

The province of Piura first, followed by neighbouring Tumbes, associated its name with the production of white cacao, although this variety is by no means exclusive to the region. White cacao grows throughout the Amazon region, where there are dozens of varieties of greater or lesser purity and different characteristics. The best-known relative of white cacao is Porcelana, a variety identified with Venezuela, where it is widespread and standardised. But Piura successfully took advantage of the crisis affecting Venezuelan cacao plantations to strengthen and expand its presence in the market, and has now become the leading quality Peruvian cacao and one of the most sought-after in the Amazon region. Piura is now the darling of Latin American cacao producers.

Cacao in Piura

Located in northern Peru, Piura is a small region traditionally associated with cotton, rice, lemon and mango farming. While the cacao plantations of Piura draw the attention of chocolate-makers, they cover such a small area of land, ranked tenth among the country's producing areas, that Piura is included in the section 'other regions' in the statistics published by the Ministry of Agriculture for cacao production in 2016. It is estimated that about 1,400 hectares are devoted to cacao in the region. Most are in the province of Morropón, in the upper and middle stretches of the Piura Valley, where Buenos Aires is located. This is a very small part of the 108,700 hectares of cacao plantations recorded in the country, but the value attributed to it by the market is higher than that of all other areas. It is the most sought-after and also the best paid cacao. New plantations are covering an increasingly larger area.

Nobody had seen a cacao tree in the fields of Piura until about 150 years ago. The warm and dry climate favoured citrus, particularly the small, round and green fruit known in Europe as 'lime', but simply referred to in Peru as *limón*, 'lemon', which is the heart and soul of ceviche. I am told that the change began with the boom in rubber and the influx of rubber tappers, and everything that they brought with them. Piura kept some of the good things. There was no jungle to exploit or native communities to enslave and decimate, and the region was the natural outlet for rubber bound for Europe. It became a gateway for this sticky white sap, latex, collected in the jungles around Iquitos, the great rubber centre of the Peruvian

Amazon. The first cacao trees are believed to have arrived in this land with the convoys of carts and wagons that carried the rubber, and here they stayed, associated with banana-growing.

The rubber boom reached the Peruvian rainforest in 1885 and lasted until 1907 when production hit its peak. It is highly likely that the introduction of cacao in Peru was no coincidence. Seventy-five years before, François Louis Callier had opened the first chocolate factory in Vevey, Switzerland, and since that time, the local chocolate industry has never ceased to grow. World demand for cacao increased, and Piura, like the Vinces district of Ecuador, offered opportunities for plantations close to ports from where it could be shipped. By the end of the century, African cacao had become an indisputable reality, and it was cheaper to ship to the factories in Europe. The market changed direction. The plantations of Piura remained, consigned to oblivion, in the hands of small-holder farmers who barely produced enough to survive. Arturo Aguirre, the son and grandson of cacao growers, explained it to me in a nutshell. 'My father practically gave the cacao away; sometimes it was left on the tree because nobody would pay for it. Middlemen

LOCATED IN NORTHERN PERU, PIURA IS A SMALL REGION WHERE COTTON, RICE, LEMON AND MANGO ARE TRADITIONALLY GROWN.

would come and pay what they liked for it. They took it to the market in Chiclayo, and that's as far as it got.' That is how it played out for his father, and for Arturo and other hundreds of growers in the area. They managed on bananas, making losses on cacao... And chocolate? There were infusions of dried and ground cacao, like in the old days, mixed with milk; two or three cups of hot chocolate to celebrate Christmas; and chocolate with milk for nursing mothers. As dictated by tradition.

The change came with the reaction of small-scale producers. They united, formed cooperatives and began to change the model of their relationship with the market. The first step was to avoid the buyers. The second was to transform the cacao plantations. Their cacao had begun to draw the attention of the European chocolate manufacturers. Producers in Buenos Aires jumped on the bandwagon and founded Asprobo in 2007. For our first meeting, in October 2011, they were already embarking on the task of standardising their cacao plantations and concentrating their work on the plant, in search of the highest possible purity. There are now close to 100 members who manage 85 hectares of cacao plantations, which in good years achieve harvests of 30 tonnes, and 150 hectares of banana plantations.

I return with Jordi Roca a little under six years after the first visit, and we tour plots where the cacao is at a level of 80–85 per cent purity. This means that of every 100 beans produced, 80–85 are completely white, while the remainder continue to have a purple tint. Some microbatches produced by Alfonso García are practically 100 per cent pure, although you can never tell. As a testament to this uncertainty, Alfonso pulled off a nearly ripe cacao pod from a tree noted down as being fully pure. We split it open and separate and cut out the beans one at a time. Three are purple. 'Nothing is certain with cacao,' he declares. 'The trees behave rather strangely, and if you want to understand them, you have to monitor them for at least five years. We have georeferenced the entire plot, but El Niño in 2017 disrupted all the work we did, and we have to georeference everything again, because surprises like this one are appearing. There's no end to the work.'

Ungrafted trees predominate here, born from the germination of a seed – the cultivation technique is known as *muca*, and consists of planting two or three beans directly into each hole. However, there are still growers who keep ungrafted Trinitario trees or hybrid strains, such as CCN-50 and CCN-51, or ISB-90 from Trindad and Tobago. Most have had scions of very pure white cacaos grafted onto them, but we have to keep working with new grafts in order to improve their genes.

The roots of chocolate

Chocolate is putting down roots in the countryside. Arturo Aguirre insists on the idea to justify the scope of work being carried out on the farm. 'Chocolate is born in the countryside, with the grower. The first thing is the soil, and then feeding the tree … Everything we're seeing ends up coming out in the chocolate bar,' he says while pointing to the ground, covered with dried leaves and a few fallen branches. 'This is protection in times of heat, and when the rains come, they rot and disappear; they become part of the soil and provide organic material. It's called "coverage", and serves to stabilise it.' The soil, the feeding and care of the tree, the protection of the trunk, the pruning to reduce its height, phytosanitary pruning, feeding the tree, fumigation – mixing the ground seeds of the neem tree with very hot rocoto or Pipí de Mono chillies – the addition of natural fertilisers to the soil, selective harvesting … everything goes into the chocolate bar. For better when applied wisely, or for worse when omissions build up. It is very likely that this is the reason for such aggressive roasting of beans when some chocolates are made.

All of this is called the 'technological package' and it provides a footing for this and other groups of farmers. 'You can have a cacao that's a hundred per cent white, but without the technological package, the yields will change. You're going to get very white pods but the quality of the beans will be much lower, second rate, or very white with small beans. The ideal is to have a plant properly classified as white, which gives you about 200 fruits per harvest, and with beans that weigh between 2.5 and 3 grams. This is what the market will pay for. Quality and volume,

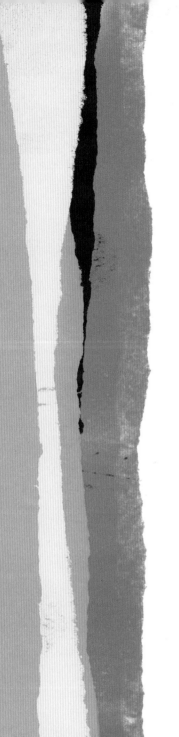

and quality is measured by the size of grade one. They'll buy grade two from you for a different price, regardless of how organic it is.'

We land in Piura in early September, and it is the low season for cacao. High season will begin in a few months, in late December or early January, and it will last three more months, until the end of March. The yield is greater and the fruits are bigger. Low season, which is also called the 'second campaign', began a month ago, in August, and will end at the end of September. High season also coincides with the rainy season, which at these latitudes equates to summer – summer in the southern hemisphere coincides with the European and North American winter – and the tasks of harvesting and particularly drying, after fermenting, is made difficult. Good facilities are required to reduce the moisture in the bean to 6.5 or 7 per cent in rainy and humid conditions.

There are few fruits on Alfonso's plantation, but harvesting continues every 15–20 days, as in the high season. The trees we are seeing can yield up to 600 pods a year, and fruits and flowers can occur at the same time. The fruits are the reality of the current harvest, while the flowers show the promise that comes with the new year. The flowers are clustered along the trunk and widest branches, forming protruding structures called 'flower cushions'. If the tree is treated well, up to 15 pods can grow from the same flower cushion. The fruits that grow directly from the trunk weigh more than those growing from the branches.

From the time the campaign begins, harvesting is selective. Only the ripe fruits are gathered every 15 or 20 days. The rain and high temperatures encourage ripening, and not much time can be allowed to lapse. When the cacao pods are ready, they turn a bright yellow colour and produce a hollow sound. The colour is a sign that it can be harvested. The fruit that are still changing colour, for which the ripening process is incomplete, are left on the tree. When overripe, there is a risk of germination occurring inside the pod. The embryo growing from the seed inside the pod reduces the volume of sugar. As it ferments, the embryo is destroyed, leaving a gap in the bean that is open to infestation by moths. Whenever this happens, the cacao is only sold on the domestic market.

A niche product

Piura cacao is decidedly a niche product. So much so that Asprobo no longer mixes all the cacao delivered to its fermentation and drying plants by its members. If the plots where it originates have a high percentage of purity, the pods are processed separately. High-quality Piura cacao is sold by microbatches. The name of the grower and the estate are gaining weight in a market that is constantly in

THE HIGH SEASON LASTS ABOUT THREE MONTHS AND IS THE MOST PRODUCTIVE. IN PIURA IT BEGINS IN LATE DECEMBER OR EARLY JANUARY.

search of greater identity, meaning and substance. Few could have imagined only ten years earlier that details like these, disregarded at the time, would determine the new direction taken by the markets. Most Piura cacaos are organically grown, which involves an impressive commitment. There is more work and lower yields, and the price paid tends not to take into account the difference. However, with the market niches that are opening through the bean-to-bar movement and small-scale chocolatiers, things are changing quite quickly. Cacao starts to generate value-added when you tend it well and if you are able to establish a permanent dialogue with the new markets. Arturo Aguirre explained this to us. 'We've also begun to change. Our customers tell us "we want this", and we go in search of the flavour profile our customers request.' The more consolidated growers work in the opposite direction; the market pursues them, as is Alfonso García's experience. An American chocolate manufacturer has bought two tonnes of select cacao from him this year.

Life-changing cacao and chocolates

The new times enjoyed by cacao has changed life in Buenos Aires, although seen from the outside, the changes seem insubstantial. There are no grand buildings, parks or big businesses. Nor can luxury brand SUVs be seen in the streets, only motorised rickshaws, a few mopeds and a number of dusty-covered old pickup trucks with a few farming utensils in the back. Prosperity here comes in the guise of simplicity: a motorcycle to take to the country, leaving the bicycle permanently parked; or Internet for a town where a television signal could scarcely be picked up. Despite the apparent modesty, they are more than eloquent symptoms of a new state of things. Other achievements are far-reaching. 'We now have the financial capacity to send our children to college to study a basic degree,' says Arturo. This was unthinkable less than six years ago.

The abruptness of this change was confirmed the day they understood that the contribution of value-added to cacao went beyond the changes made to the forms of cultivation; it was in the chocolate and confectionery, to start with, but also in other products that were increasingly in demand on the market, such as the nibs and cacao paste, also known as cacao liquor. The export market has changed its perspective. Previously, there would be an order for 20 tonnes of beans, but now the order is for ten tonnes of beans and another ten tonnes of processed products.

THE NEW TIMES ENJOYED BY CACAO HAS CHANGED LIFE IN BUENOS AIRES, BUT PROSPERITY HERE COMES IN THE GUISE OF SIMPLICITY.

Initiatives are growing in Buenos Aires. These can come in individual form, such as Kayul, a brand of confectionery – chocolates made with local fruits and truffles, among others – created by Arturo Aguirre himself, which is a good example of tree-to-bar thinking, but there are also collective initiatives. The Association of Women Entrepreneurs is one of them. They were already active six years before in a primitive workshop where they made cacao paste and chocolate bars with which to pay for the 'glass of milk at school' project (a glass of milk to supplement the diet of local school children), and they continue with their cause. The association comprises 17 women who process their own cacaos. They have modernised the machinery and produce confectionery, cacao paste and chocolate bars, which helps to supplement their family income.

Cacao in Peru

Cacao has always been a part of the Peruvian rainforest, distributed among farms and fields drawing little attention. There were moments when cacao cultivation brought an inkling of prosperity, but they were fleeting, little more than a mirage. It was difficult to develop in a region that was practically cut off from the rest of the country. The war against the Sendero Luminoso (Shining Path) revolutionary movement, first, and the subsequent dominance of the coca plantations kept the cacao plantations of Peru in a state of hibernation The cacao was there, but there were few who worked to grow it and even fewer paid any attention to it.

The statistics kept since the beginning of this century are a clear indication of the evolution of cacao-growing in the country. The 41,300 hectares of cacao plantations and 24,800 tonnes of cacao produced as recorded by the Ministry of Agriculture in 2000 grew to 108,700 hectares and 120,400 hectares, respectively, in 2016. The incredible expansion of the plantations was accompanied by even greater productivity, which has grown fivefold. This information is an important start to explaining the growing weight that the cacao industry has in Peru, growth that has subsequently been consolidated by focusing on new crops on the CCN-51 hybrid. The idea was to free the inhabitants of the Amazon regions from the tyranny imposed by the coca plantations. For this, strains that were highly resistant to disease and able to generate income in the shortest possible time were needed. San Martín is the best example. This region in the heart of the Peruvian Amazon, which in 1985 had barely any cacao plantations, today accounts for 43 per cent of the country's cacao production, mainly obtained from CCN-51.

Cacao was for a long time a marginal crop in the context of Peru's agricultural output. Such was the case that Ministry of Agriculture statistics show no exports of cacao beans until after 2000. Today they account for 70 percent of output. Even so, Peruvian cacao production barely accounts for two per cent of the world market. The crop has expanded and become consolidated in regions such as San Martín, Junín, Cuzco, Ucayali, Ayacucho, Cajamarcas and Amazonas. The La Convención Valley, in the Cuzco region, is set apart by its plantations of Chuncho cacao. Domesticated by the indigenous Machiguenga communities and spread more than a century ago in the form of plantations of ungrafted trees, Chuncho is a variety that produces rounded fruits that are smaller than other varieties and with a thinner skin, which makes it more sensitive and more difficult to tend. This cacao, however, is elegant, delicate and floral. It has come under siege from CCN-51 in recent years. A little over a decade ago in San Ignacio, the plantation owned by Faustino Colala produced the surprising discovery of two trees of one of the most prized varieties of Ecuadorian Nacional cacao, which had been considered extinct since the turn of the twentieth century. Researchers from USAID assigned it with a name referencing their work camp, a name that stuck: Fortunato No. 4. Finally, there are the regions of Piura and Tumbes, with their white cacaos.

There are other areas in which native cacaos are beginning to flourish, with the expansion of those plantations and reaping the benefits of the factors that set them apart from CCN-51, particularly their value-added that this hybrid strain cannot give. Satipo and Pangoa in the department of Junín – at the entrance to the VRAEM (Valleys of the Rivers Apurimac, Ene and Mantauro) region, the main coca-growing area of Peru – are among them. The plantations are run by a number of indigenous communities, such as the Ashaninka and the Not-Machiguenga, and their cacaos trade for higher prices. Also worthy of mention are the Wampi and Awajún communities of the Alto Marañón region, centred on the provinces of Bagua, Utcubamba and Condorcanqui, in the department of Amazonas, whose main production areas are in the vicinity of the localities of Imazita, Chiriaco, Santiago and Santa María de Nieva.

Liquid jelly
400 g water
100 g glucose powder
5 g agar-agar

Chocolate²

CHOCOLATE CREAM

For the liquid jelly
Mix all the cold ingredients together in a saucepan. Bring to the boil and remove from the heat. Leave to cool at room temperature. When set, whisk to the consistency of crème anglaise.

For the chocolate²
See the process for making 250 g on page 252.

Assembly and finishing
Heat both the chocolate and the liquid jelly to 40ºC. Whisk the jelly with the chocolate to make the cream. Pour into small glasses and chill in the refrigerator for at least 2 hours before serving.

JAÉN, THE ENDLESS JOURNEY

JAÉN IS THE LAST BIG TOWN in the department of Cajamarca before you reach the rainforest, but it is almost nothing like what you would expect to find. Rice paddies are everywhere, encircling the town as far as the eye can see. You would never guess that Jaén is in rice country until you look out over the horizon where there is little to tell you otherwise. You expect something else. However, much has changed on the edges of the jungle over the last 20 years. Rice dominates the landscape and the lives of the inhabitants of Jaén, with their terraces and low dirt walls. Its presence is overwhelming. Even more so if you consider that the land was covered in cacao plantations only sixty years earlier.

Catastrophe struck when an ice-cream manufacturer and confectioner from Lima bought up 300 hectares of cacao plantations to supply his chocolate-making operations directly. The head of the project decided to replace the native varieties in the area with new plants brought in from Brazil. With them came diseases and pests, starting with 'witches' broom', which would eventually devastate the cacao plantations in the area. The cacao was diseased, whereas rice would give two harvests a year that could be turned into hard cash – little, but money no less. The banks supported the transformation, and the valleys were turned into rice paddies.

Slowly but surely, cacao is reclaiming the land, and it is doing so one farm at a time, like a drip, in what seems to be an unstoppable process. There is no other way out for people wishing to escape the tyranny of rice, the symbol of the poverty typifying life in this region. The figures speak clearly: one well-managed hectare under rice can provide a net income of 12,000 soles a year (about 3,700 US dollars in mid-2018). If that were not enough, it also causes high levels of pollution owing to pesticide use and chronic health problems among farmers, who are forced to spend half their lives knee-deep in water. On the other hand, a well-managed hectare under Criollo cacao can generate between 25,000 and 35,000 soles each year if bananas are planted as a secondary crop. There is no pollution – local cacao plantations mainly use organic methods – and less work is required. The old rice paddies provide flat, delineated and fertile terraces, ready for planting with very little additional investment required. The figures speak and people are starting to listen and, more importantly, to understand. There is one last point that tips the

scale towards cacao: the large amounts of water needed to grow rice. Cacao offers a natural, environmentally friendly alternative to the aggressiveness and wasted resources involved with rice cultivation.

Jorge Troya was one of the people who heeded the call of cacao. We arrive at his plantation by travelling over a compact dirt wall raised a few centimetres above ground level, forming the boundary between his farm and the neighbouring paddy field, the frontier between two worlds. On the right is the paddy, a flood of green, with the rice grown so high that the water can scarcely be seen. On the left is the certainty of a different universe: trees, height, lush vegetation and identity, comprising a landscape showcasing the sheen of prosperity, turning into a virus that is beginning to infect other farmers. Jorge's brother and a few neighbours take pride of place among the newly converted.

We are in the Shumba Valley, a few kilometres outside of Jaén. Within the boundaries of Jorge's cacao plantation two different realities coexist. One row, sometimes two, of trees bearing red cacao pods, and another row mixing yellows with greens and purples. The red reveals the presence of CCN-51; the others are a native variety of cacao that Jorge chose for the parcels of his estate. It is called Marañón-15 and is one of the 188 varieties of Marañón cacao classified and stored in the germplasm bank founded a few years ago by a development assistance agency in Jaén. It collects samples of native cacaos from the area compris-

RICE DOMINATES THE LANDSCAPE AND THE LIVES OF THE INHABITANTS OF JAÉN, WITH THEIR TERRACES AND LOW DIRT WALLS. FIFTY YEARS AGO, THE ENTIRE AREA WAS UNDER CACAO.

ing San Ignacio, Jaén and Bagua, and it was the first step in the mission to revive cacao cultivation in the district. Jorge chose Marañón-15 because he felt it was a high-quality, fine cacao that gave good yields.

The cacao farm owned by Jorge Muñoz is embarking on a new stage of what seems to be a journey without end: the transformation of the hybrid cacao trees, mainly CCN-51, into Criollo trees. He began his undertaking two years ago by grafting new scions onto the trunks of the trees. A tree will miss out on producing for one year, after which it will yield cacao of the new variety. Jorge is not alone on this new stage of the journey. His travelling companion is Óscar Velásquez, a gaunt man accustomed to swimming against the tide. Óscar, the son and grandson of cacao growers, has been involved since the 1990s in the battle for cacao, which started out as a war against rice and later became a quest for purity. He focuses his work on the Shumba Valley and other neighbouring valleys. The title deed of the

JORGE TROYA AND ÓSCAR VELÁSQUEZ AT THE FORMER'S CACAO FARM, PLANTED ON FORMER RICE PADDIES IN THE SHUMBA VALLEY.

land he now farms, bought by his grandfather in 1914, mentions a piece of land devoted to pasture and cacao plantations.

Óscar Velásquez makes a living from cacao. He grows it and sells it; he advises and offers technical assistance to other growers; and he buys part of their production and sells it on to chocolate manufacturers. What he does most is offer technical advice to new growers, in collaboration with the Cepicafé cooperative, whose activities are diversified between coffee and cacao, which has indirectly led to his involvement in other activities. His first mission was the revival of cacao-growing in the district. Then came its transformation, with the grafting onto low-quality trees of fine Criollo varieties, into which he puts blind faith. The next thing was to start up a programme, which he describes as the 'genetic recovery of ancestral cacao plants with a fine aroma', designed to rescue the cacao varieties native to the area. With help from the cooperative, he has been combing through old cacao trees, until he managed to select 68 varieties that he tends in a nursery while he seeks funding to allow him to study them and see which ones are best suited to the district. Only three years would be needed, with some sacrifice from growers, in order to graft the existing trees and transform the cacao plantations of Jaén, and in doing so the landscape of and life in the district.

'We're trying to produce cacao with a fine aroma, like it was in the past,' he explains while showing us how to graft a scion of a white cacao he brought back from Piura onto a hybrid tree stock, from which a new tree will grow. 'Here, there used to be plantations of cacao of excellent aromatic quality that have practically all been lost. Very few trees survived, and we're trying to rescue those plants, which have remained as relics, in order to propagate them again and bring back the wonderful cacao that was once found in north-western Peru. I find relics, because I have the privilege of entering very old plantations and dealing with people who want to bring in new cacao.'

Óscar has gradually started to thrive, thanks to his work and the small margins he makes from trading in cacao. His relationship with the growers in the area allows him to spot the best quality parcels and gives him access to buy their fruits. It looks easy, but the economy of the area is not exactly booming, and access to finance that enables him to purchase crops tends to be out of reach. The big banks turn their backs on small-holder farmers. He is able to trade by means of the microloans provided by the financial institution Financiera Confianza, which the locals call Caja Confianza ('Trust Bank'). Peruvian farmers prefer simplicity, even when doing business.

Vanilla sponge
9 fresh eggs
180 g sugar
2 vanilla pods
180 g plain flour

Ginger filling
200 g egg yolks
150 g sugar
1 kg cream
4 gelatine leaves
Ginger extract

Mango mousse
650 g cream
360 g egg whites
175 g sugar
30 g powdered egg
  white
175 g glucose
80 g water
4 g pectin
11 gold strength (200
  bloom) gelatine
  leaves
1 kg mango purée

Red paint
600 g white couverture
  chocolate
300 g cocoa butter
Fat-soluble red food
  colouring, (as
  needed)

*Assembly and
finishing*
Mini meringues
Red-fruit powder

RED VELVET CAKE

For the vanilla sponge
In a mixer, beat the eggs with the sugar and the seeds of the vanilla pods.

Very gently add the sifted flour a little at a time while mixing.

Divide the batter into two Koma baking trays (40 cm x 30 cm) and smooth with a palette knife to a uniform thickness. Bake at 170ºC for 8 minutes in a dry oven on fan setting 3.

Transfer to a clean tray, freeze, cut out to desired shape and set aside.

For the ginger filling
Combine the yolks well with the sugar. Bring the cream to the boil and pour over the yolks. Cook to 82ºC, as if making crème anglaise, and add the softened gelatine. Strain and cool.

Whisk the cold mixture and add the ginger extract. Pour into moulds and freeze.

For the mango mousse
Whip the cream to soft peaks and set aside. Make an Italian meringue by whisking together the egg whites, 25 g of sugar and powdered egg white with a hand-held blender.

Combine the glucose, 125 g of sugar and the water in a saucepan and cook to 121ºC to make a syrup. When this temperature is reached, drizzle slowly into the beaten egg whites while whisking. Continue to whisk until the meringue cools to lukewarm.

Heat the purée, add the pectin mixed with 25 g of sugar and bring to the boil. Dissolve the softened gelatine and leave to cool a little.

Fold the meringue into the mango purée in a large bowl, and then fold in the cream. Fill piping bags.

For the red paint
Melt the couverture with the cocoa butter and red food colouring, and mix. When the temperature of the mixture reaches 40ºC, strain and fill a paint sprayer.

Assembly and finishing
Fill the moulds to one-third with the mousse. Position the ginger filling insert in the middle and cover almost to the top of the mould with the mousse (leave a space of 1 cm). Cover with the sponge and freeze.

When frozen, unmould and stand cakes on a tray. Turn on the air compressor and spray the cakes with a fine coat of the paint. Decorate the individual cakes with mini meringues and freeze-dried red-fruit powder.

THE GUARDIANS OF THE JUNGLE

UUT IS IN THE MIDDLE OF NOWHERE. A dozen humble, rudimentary houses scale the slope overlooking the countless meanders of the River Marañón, an hour and a half by boat from the river port of Imazita. The first houses are high enough above the river to be out of reach by flooding during the rainy season. From above, the view is breathtaking. The river below cuts through the uniformity of the jungle, which dominates the horizon. All is green as far as the eye can see. Beached on the stones and mud of the riverbank are four typical boats, known as *peque-peques*. These long and narrow canoes provide the main form of river transport. They used to be carved out of a single tree trunk, but now they are assembled using wooden planks, although the shape is the same. Sometimes a small trunk is split to form the base, and the structure is built up with planks. The larger trees disappeared as the lands along the river became developed and its people were uprooted. The name of the boat imitates the sound of the small outboard motor, resembling that of a lawnmower: peque... peque... peque...

Carlín Paati is the *apu* of Uut, the chief of the village, and he awaits us on the bank. About 40 years old, he belongs to the new generation of Awajún leaders. In recent years, young people have been replacing their elders as leaders of their communities in order to set a new pace, and to deal with the profound changes they have been experiencing for the last 60–70 years, when the once nomadic societies comprising a handful of families were made to live in permanent settlements. The process began with the arrival of evangelising missions, interested in bringing together the inhabitants of the region to ensure control over their society and the introduction of new beliefs, in addition to providing services such as healthcare and education. Evangelical Christians arrived in the 1920s, through the Summer Institute of Linguistics, while the Jesuits came in the 1940s. Recognition of the indigenous lands by the Peruvian state and the official creation of native communities came in 1974, with the passing of the Native Communities Act, which fosters, consolidates and regulates this process.

Uut is home to 680 inhabitants, who are evidence of the new way of life imposed on Awajún society. They were forced to leave behind the thousand-year-old traditions of a people who hunted, fished and gathered for their subsistence, to become farmers and poultry breeders. Hunting and gathering are unthinkable in the

THE AWAJÚN PROCLAIM THEMSELVES TO BE THE LAST GUARDIANS OF THE JUNGLE. THEY ARE A PROUD PEOPLE, AND THEIR PRIDE IS MORE THAN JUSTIFIED.

new reality faced by the Awajún people. They were possible when they lived in small groups and wandered the rainforest, moving their dwelling places to new areas so that life in the areas they left behind them could recover. There is barely any wildlife in this part of the Amazon today. Any young person in Uut who decides to go out and hunt has to cross the Marañón into the jungle and hike for two or three days. Agriculture rules the new Awajún reality, and it is practised in tune with their understanding of their relationship with the forest: with the greatest possible respect for the natural environment. 'Because God gave us the land, we work it and produce the way we do,' *apu* Carlín Paati explains. Whether it is out of obedience to divine command or owing to the extreme poverty in which they live, no chemicals or pesticides are applied to any of their crops.

The Awajún are a proud people, and their pride is more than justified. They proclaim themselves to be the last guardians of the jungle, drawing from an understanding of the universe that upholds the significance of the role they have been given in the scheme by which the relationship of humans with nature is governed. Their view of the world is based on the duality of the souls housed in each individual – the one that rises to heaven and the one obligated to remain on the Earth – becoming incarnate in trees and animals that are able to take on the appearance of small demons, which only attack the enemies of nature. The jungle is the Earth, and the gods entrusted them with its care even after death.

The spirituality and mysticism that encompasses their life is largely based on ayahuasca and other plants, such as toé, which defines the life of the individual through ceremonies of introspection. When I ask Otoniel Danducho, mayor of the Imazita district, about how Awajún leaders are chosen, he points me directly and unwaveringly to the ayahuasca ceremony. 'It's the result of an extraordinary clarity that you get through the visions obtained through hallucinogenic plants – ayahuasca, toé and others – and there you see your future. As of that moment, you strive to achieve what you saw with the hallucinogenic plants. And that's very important. All our leaders have taken them, and the people who haven't taken them have practically no vision.' He continues. 'They're ritual sessions that can be led by an elder who knows how it works and helps you to have visions. And if you don't see, you have to fight, and to continue taking them as often as it takes for you to be able to see. When you have the vision, you can stop taking them, but if you lose your power, you have to keep taking and taking them.'

It cannot be easy to reconcile this mystical view of the past and the spirits with the new religious relations with the Evangelical churches that are flourishing

THE CACAO IN UUT IS COVERED WITH
BANANA LEAVES AND HESSIAN SACKS
TO KEEP IN THE HEAT FROM THE
FERMENTATION PROCESS.

THE AWAJÚN HAVE RETAINED THEIR TRADITIONAL CUSTOMS. SURI, THE GRUB THAT LIVES IN THE HEARTS OF CERTAIN PALM TREES, IS CONSIDERED A DELICACY.

in this part of the Amazon. I ask the pastor of Nuevo Salem, and he offers an interesting account of the way in which the two beliefs are reconciled. He does not accept the use of ayahuasca, but he does not condemn it either. He calls it destructive, but admits that he used it twice before finding his path: He does not believe he will use it again, but neither does he rule it out. Nothing in this land is straightforward.

Our arrival in Uut brings with it the repetition of a ritual shared with all the communities in this part of the Amazon rainforest I have visited over the last four years. The presence of strangers is an occasion for a communal gathering, to which all inhabitants, including women and children, are invited. Visitors must introduce themselves to the community, explain who they are, where they come from, what they do, and why they have come. The assembly decides if their presence is accepted or, if not, rejected. The meeting is a mere formality today, there were a few times in the past when things got tense, and I was made to turn around and leave. The gathering is held in the open air, in a clearing next to the village, far from the communal hall that is the hub of life for these peoples. That is where they meet to debate and also to deliver penalties and punishments. The *apu* is wearing a *tawa*, a striking headdress of feathers, in this case from the tunki bird,

also known as the Andean cock-of-the-rock, a sign of rank. As you rise through the ranks, the source and number of feathers change. They used to be toucan feathers, but given the increasingly rare and protected nature of the species, new *apus* have had to seek other birds from which to make them. However, finding tunki birds in this area is no longer easy. A few of the attendees demonstrate ritual paintings, while a small group wear traditional garb – red tunics for the women, necklaces fashioned from seeds, and belts from which hang pieces of shell from the kunku snail, the world's largest land snail. The men wear anklets, known as *shakab*, which tinkle like tiny bells when they walk. Agreement is reached; the assembly is over quickly and it ends with the sharing of a bowl of masato – the ritual beverage made from fermented cassava – a dance with the newcomers and a communal lunch. Today they have stewed one of the chickens that roam freely about the village, and cooked a few pieces of chonta, which is the tenderest part of the heart of the palm. If there is chonta, it also means that there will be suri, a large, buttery grub that lives in the heart of palm. It is a cream colour, and its head is hard and black. Freshly cooked over embers, it is a succulent delicacy, creamy on the inside and crunchy on the outside.

Uut is a small community, but the inhabitants use their own facility to ferment

THE INHABITANTS OF THE AWAJÚN COMMUNITIES SURROUNDING CHIRIACO AND IMAZITA GATHER IN PAKÚ TO SHOW US SOME OF THEIR TRADITIONAL CRAFTS.

PAKÚ IS ACROSS THE RIVER FROM CHIRIACO. YOU CAN CROSS BY BOAT OR IN THIS CAGE PUSHED FROM ABOVE.

and dry cacao, fruit of the development programmes that have passed through this place. They have three fermenting boxes set up at the same level, although as the low season has just finished, only one is full today. It is covered with banana leaves and hessian sacks to keep in the heat and make use of the bacteria living under the leaves to encourage fermentation. They also tend to the drying, but the humid conditions complicate their labour. The inhabitants of Nuevo Salem, practically across the river from Uut, do not have their own facility. They used to cross the Marañón with their cacao to ferment it in Uut, but relations between the two localities are a little strained now, and this crossing has been interrupted. There was a time when they came to an agreement with a Peruvian company that paid them four soles for each kilogram of baba, and they had no need to ferment or dry the beans. It was a good price, but well-intentioned companies come and go in this land, just like NGOs – few last more than one or two years, but after this time, aside from token changes, things tend to go back to how they were before their arrival – and they were once again preyed on by cacao buyers. They continued to be paid four soles, but this time for each kilogram of dried cacao, which meant a cut of 40 per cent in the purchase

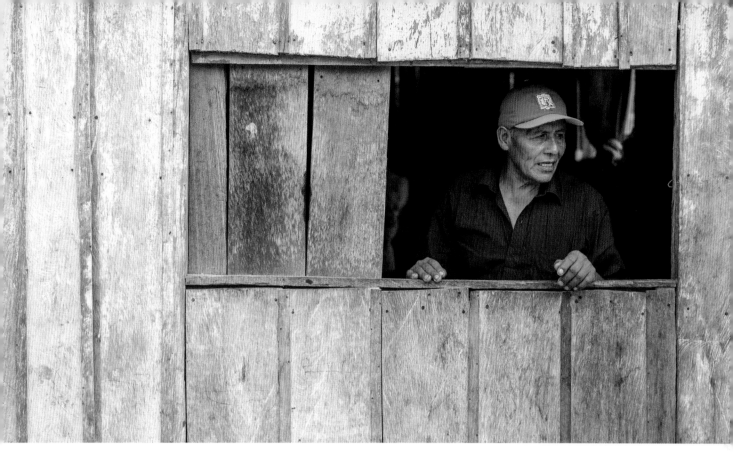

price and a noticeable increase in costs.

Thirty-five families live in Nueva Salem, which is significant demographic growth; there were only eight in 2000. Prior to then, the only inhabitants were the family of Víctor Kining, responsible for transforming the place. An Evangelical Christian church was built in 1999 and the settlement began to grow. Now with 35 registered households, there are sufficient numbers for a local school. There are 46 students in primary level and 20 in infant education. Víctor's farm covers a hectare planted with cacao and banana, and he has little hope of increasing its size. Obtaining land in the rainforest is no mean feat. The sustainable management of the environment and control of the frontier forest are practically insurmountable barriers to the expansion of farmland. He discovered this when he married a girl from Uut. He crossed the river to live with her, but had to cross back because there was no available land to farm on her side. Here he has a hectare of land with which to feed his family. He grows cassava, which is their staple food, and other subsistence crops, together with cacao and banana. It is not much when you live together with three of your eight children and two grandchildren, but they make do. The income from the three years

VÍCTOR KINING WAS THE FORCE BEHIND THE GROWTH OF NUEVO SALEM. HE CULTIVATES A HECTARE OF CACAO AND SOME YUCA, WHICH IS HIS FAMILY'S STAPLE FOOD.

during which he worked as a team leader on the Tajimat Project allowed him to start up a turkey farm and to build a 700-square-metre fish farm, which produces the native black prochilodus and other varieties. Symbolising his prosperity is the television, which takes pride of place in the main living area of his home and which runs on a generator. Solar panels only cover the basic necessities.

Cacao is the focal point of life in Nuevo Salem. 'We can't give it up because it's our livelihood; without cacao and without bananas, we couldn't live,' says Víctor as he dreams of being able to make his own chocolate. He took courses in Santa María and Tarapoto to learn the secret of the transformation the cacao bean undergoes, but the machinery he would need remains out of reach.

The road to the future is being carved out on this cacao plantation, which is so very different from the one we encountered a few days earlier in Piura. While the cacao there flourishes in the fields, here it is hidden in the forest. The people live and work in the rainforest, and the environment determines both the way this work is performed and its result. The rainforest looms over everything, and while this does not make it better or worse, it complicates things a little, although it also makes others easy. It is not easy to overcome postponements or to change the basic structure of the lives of the Awajún communities. The environment in which they live out their lives marks the starting point for the road that will bring these growers closer to niche markets.

Awjún territory

We are in the province of Bagua, one of the seven that comprise the department of Amazonas, in the north-west of Peru, close to the border with Ecuador. Bagua and the neighbouring province of Condoranqui are home to most of the members of the Awajún ethnic group in Peru – some sources mention 55,000, while others raise the figure to as many as 80,000 – although the ancient peoples of the jungle are not governed by contemporary administrative boundaries, but by the territories defined by the basins of the rivers that flow through the region. It would be more precise to say that the Awajún occupy the basins of the middle reaches of the rivers Santiago, Dominguisa, Marañón, Nieva, Chiriaco and Cenepa. There are a few offshoots in the neighbouring Cajamarca province, on the border with Ecuador, in San Martín, close to the River Mayo, and in Datem de Marañón, in Loreto. The name they give themselves is *Aents* ('people'), and together with the Shuar and Achuar peoples they form the larger family of Jivaro ethnic groups. The Shuar (a name that also means 'people') are mainly found in the south of Ecuador, along the border with Peru. It is estimated that they exceed 80,000 members, part

of whom inhabit the Peruvian side, along the upper reaches of the River Santiago, where they are known as the Wampi. The Shuar inhabit the cantons of Pastaza and Morona. The three are warrior peoples, who had already established relations with the Mochica people of northern Peru, and would end up holding out against the Incas, and later the Spaniards.

We have entered the jungle via the highway that takes us to the River Marañón as it leaves the National Sanctuary of La Cordillera de Colán, close to 40,000 hectares of virgin rainforest enjoying the greatest possible protection for a natural park. This is the only road that crosses it, and there is no way to enter the park. Here the rainforest becomes misty and damp, as it is constantly blanketed by low cloud that clings to the ground, at times cutting the mountain in half. Jaguars are still thought to live here today. They have a special significance for the Awajún, and are a sacred part of their lands. The scenery is breathtaking. A succession of forested mountains and a web of watercourses that interconnect to gorge the Marañón with their waters. Much further downstream, between Iquitos and Nauta, where the Marañón joins the Ucayali, the resulting river is given the name Amazon.

In two hours we will have reached Chiriaco, and from there to Imazita, beside the river, it is only about 20 minutes by trail. Our journey into Awajún territory,

WHILE THE CACAO IN PIURA FLOURISHES IN THE FIELDS, HERE IT IS HIDDEN IN THE FOREST. THE ENVIRONMENT DETERMINES THE WAY WORK IS PERFORMED AND ITS RESULT.

however, starts out even before we reach their domain, in the midst of an almost desert-like area – technically a dry tropical forest – a few kilometres before reaching Bagua, the provincial capital. We pause at kilometre 201 of the 5-N, the great Amazon highway that runs along the edge of the jungle, at a place called Curva del Diablo ('Devil's Curve'). There we have an appointment with Max Drusche, a German who has lived his whole life in Peru and today is one of the leading players in the development of the district we have come to visit, centred on Chiriaco and Imazita. The space where we have stopped is where one of the most dramatic events in Peru's recent history took place on 5 June 2009.

Max explains. 'In 2009, national laws were passed that the indigenous peoples interpreted as a threat to their control over their lands. They began a protest movement and blockaded this road for 55 days. The negotiations were deadlocked, and one day before they were supposed to lift the blockade, the Peruvian government decided to act to break the blockade with a police offensive, causing a clash in which 23 Peruvians died, both police and indigenous. On the same day, 11 more police were killed at a pumping station owned by Petroperú, inside the rainforest.' The terrible outcome caused a huge scar that still has not healed, and reflected at this very curve by the 23 white crosses with the names of the 23 victims in black. On the other side of the road, an Evangelical Church has raised a huge hoarding with a new name proposed for the place: Curve of Hope, with Jesus. Everybody continues to identify it as the Devil's Curve.

Max Drusche had proposed starting the journey here, 'because this is where our involvement with the indigenous communities began'. As he explains, 'We were invited to take part in a series of talks and to assist with the process of analysing what had happened, and how we had come to the bloodiest confrontation in the recent history of the Republic of Peru. In this context, both mestizo (mixed-race, the majority ethnic group in Peru) and indigenous communities concluded that a shared discourse engaged with a market logic was in their interest. They have a rather restricted economy; however, their opportunities for subsistence on hunting, fishing and gathering are increasingly less feasible. It was a time when their transition to family farming was still in its early days but increasing in importance, especially for the young. When we saw the importance it had, we took on the challenge of working together with them on a project that they themselves christened Tajimat, which means 'living well', to improve and strengthen two value chains, native cacao and organic bananas.' Bamboo has been incorporated today as a third element.

Cacao means opportunity in the land of the Awajún, and bananas are their ally. There was always naturally growing, wild cacao here, but it could not be turned into chocolate. The fruit are too small, the yield in beans is insignificant and there

HERE THE JUNGLE BECOMES LOWLAND FOREST, WITH LITTLE VARIATION IN THE TERRAIN AND A GREEN AND UNIFORM HORIZON.

were no benefits to consider. The new settlers place the first arrival of domesticated cacao at the beginning of the 1980s, attributing to their parents the responsibility of the boom in its cultivation, although this turned out to be somewhat ephemeral. Plantations flourished using native varieties and their produce found good markets, changing the lives of the growers' families. However, the appearance of the *Moniliophthora roreri* fungus and witches' broom disease wiped out the cacao in little under the time the boom had lasted, leading to the abandonment of cacao-growing for the next 25 years. The cacao did not disappear; it just stayed there, waiting to be rescued. Twenty-one communities scattered throughout the Alto Marañón and Bajo Marañón regions and around the headwaters of the River Nieva were involved with the Tajimat Project. At that time, the communities' relationship with cacao was one of mere subsistence, and average yearly production did not even reach 90 kilograms per hectare, when the national average was about 800 kilograms.

Tajimat focused its work on improving crops through training the members of the communities. It began by training members of the actual communities to be team leaders and hiring them to oversee the work in the field, enabling cultivation techniques to be improved, encouraging work in cacao production and improving productivity. Then came the identification of varieties, and although the genetic analysis of each one of them could not be conducted, a total of 1,000 parcels were georeferenced. At the time the Tajimat Project was officially closed – at the end of the time established for the duration of the project by its sponsors the Inter-American Development Bank the Peru-Ecuador Binational Plan – production had risen to between 300 and 350 kilograms per hectare; commercial links had been forged, which included exports to Italy; and continuity of part of the work was guaranteed by the development programmes implemented by the municipality of Imazita.

Women of Sukutín and Kunchín

We have come to visit some of the communities of the Alto Marañón region with whom Tajimat was working, whose centres in Chiriaco and Imazita channelled the fruit of their labour through the ports located in each locality, one on the River Chiriaco, and the other on the Marañón itself. These centres are where commercial and administrative relations with the inhabitants of the area are conducted. The first visit is always to Temashnum. It lies 15 minutes upstream from Imazita. It is the closest, best organised and most populated of the villages we will be visiting. There are about 800 inhabitants and some 130 families who live on a plain, a few metres above the level of the river. We arrive during class time and there is plenty

LIKE OTHER WOMEN IN MANY
VILLAGES, LIDIA CUNGUMAS OWNS
HER OWN FARM IN TEMASHNUM.

of activity in the school, which has over 100 children enrolled. It is supplied by solar energy and has a mobile telephone mast with limited service, but it offers a better signal than the one in Imazita. There is a prosperity that is not to be seen in other villages.

In Temashnum we are received by a few of the Awajún team leaders trained under the Tajimat Project who have come from Kunchín and Sukutín, two communities that have become legendary. There is little more than an hour's walk separating the two localities, which are the two most productive centres of the project. They were the first to ferment and dry their own cacao beans, and to produce the highest quality product, but they are practically impossible for us to visit. There are no conventional paths leading to either village, as most trails rise and fall abruptly, making any journey an adventure. The native porters can make the journey on foot in seven or eight hours, depending on how laden they are, but it would be much more difficult for us. Inés Paape and Teófilo Paape, respective presidents of the separate cacao growers' associations for men and women in Kunchín, and their two companions left the village yesterday morning at eight o'clock and reached Temashnum nine hours later, at five o'clock in the afternoon. Inés carried her young daughter. The path to Temashnum coincides with the journey made by the cacao to the river, on its way to be sold. It is carried by professional porters who carry sacks weighing between 30 and 40 kilograms each, and they take eight hours to cover the distance. They take advantage of the journey back to deliver essentials needed in the village, but they are lighter on their feet and make the trip in six hours. 'How long would an outsider take?' I ask Teófilo. 'Outsiders would take more than 12 hours; the way is really bad.'

Sukutín and Kunchín lead the field in many areas: they harvest larger volumes; they control the fermentation process; they dry the beans; and they have a quality product. They managed to produce 1,000 kilograms of dried beans one season, but the *Moniliophthora roreri* fungus and witches' broom disease hit hard, meaning that they could sell no more than 560 kilograms of their last harvest. This may seem little, but the income it brings in is a determining factor of life for these small communities (Kunchin has 180 inhabitants, while Sukutin has 430). And then there are the women, who are a role model for the entire district. Inés and another 32 women of Kunchín founded the Women Cacao Growers' Association in 2016, while the women of Sukutín created their own, the Nugkui Association. They are the only two initiatives of their kind among the Awajún and among the very few existing in the entire cacao-growing areas of Peru.

The Cacao of Amazonas

The cacao produced in the department of Amazonas has been protected by special protected designation of origin status since August 2016, when the Cacao de Amazonas Denomination of Origin was created. It includes, distinguishes and, on paper at least, protects close to 12,000 hectares of cacao plantations registered to 1,239 growers in the provinces of Bagua and Utcubamba, excluding the plantations of Condoranqui owing to the predominance of hybrid varieties there. It is the tenth such denomination of origin created in Peru and suffers from the same drawbacks as the earlier ones. They were imposed directly by the government, top-down, instead of following the path taken by the product from the bottom, from the growers, which creates doubts and leaves certain gaps. But it is a good support system for the cacao plantations of a region which has become committed to native varieties, setting the quest for quality above yields. It is also a good starting point for a region determined to consolidate its native cacaos to gradually convert the remaining varieties to natives. The regional government has passed a resolution making it compulsory for 80 per cent of new plantations to be stocked with native cacao varieties.

Makes 25

*Hazelnut and
chocolate mousse*
150 g milk
75 g egg yolks
37.5 g sugar
560 g cream (35% fat)
6.5 g gelatine leaves
125 g hazelnut praline
125 g milk chocolate
250g cream

Hazelnut sponge
114 g eggs
15 g egg yolk
80 g sugar
76 g egg whites
28 g plain flour
80 g ground hazelnuts
0.4 g salt

Lemon cream
131 g lemon purée
131 g sugar
87 g egg yolks
2 g gelatine leaves
174 g unsalted butter

*65% cacao chocolate
cream*
56 g egg yolks
28 g sugar
140 g milk
140 g cream (35% fat)
134 g 65% cacao
  chocolate

Neutral glaze
167 g still mineral
  water
84 g glucose
117 g sugar
5 g pectin NH
0.8 g citric acid

MILK CHOCOLATE, LEMON AND HAZELNUT CAKE

For the hazelnut and chocolate mousse

Make a crème anglaise by heating the milk in a saucepan, whisking the egg yolks with the sugar separately, and mixing everything together in the pan before folding in the cream. Stir the mixture over the heat until it reaches a temperature of 85°C. Remove from the heat, strain and add the softened gelatine leaves. Pour the mixture over the praline and chocolate. Whisk well and cool to 33°C. Finish by folding in a small amount of cream whipped to soft peaks, followed by the remainder.

For the hazelnut sponge

Beat the eggs and the egg yolks in a bowl, adding 50 g of sugar, to ribbon consistency.

Beat the egg whites with 30 g of sugar to stiff peaks.

Mix the two mixtures together, and then fold in the flour, ground hazelnuts and salt.

Fill a 60 x 40-cm baking tin and bake for 8 minutes at 220°C.

For the lemon cream

Mix the lemon purée with the sugar and egg yolks in a saucepan and bring to the boil. Add the softened gelatine leaves and mix thoroughly. Cool the mixture to 40°C and add the butter at room temperature. Whisk the mixture, fill (4 cm diameter) moulds and freeze.

For the 65% cacao chocolate cream

Whisk the egg yolks with the sugar, heat the milk, and mix together before incorporating the cream. Pour over the chocolate and wait for a few minutes before whisking. Transfer to a container and set aside in the refrigerator for 12 hours.

For the neutral glaze

Heat the water with the glucose in a saucepan to 60°C. Gradually add the sugar mixed with the pectin. Bring to the boil, add the citric acid and bring back to the boil. Skim off any impurities from the mixture and set aside in the refrigerator.

For the soft praline shortbread

Add the sugar to the softened butter. Whisk until thick and pale in a mixer fitted with a flat beater.

In the meantime, lightly heat the milk and mix briskly with the praline until elastic and glossy.

Add the milk and praline mixture to the softened butter and add the sifted flour.

Chill the pastry for an hour in the refrigerator and spread out to a 2–3-mm thickness on a tray. Freeze. When frozen, cut to the desired size and bake at 160°C for about 12 minutes.

*Soft praline
shortbread*
58 g sugar
147 g unsalted butter,
  softened
39 g milk
60 g hazelnut praline
196 g plain flour

Microwave sponge
83 g hazelnut butter
125 g egg whites
83 g egg yolks
83 g icing sugar
26 g plain flour

Praline crunch
240 g 45% cacao milk
  chocolate
340 g hazelnut praline
156 g hazelnut butter
113 g feuilletine flakes

For the microwave sponge

Whisk all ingredients together with a hand-held blender. Strain and fill a siphon.

Pipe the mixture into 33-ml plastic cups, filling halfway, and cook for 40 seconds in the microwave on the highest power setting.

For the praline crunch

Melt the chocolate and mix with the hazelnut praline and hazelnut butter. Next, fold in the feuilletine flakes. Spread the mixture over the hazelnut sponge and chill in the freezer for a few minutes.

Assembly and finishing

Assemble the cake in reverse order. Fill the mould halfway with the hazelnut mousse. Next, add the lemon cream insert and cover with a little more mousse. Finally, close the mould with the crunch-covered hazelnut sponge. Freeze, unmould and brush with the neutral glaze. Place on top of the shortbread. Decorate with a little microwave sponge and a quenelle of chocolate cream.

CACAO CAME FIRST

ON GLADYS MARÍA MESTRE'S FARM there is a tree that bears the whitest, strangest and most striking cacao pods I have seen until now. Its skin is tinged with a very light and muted green, but the surface is white and rough – very rough – and covered with bumps, as if suffering from a rash. It is not very big, more medium sized and rounded. Two pods hang from the trunk, and we are allowed to split one open, seeing it is nearly ripe. It has a few seeds, which are wide and a good size, and they are completely white when cut open. The pulp is sweet and aromatic, and when you taste the bean, it is soft, subtle and fragrant. This tree was grafted with a scion of another found a few years ago on a mountainside in the Sierra Nevada de Santa Marta mountains, and it is one of the few that have survived on the farm after the tremendous drought experienced three years before. It was able to survive thanks to the plastic soda bottle hung next to it, providing it with one drop of water at a time. I have seen photos of similar fruit in the Suchitepéquez region of Guatemala.

Gladys's white cacao has spent more than two years under intensive care and now has two pods. It overcame one of toughest and most devastating droughts ever recorded in this land, at a time when there were more than 500 cacao trees on this farm. Now, little more than one year later, barely a few scatterings remain.

There is nothing random about our encounter with this cacao of post-apocalyptic appearance and unique qualities. We have been brought here by Mayumi Ogata, a Japanese woman who founded and is one of the partners of Cacao Hunters, a leading

ON GLADYS MARÍA MESTRE'S FARM IS THE STRANGEST CACAO TREE THAT I HAVE EVERY SEEN. ITS WHITE AND ROUGH PODS ARE TINGED WITH GREEN.

THERE IS A LITTLE OF EVERYTHING ON THIS FARM. WHITE CACAOS, CRIOLLO VARIETIES AND REGIONAL CACAOS.

brand in the new Colombian chocolate scene, and a defining figure. Mayumi has worked for six years on rescuing cacao-growing in Colombia, but she has a very special relationship with the Arhuaco communities in these mountains. She has trekked through the areas most suited to growing cacao, identifying and noting down practically every tree. She found the original tree a few years ago, and she brought back a few cuttings to graft.

There is a little of everything on this farm. We come across what Mayumi classifies as regional cacaos, growing next to Criollo varieties and a few white cacaos, although here they are known as 'sweet cacaos'. White cacaos are quite distinct, sometimes as remarkable as the whitish and rough specimen we have just opened, but we are yet to see any two that look the same. These cacao plantations are a sort of genetic Tower of Babel. There is a bit of everything, and it is sometimes difficult to find harmony. This morning we are visiting the farm owned by Victoria Torres, on the bank of the River Don Diego. There too we find diversity, including the hybrid strains promoted by the development plans, always spearheaded by CCN-51. It is the result of the Forest Warden Families Programme, put in place in 2006 by the United Nations and the government of Colombia and designed to eradicate coca plantations, replacing them with cacao and timber tree species.

There is a proverbial abundance in Victoria's domains; more than 800 cacao trees cover the hectare of land she has been farming for seven years. Prior to this time, it could barely be identified as paddock. A very old cacao tree somehow had managed to survive in the middle of the field. Nobody knows its age, but it has a broad trunk and an exposed network of roots, treasuring the memory of days gone by. It was kept after the grass was dug up, and more cacao was planted, along with banana and some yuca.

Both Gladys and Victoria consulted Mamo Camilo before planting their cacao trees, as do other inhabitants of this part of the indigenous territory. The title *mamo* is given to the leaders of the Arhuaco communities, regardless of what careers they may have made for themselves, and Mamo Camilo is the most highly respected leader in this part of the Sierra Nevada mountains. Authorisation is essential for any activity that involves using or altering the natural environment. The Arhuaco people not only live in harmony with nature, but they see it as their life's mission to preserve the balance of all natural elements: sun, rain, wind, fire, plants, stones and animals. Any activity that implies transformation must be consulted with the communities' spiritual guides and authorised by them.

Mamo Camilo receives us in Catanzama, located on the slopes of the Sierra Nevada de Santa Marta, an impressive mountain range in the north of the country, rising to over 5,700 metres. It is amazing to see snow by the shores of the Caribbean. And between the snow and the sea is a whole world of microclimates and natural spaces which have largely remained untouched by human activity. Catanzama is close to Perico (between Buritaca and Palomino), on a tongue of land jutting into the sea that is considered sacred by the Arhaucos and three other indigenous communities – the Kankwamo, Wiwa and Kogi peoples – who have always shared the lands contained in the Sierra Nevada de Santa Marta National Park, which was declared a biosphere reserve in 1979. It is the world's highest coastal mountain range, and the lands inhabited by the four ethnic groups that comprise the Tayrona Indigenous Confederation. And it is here, in Catanzama, where their representatives gather to reconcile their relationship with the space in which they live. 'Here is where we live and where the reality of the indigenous peoples is preserved,' the *mamo* explains. 'We believe that everything has life – the trees, the water, and all the elements that surround us – and that the land is like our mother, because if it didn't exist, neither would we exist. We depend on it, and we make our living from it, which is why we should protect it.' Catanzama in the Arhuaco language means 'root of thought', which is in tune with their basic beliefs about the origins of the

WHITE CACAOS ARE QUITE DISTINCT, SOMETIMES AS REMARKABLE AS THE WHITISH AND ROUGH SPECIMEN WE HAVE JUST FOUND.

world. The Arhuacos and everything around them existed in thought even before the creation of the universe. They are the older siblings, and they live at the centre of the Earth, which they share in peace with the other three native peoples. Other human beings came later. We, the younger siblings, are like a fleeting accident, and we seem to be more interested in altering the natural order than anything else. The Arhuacos tend to use the word *iku*, meaning 'person', to refer to their people.

Mamo Camilo is a striking figure. He receives us seated under the largest tree in the village, some sort of energy hotspot provided by nature. He is dressed completely in white, like everybody we come across – whether man, woman or child – although his is the whitest of all. He wears a knee-length tunic, gathered at the waist by a woollen belt, also white, and calf-length trousers. His hat resembles a hard helmet in the shape of a truncated cone. It rounds off an immaculate outfit which is complemented by two sling bags that every Arhuaco tends to carry, a large bag for their personal items, and another smaller bag for coca leaves. There can be a third, for food, but today it is at home. Most Arhuaco bags are made of wool, but those worn by the *mamo* are much finer, possibly made from cotton or a plant fibre known as *fique*, traditionally used in Colombia until the introduction of wool. They are also missing the traditional geometric patterns of Arhuaco bags, featuring lines reflecting the lines of thought: long and relatively straight for men, and broken and shorter for women. Arhuaco culture reserves thinking and work on the land for men, relegating women to everyday chores. Men carry a strange utensil, cream in colour and with a stick inserted through the top. It is a *poporo*, a type of container that collects the thoughts of the Arhuaco man. It consists of a dried and hollowed-out gourd with a hole at the top and filled with a powder made from ground sea shells. Arhuaco men always carry one from the time the *mamo* decides that they have reached adulthood, and it is associated with the coca leaves they typically chew. When a man has a thought, he wets the end of the stick with saliva and dips it into the shell powder and draws lines around the gourd, which grow with every new thought. The *poporo* that the *mamo* is holding already has a powder coating some five centimetres thick, and he will continue to use it until its size and weight makes it difficult to hold. Each man keeps his *poporos* at home, in case there is a need to go back over past thoughts.

Catanzama is the centre of the universe. This is the land inhabited by the first peoples, and cacao is an intrinsic part of it. Everything here is imbued with a halo of transcendence that turns each surprising detail into food for thought. His garments are a good example. 'These clothes weren't invented by my grandfather or my great-great grandfather, or by his,' the *mamo* explains. 'They were also made

MAMO CAMILO IS A STRIKING FIGURE. HE RECEIVES US UNDER THE LARGEST TREE IN THE VILLAGE, SOME SORT OF ENERGY HOTSPOT PROVIDED BY NATURE.

GLADYS MESTRE'S CACAO TREES HAVE NEVER BEEN VERY PRODUCTIVE, AT TIMES YIELDING THREE OR FOUR PODS PER TREE. THEY ARE OFTEN AS SMALL AS THIS.

at the beginning, when the creator left us this culture of great knowledge. The hat represents the snow of the Sierra Nevada, and we dress this way because we're always in a spiritual connection with Mother Nature, with the spirit of the snow and with the sea, and with the other components that are a part of nature.' You cannot visit Catanzama without an invitation. This small community, with sixty permanent inhabitants, growing to more than 200 at times of important gatherings, is off limits to outsiders.

Cacao is an essential part of the view of the world held by the Arhuaco communities. It was with them in the beginning and is born with them, handed down by a spiritual father they call Terunna or Tayuna. He was the one who gave them this crop, and they have been faithful to his command, although with a few highs and lows. The *mamo* tells us about the time when the younger siblings came and forced them to move to the plateau, distancing them from their natural settlements. It takes me a while to realise that he does not refer to the Capuchin missionaries who entered these lands with the intention of destroying their beliefs and way of life with blood and fire; nor does he refer to the settlers, who appeared with the highway built by the government, bringing with them crops of marijuana first, followed shortly afterwards by the large-scale planting of coca and by the war brought by it. His conversation is in fact leaping back 500 years in time, to the arrival of the Spaniards, which he presents as a temporary event. These people, who can be anything other than belligerent, believe that they are marked by fate, and they know that this is their place and they will always find it again. 'It was time for us to move away a little, but knowledge is always preserved,' Mamo Camilo concludes. They partially achieved this in 1973, when the Resguardo Arhuaco, a 'reserve' or collective indigenous territory, was officially created. It was cemented in 1983, with the enlargement of the area to cover close to 200,000 hectares of the Sierra Nevada de Santa Marta, spanning the departments of Magdalena and César, and they again consolidated their position over the last decade with the eradication of the coca and marijuana crops. Cacao has become a decisive factor in this process of the Arhuaco returning to their roots, regaining their natural space and reasserting their quest for balance with nature.

With time, they were able to restore the slopes and foothills of the mountains, the areas most suited to cacao-growing. Over the course of the last ten years, they rescued the trees that had managed to survive the passing of time and neglect, and they have come to embrace new growing techniques that will help them to change their relationship with the market. The *mamo* also grows cacao. According to Mayumi Ogata, his farm has a different sort of energy. When the *mamo* took over it, there were many cacao trees and many of them were very old. They are still researching the varieties, but Mayumi thinks that the property has a great deal of potential.

The role of cacao in the view of the world that sets this people apart can be summarised in one sentence expressed by Hernán Villafana as we go to visit the school in Catanzama, where lessons are given in Arhuaco and future *mamos* are being trained: 'The white cacao bean is the brain of nature.' Mamo Camilo would later explain this concept a little further: 'White cacao produces thought in us.'

Distinction is made in this district between new cacaos, which are the hybrids that came with the anti-coca programmes, and the old cacaos, which encompass Criollo cacaos and white cacaos. The latter form a separate family whose members are locally referred to as sweet cacaos. We had already found white cacaos in the jungle of Peru, and the cacao plantations of Venezuela had turned a few more into benchmarks. In order to do so, there was a period of genetic selection prior to choosing the varieties that would end up as a monoculture. Here, work has barely begun on locating and noting down the varieties. Mayumi Ogata, our companion and guide for this part of the journey, is behind this work. The Arhuaco lands

THE SIERRA NEVADA DE SANTA MARTA IS AN AMAZING WORLD OF MICROCLIMATES AND NATURAL SPACES THAT ARE STILL UNTOUCHED BY HUMAN ACTIVITY.

have become a second home for her since her second visit to the cacao-growing lands of Colombia. Her first visit took her to many areas, including some in the vicinity, but she did not make it to the farms of Sierra Nevada de Santa Marta. The Arhuacos are a very reserved people and a great deal of negotiation was required. That was in 2009, and she had not found anything she thought to be particularly worthwhile. Four months later, she retraced her steps and finally managed to obtain permission from the Arhuacos to enter their sacred lands. There she found varieties of white cacao that she had never heard of.

'At that time, they knew very little about white cacao; they even thought it was a disease affecting the cacao and they were cutting the trees down. They had no idea of their value. We explained that part and asked for permission to look for more cacao and to teach them how to preserve it. They knew nothing about the crop, or how to improve production or the way to prevent diseases affecting the plant. We spoke to the *mamo* and the group, and gradually managed to get permission to do this work.' It took a long time, but in 2015 the first bars of Cacao Hunters brand Arhuaco chocolate came onto the market. The chocolate contained 72 per cent cacao, and its wrapper bore the name of the Arhuaco community.

Mayumi has been helped in her search by the children of the different villages. They are the people who best know the countryside and who tell her about the discovery of new trees. Today we are accompanied by Fredy, Victoria's son, who has come to find us riding the horse he sometimes uses to go to school in Catanzama. The journey holds many firsts for us. Mayumi Ogata turns the tour of the farm into a lesson in applied botany. When she finds a flower, she tells us, 'The cacao flower comes in different colours, but the flower of some cacaos is really

FREDY, VICTORIA TORRES'S SON, AND SEVERAL CLASSMATES FROM REMOTE FARMS RIDE HORSES TO THEIR SCHOOL IN CATANZAMA.

white. It has five petals, and it always points downwards because it has an olfactory molecule we aren't capable of smelling. But it weighs so much that it bends the flower over.' Each tree has dozens of them at a time. She explains the condition and shape of the trunks, and she speaks at length about the fruit. She describes the shape of the pod, the type of neck it has, the rugged skin, the colouring – 'A lot of the pods here are green, but they turn yellow as they ripen'. She goes on to explain that when different varieties interbreed, the colour and the glossiness of the skin ends up changing. There is an explanation for everything, or a chapter in this encyclopaedia she keeps in one or other part of her memory. And then there are the leaves, which differ so much between the different cacao varieties that if I had not seen how she cut them, I would think they were from a different species altogether. She has been setting aside pods from a number of clearly distinct trees, and cutting a leaf from each tree. They are completely different; some are long and pointed; others small and round; others are serrated … None of them resemble any of the others. Leaf shape is part of the identification process she has developed for when she visits the countryside outside of harvest times. 'The first thing I do is look at the tree, and then the flower. Next, I look at the leaves and the fruit,' she

THERE IS A PROVERBIAL ABUNDANCE IN VICTORIA'S DOMAINS; MORE THAN 800 CACAO TREES ON A HECTARE OF LAND. ONLY SEVEN YEARS AGO IT WAS A PADDOCK.

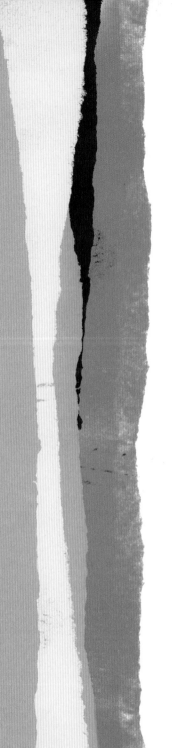

explains. 'I split it open and smell the part without any seeds first, which is where the purest aromas are, the notes that are most like cacao. I split open the seeds to see their colour and I taste them to determine the level of bitterness and astringency. I store it all in my head, and with that I can more or less understand any cacao tree without fruits. The leaves of the white cacao tree are smaller, rounder and wider,' she adds later, while we split open the pods and inspect the beans.

It seems as we tour Victoria Torres's farm that she knows each and every tree. 'This one has a graft, but there is no fruit… This one is a local variety of cacao, but it isn't white cacao because its surface and flower are different… This one is over twenty years old; it isn't ill, but it needs a good tidying up. When the tree isn't tidy, there are no flowers …' These cacaos have never been very productive. Three or four fruits for each white cacao tree, although there may be as many as six. Low yield is one of the drawbacks that determine whether or not the white cacao trees survive, and explains why they have been replaced by hybrid strains in other areas. It is one of the flaws in the process of introducing new crops in the fight against coca leaf cultivation. In order to compensate for the income from coca leaf, high-quality cacaos are needed that can generate higher incomes. Until 2015, all the growers in the Catanzama area sold their crop to cacao buyers at their set prices. Since then, they have been delivering most of their production to Mayumi's company, which has already marketed a chocolate called Arhuaco. They receive a fair price, and it has brought them the recognition of the international market.

The Arhuacos in this part of the mountains have created their own *beneficio* – a collectively owned collection, fermenting and drying plant – on Gladys's farm. It is very small and they run it themselves. The fermenting boxes are arranged in a row over the floor, and not all of them are full. The low season means the pace is less demanding, but there is still work to be done. We remove the plastic and hessian covering the boxes, keeping in the warmth, and we plunge our arms elbow deep into their moist and sticky contents. When we take them out, our hands smell strongly of rotten fruit, alcohol and even vinegar. Each box has a different smell, depending on the variety of cacao it contains and the farm it comes from. Distance determines how long it takes the beans to arrive, and this affects how the fermentation process develops.

Mayumi and her team advise and train local team leaders. Hernán is one of them. He tells me that he was led to cacao twenty years earlier with the younger siblings, and that he has been furthering his knowledge on cultivation methods for four years. He is entrusted with the task of helping the inhabitants of Catanzama to understand the importance of routine and the dynamics of the cacao plantation.

He is also an enthusiastic promoter of white cacaos, although this is difficult at times 'We older siblings have been working to recover our lands, although it seems that cacao is something new and that some Arhuacos have little knowledge of the history of cacao. I don't want to speak ill of the younger siblings, although little by little, we older ones have been regaining our ancestral lands and we've managed to make use of the trees in the mountains, where the seeds were taken from. These are our cacaos, the cacaos of our ancestors that were always the beverage of the older siblings.'

The Arhuaco cacao-growing area is, in Mayumi's words, 'cacao soup', an absolute mishmash of varieties and families. Although lacking the genetic analysis, most appear to be Criollos, many of them white, and they are always different, but that is all that can be said. Sometimes the differences are astonishing. Mayumi points this out while telling us about the colour of the flowers, which are always tinged with different hues other than white. She has only ever seen three completely white cacao flowers, the three in Sierra Nevada de Santa Marta.

Mayumi Ogata, cacao hunter

'It's experience; I'm reading the cacao,' Mayumi tells me as we inspect the shapes of leaves and pods from a number of cacoa trees she has been choosing on a farm in the Sierra Nevada de Santa Marta mountains. Experience is everything in the career of this woman whose job description nobody has ever used until now, that of cacao hunter. The experience that the reading gives her tells her that the key lies in genetics. It is the great obsession that she has carried with her in her travels through the world of cacao. She started out in Colombia in 2009, and for the next four years she journeyed through another 13 cacao-producing countries, until she had gathered enough information to allow her to decide that her destiny was, in fact, to return to the place where she began. She has lived in Colombia since 2013, where she has created her own brand of chocolates, Cacao Hunters, in partnership with the Cacao de Colombia company. Since that time, Mayumi has been touring the Colombian cacao-growing regions identifying, grading and classifying the cacaos she comes across.

Mayumi Ogata is from Sagamihara, a city in Kanagawa prefecture, close to Tokyo. She could never have imagined that life could have taken her so far away from Japan. She studied nutrition, and her first job was in a food-processing company where she created recipes with chocolate for the company and her own clients. Until one day she began to realise she had been living in the dark. 'I had nothing real in my hands.' She had spent six years shut away in her laboratory in Tokyo,

MAYUMI HAS BEEN HELPED IN HER SEARCH BY THE CHILDREN OF THE DIFFERENT VILLAGES. THEY ARE THE PEOPLE WHO BEST KNOW THE COUNTRYSIDE AND WHO TELL HER ABOUT THE DISCOVERY OF NEW TREES.

until she took advantage of an invitation from her current partner Cacao de Colombia to visit the country. That trip became the trigger for a radical change in her life. She left the company she worked for and set off to discover the world of cacao. First Madagascar – 'I was told that much of the best cacao in the world is from Madagascar' – and later Mexico and Guatemala – 'The Mayans were so important in the history of cacao' – and so forth until she completed a journey that began with the aim of discovering the world of cacao. She continued on her quest to find a way to approach cacao growers, which ended up with her gaining great knowledge of the nature of cacao.

Nine years after that first trip, Mayumi Ogata has a more than fluent dialogue with Colombian cacao. 'I'm speaking with the cacao and it's telling me things.' What does it say? 'Look inside my heart. It's a little difficult, but it's an experience. I've seen and tried many kinds of cacao, and besides taking notes, I memorise the information. And this experience is helping me to classify the cacao.' She sometimes makes a mistake and starts again from scratch. She understands chocolate to be the result of her work, but the cacao always comes first. 'It's the subject of my life. People can live without cacao and without chocolate, but with cacao and with

MAYUMI OGATA IS FASCINATED BY THE WHITE CACAOS SHE FINDS IN THE MOUNTAINS FOR THEIR SPECIAL QUALITY, AND BECAUSE THEY REFLECT HER WAY OF UNDERSTANDING CHOCOLATE.

'PEOPLE CAN LIVE WITHOUT CACAO AND WITHOUT CHOCOLATE, BUT WITH CACAO AND WITH CHOCOLATE, PEOPLE ARE HAPPY. AND WHEN THE CACAO ISN'T HAPPY, THE CUSTOMERS AREN'T HAPPY EITHER.'

chocolate, people are happy. And when the cacao isn't happy, the customers aren't happy either.'

This happiness from chocolate is the starting point for her current view of the world and a perspective on life that is full of surprises. Perhaps it is the reason why she has such a special relationship with the Arhuacos. Together with them she has combed the slopes and ravines of the Sierra Nevada de Santa Marta mountains to find unique specimens, such as the ones she has shown us on this journey. Her relationship with the Arhuacos was born out of her interest for white cacao, but there is clearly more between them than that.

Mayumi Ogata is particularly interested in white cacaos. The reason is their special quality, and because they reflect her way of understanding chocolate, in which subtlety and aromatic, floral and fruity notes outweigh bitterness and astringency. Here she found the white cacao she had been looking for, above all, one of extraordinary genetic diversity. She also identified deficiencies in the fermentation techniques, allowing her to improve the quality of the product, and the lives of growers scarred by the post-conflict situation, the troubles caused by cocaine and the short-term thinking behind the government's strategy. 'There's room, I thought, for me and to do something for the growers.'

Cacao always comes before chocolate. Practically every conversation we had with Mayumi Ogata about cacao or chocolate led, one way or another, to the subject of genetics. 'There still needs to be research into genetics. For example, in Peru in 2008, the government began intensive research into the genetic side and there were results between 2010 and 2016. Things are gradually happening, but when we look at genetics in the world, there's still so much research to be done. Lab work is needed.' There is also a need for finance and a necessity to understand the position cacao holds among the country's strategic products. She insists on the need to speak about genetics with regard to a product that is so easy to interbreed like cacao, although without it, there is always experience. 'Without genetics I can't know what cacao I have, but experience allows me to know whether or not it has potential. It helps me with the shape of the leaves or of the pod, or the flavour and aroma of the beans. I can always tell whether or not it's more aromatic when I try the cacao nibs, and finally, we apply fermentation and drying techniques that sometimes allow us to conceal some things and to enhance others. In the end, technique is as essential as genetics.'

Mayumi Ogata is fascinated by the white cacaos she finds in the Sierra Nevada and agrees with people who rank them among the finest, which takes us back to genetics. 'Many people say that white cacao is the best in the world, but when I

ask why there hasn't been any genetic research, they tell me that nobody has done it, and that it makes no sense. That's what the world of cacao is like; we're going around half-blind. In genetic terms, cacao is much more valuable, because cacao will always want to interbreed. This is why 100 per cent white is more valuable. Besides, the flavour, aroma and colour are always different.'

Chocolate was the beginning of an adventure that led Mayumi Ogata to change her life. She started with it, arrived at cacao, and then returned to chocolate with her company Cacao Hunters. We have spent three days speaking about cacao and we have barely mentioned chocolate. 'What do you want from your chocolates?' I ask. 'When I make chocolate, I don't like strong bitterness or strong astringency. From this point of view, I go back to genetics and prefer cacao without a strong flavour and which offers more aromas.' The personality of a single cacao or a blend of cacaos? 'It depends on what we want to do. If I'm looking for a long aroma, I mix several cacaos. There's no right way in the world of cacao; I always think of it as if I want to draw it, and if I make a mistake, I start over.'

'What is chocolate?' 'It's the result of our work; cacao always comes first.'

Macondo and the cacaos of Aracataca

Diversity is a given on Colombia's cacao plantations. While awaiting programmes that allow the genetic study of the cacao to be conducted, creating a map of the varieties that will enable progress in the definition of long-term pathways, the only thing left is a labour of trial and error – testing each variety separately, including harvesting, fermentation and drying, in order to transform it into chocolate and study its possibilities and, more particularly, its potential for today's market. We will see this at the Macondo Cacao School, founded by Cacao de Colombia, the company supplying Cacao Hunters, near Aracataca, a town to the south of the Santa Marta and bordering on the Sierra Nevada mountains.

Eduardo Rodríguez is waiting for the results of one of those tests. He is a farmer from the *corregimiento* of Cauca, not very far from the town of Aracataca, where he has a plantation that he is reviving after some difficult times. He sets great store by a variety that he has grafted to a dozen or so *palos* or 'sticks', the local name for the cacao trees. We split open a pod and the result is very floral, and also extremely fruity, with notes of green apple, lemon and, more particularly, mandarin. Nine pods had been picked and their beans subjected to a micro-fermentation

EDUARDO RODRÍGUEZ RUNS THE FARM THAT BELONGED TO HIS FATHER-IN-LAW, WHO WAS MURDERED BY A PARAMILITARY GROUP IN 1995 WHILE WORKING WITH HIS SON AND SON-IN-LAW.

ON EDUARDO RODRÍGUEZ'S FARM, IN THE VILLAGE OF CAUCA, A KITCHEN HAS BEEN BUILT MAKING USE OF THE STRUCTURE AND SHAPE OF TWO TERMITE NESTS.

process that has not yet concluded. Eduardo asks about the result to see whether he should go ahead with the grafting, but they are not ready yet. You have to dry the bean and turn it into chocolate in order to see its real potential, and to test it to confirm whether there is a market for it.

Eduardo's farm is squeezed in between two enormous oil palm plantations, the tree that is devouring the world's last tropical rainforests. He and neighbouring farms have been experiencing a round trip that is beginning to reach its end. The starting point can be found at the end of the nineteenth century, when the administrative divisions of the area were defined, also consolidating changes made to the uses given to the local plantations, previously dominated by tobacco. The new administrative division split the municipal area of Aracataca into *corregimientos* and *veredas* – villages and rural districts, respectively – and christened one of the latter as Vereda Theobromina, a testament to the existence of a large cacao plantation. There are few written records from subsequent years, but there is evidence of large plantations in the 1960s and as late as the 1970s, when the *Moniliophthora roreri* fungus struck, catching cacao growers unprepared. If the fungus is treated, other than debilitating the tree, it does not pose a problem for its survival. However, the lack of knowledge and training led to a shift in crops towards banana, and later palm oil. Then came the violence, brought by the guerrilla movement and prolonged by the paramilitaries who ravaged the countryside around Aracataca.

The farm did not belong to Eduardo, but to his father-in-law, who was murdered one afternoon in 1995 by the United Self-Defenders of Colombia paramilitary group. He was with one of his sons, a daughter and his son-in-law. The daughter managed to escape carrying her newborn son in her arms. Eduardo's father-in-law and his two brothers-in-law died right there, in front of the house in which we are now speaking. Eduardo took charge of the farm after that. None of the sons wanted to return to the farm for years, and when one of them does come back, he only stays for the day. Nobody lives in the house where the massacre took place.

Aracataca now has six *corregimientos*, ten *veredas*, four *caseríos* or hamlets, and 38 *barrios* or urban neighbourhoods. The awakening of the cacao plantations is a recent phenomenon, and it offers a new view of this 'cacao soup' that is replicated all over the country. The neglected Criollo cacao trees have been interbreeding, creating new varieties and even new families, mixed with the new cacao varieties introduced by the development programmes.

ON LUCHO'S FARM, WE FIND FRUITS THAT CHANGE COLOUR FROM GREEN TO DARK BROWN ARE GIVING GOOD RESULTS.

The Macondo processing facility receives cacao from 26 farms in the area, while its leaders work to train the growers and to work out a very basic map of the different varieties. There is a treat in store for us at Lucho's farm. There is a bit of everything and something for everyone. Trees that have been standing for 40 or so years are together with others that have barely seen a decade, and between the former and the latter, cacao pods whose differences can be spotted immediately. There are pods that are still green – which will turn yellow as they ripen – together with purplish ones, and scattered about are the bright red pods that characterise CCN-51. There is also a tree whose fruits change in colour from green to dark brown, while the seeds from the melon-shaped pods are giving very good results. If we compare them to the white cacao trees of the Arhuacos, which only produce nine pods at most, these trees with their yearly yield of 200–300 pods are a panacea.

Cacao production in the department of Magdalena is being reborn, encouraged by the new interest aroused by the cacaos of the Sierra Nevada de Santa Marta mountains, and is also expanding in the areas of the department of César and around Aracataca. These are two of the many faces of the round trip journey made by cacao-growing in Colombia over the last 400 years. It knew splendour for 200 years, before waning in the course of the twentieth century, but now, at this particular time, we are starting to see its rebirth, which may be definitive.

The development of the European chocolate market in the first half of the seventeenth century, buoyed by its gradual introduction into the courts of the European royalty, led to the founding of the first cacao plantations in these lands and their later expansion throughout the country. Cacao, domesticated at times and also wild, was part of the daily life of the Yukpa, Bari, Arhuaco and other native communities that comprise the present-day Tayrona Indigenous Confederation, but historians agree in pointing to the Jesuits as the driving force behind its propagation as a crop. They were so successful that what was then the Spanish colony of New Granada became the leading supplier of cacao to the crown, and it became the colony's main export. By the end of the eighteenth century, the significance of cacao-growing could be seen in Magdalena, Huaila, Chocó, Antioquía, Caldas, Cauca… The Criollo cacao varieties, then known as 'melon-shaped' after the shape of their pods, were considered of little value, and the expanding plantations were seen to be planted with seeds of the Trinitario varieties.

The growth of the European coffee market in the nineteenth century led to the first great crisis in Colombian cacao production, which was subsequently aggravated by the development of cacao production in Africa. As a crop, cacao entered into a period of decline until the mid-twentieth century when the first diseases appeared, spearheaded by black pod disease and exacerbated by *Moniliophthora roreri* and witches' broom. The coffee boom of the twentieth century, followed by the armed conflict that has torn the country apart over the last 60 years and the expansion of coca leaf crops, dealt what seemed to be the final blow. Nonetheless, production began to grow slowly in the 1980s, associated with development programmes put into place in conflict zones or as an alternative to coca leaves. Growth was sustained basically by the introduction of clones, led by CCN-51, and the timid revival of some varieties from the former cacao-growing areas, largely Criollo. The harvest of 1993 hit a peak at 54,000 tonnes, followed by falls that would bottom out in 2002 at 34,000 tonnes. The almost iron-grip control exerted on the market by two companies, which set prices and conditions, were mostly to blame for this process. Exports scarcely accounted for ten per cent of Colombia's production in 2009, contrary to the experience of its neighbours Venezuela and Ecuador at the same time.

The huge mix of cacao varieties and the lack of a long-term strategy hindered the identification, classification and breeding of varieties, a process that was vital for entry into markets for quality products.

Colombian cacao production is now headed by the departments of Santander, Arauca, Antioquia, Huila, Nariño and Tolima, followed by others such as Cauca

and Chocó. Chocolate manufacturers in search of distinction turn to Magdalena and César, in the north of the country and in the vicinity of Sierra Nevada de Santa Marta; to Tumaco, on the border with Ecuador; and to Boyacá, a department in the Colombian Andes, located close to Bogotá in the centre of the country. Exports have been growing every year, and in 2017 they reached 12,000 tonnes.

THE MACONDO PROCESSING FACILITY SEPARATELY FERMENTS AND DRIES THE CACAO BEANS HARVESTED BY 26 GROWERS IN THE AREA.

*Firm bitter orange
ganache*
200 g 70% XMC
   chocolate
140 g bitter-orange
   purée
60 g sunflower oil

Beetroot jelly
55 g beetroot juice
1.5 g pectin NH
30 g sugar
40 g isomalt
2 g 1:1 citric acid and
   water solution

*Jasmine tea royal
icing*
5 g egg white
25 g icing sugar
5 drops jasmine tea
   essence

Black paint
25 g dark chocolate
25 g cocoa butter
3 g fat-soluble black
   food colouring

Red paint
20 g cocoa butter
30 g white chocolate
   couverture
3 g fat-soluble red food
   colouring
1 g metallic red food
   colouring

EARTH NOUGAT

For the XMC single-origin chocolate
See the process on page 256.

For the firm bitter orange ganache
Heat the chocolate with the purée in a saucepan to 40ºC.

Whisk with a hand-held blender and add the oil to make a ganache.

For the beetroot jelly
Bring the beetroot juice to the boil in a saucepan. Incorporate the pectin with 15 g of sugar and bring back to the boil. Add the rest of the ingredients and cook until the sugar content reaches a refractometer reading of 75º Brix. Remove from the heat and add the citric acid solution. Pour into a tray to a 2–3-cm thickness and leave to cool.

Cut the jelly into the desired shape.

For the jasmine tea royal icing
Whisk the ingredients together and spread over baking parchment. Dry out at 50ºC for 12 hours.

Break the dried icing into small pieces.

For the black paint
Heat the chocolate and cocoa butter in a saucepan to 40ºC. Use a hand mixer to whisk in the colouring.

For the red paint
Melt the cocoa butter with the couverture in a saucepan at 40ºC. Add the two colourings and cool to between 29º and 31ºC.

Assembly and finishing
Prepare a nougat mould (12 cm x 4 cm x 2 cm). Use a thin paintbrush to apply dots of black paint. Leave for a few minutes to harden. Use a paint sprayer to apply a layer of red paint at 29ºC inside the mould. Leave to harden.

Temper the XMC chocolate (see page 256) and spread a thin layer to cover the interior of the mould. Leave for about 15 minutes to harden.

Using a piping bag, fill the mould with the bitter orange ganache heated to 31ºC. Insert the beetroot jelly into the ganache before leaving to harden.

Heat a little of the XMC chocolate to 31ºC. Mix with the jasmine tea royal icing and seal in the contents of the mould. Leave to harden for 24 hours before unmoulding.

GRAND NACIONAL CACAO

CACAO HAS EARNED A SPECIAL NAME FOR ITSELF in Ecuador. Nacional is a variety that is one of the great jewels of Latin American cacao. It is grown on most of the country's plantations, alongside CCN-51 and certain varieties that are more widespread in particular cacao-producing regions, such as Esmeraldas, named after the province in which it grows, or Sacha, the latest find in Ecuadorean cacao which, grown on plantations in the Amazon region, offers outstanding qualities and resistance to disease. I have just tried Nacional cacao turned into chocolate at the República de Cacao factory in Quito, and I am fascinated by its fineness and nutty aroma; it is like eating chocolate with almonds. Nacional cacao is known by the nickname *Pepa de Oro* ('golden nugget'), capitalised to accentuate its significance to the life of a country in which it is estimated more than 100,000 people live directly from farming cacao, which translates into a huge labour force when you work out the size of the average farming family and the indirect employment in ancillary industries.

In figures, Nacional cacao is extraordinary, although compared to the leading Asian and African producers, Ecuador is lowly ranked in the global market. The nearly 290,000 tonnes harvested and dried during the 2017 campaign barely accounted for 4 per cent of the world's total production. But things change when you change perspective. Ecuador is the world's leading producer of fine cacaos – estimated to cover 63 per cent of the demand – and the markets think highly of this. Farm numbers are growing at the same rate as production, leading to the inclusion of new areas to the map of Ecuadorian cacao production. If you are looking for cacao in Ecuador, you can find it practically anywhere. Sucumbíos, Orellana, Pichincha, Bolívar, Cotopaxi and Amazonia, among others, join the traditional cacao-growing areas of Guayas, Los Ríos, Manabí, Esmeraldas, El Oro and Santa Elena. It is quicker and easier to list the provinces where it is not grown.

It has been a giant leap. International demand is fuelling production, which has practically tripled in the last 15 years (from 120,000 tonnes in 2003 to close to 290,000 tonnes in the most recent campaign), opening up new territories for the crop in drier regions further and further away from the traditional areas, which were established in the coastal regions in colonial times for ease of transport and marketing, and later expanded to the east of the country. While their proximity

to ports was an advantage four centuries ago, these humid regions are now more prone to the diseases that attack cacao.

Nacional cacao is at the heart of everything. We see this on Bitricio Salazar's plantation in the canton of Baba, province of Los Ríos, one of the production hubs for Cacao Arriba cocoa, together with Guayas. We are not far from Vinces, which basked in splendour at the turn of the twentieth century, when the fruits of these straight rows of trees standing seven or eight metres tall were responsible for most of the country's wealth. Nacional is the star of Bitricio's farm, as it is of all the others in the area, and his three and a half-hectare holding is dotted with cacao pods. The fruit is green, which will turn yellow when ripe. They are rounded, with a small neck, and their skin is marked by ten deep grooves. The peel is of medium thickness and encases between 46 and 48 seeds, although there may be up to 50. We split open a few pods and count them. True to form, practically all of them have 48 seeds. Each bean is bright purple, and they are not particularly bitter when

NACIONAL CACAO IS PREDOMINANT IN THE GUAYAS DISTRICT. ONCE THE PODS ARE EMPTIED, THEY ARE LEFT ON THE GROUND TO FERTILISE THE SOIL.

tasted raw; on the contrary, they are cheerful, friendly and aromatic. The legend of cacaos classified as 'fine' was built on the fruity and floral notes and elegance of Nacional cacao. Properly processed and transformed, Nacional produces distinguished chocolates of great presence.

I find cacao trees that may be more than 130 years old on the Sotomayor Brothers' farm. They were already here when his father purchased it more than a century ago. I tour the farm with my gaze fixed on the tops of a few tall, straight trees, a sight that is not easy to see on other plantations. They must be as tall as seven metres, and I am assured they are ungrafted trees, grown directly from seed. Three or four were planted in the soil, and finally the strongest of all of them was allowed to grow. When they reach the end of their productive life, they will be grafted with scions from the highest-yielding and hardiest trees. Grafting is a never-ending chore on this plantation and others in the area.

The Nacional cacao grown in the provinces of Los Ríos and Guayas is known as Cacao Arriba ('upper cacao'). The name was used to distinguish the cacao that was shipped by boats downstream along the River Guayas from the cacao grown along the coast. Things were made quite clear from the very beginning: the plantations must always be close to the port of Guayaquil and along navigable rivers for ease of transport. Cacao Arriba features a fine aroma and elegance. There was

BITRICIO SALAZAR WORKING WITH HIS SON ON HIS FARM IN THE CANTON OF BABA. MOST OF THE LAND IS STOCKED WITH NACIONAL CACAO TREES.

NACIONAL CACAO IS KNOWN BY THE NICKNAME *PEPA DE ORO* ('GOLDEN NUGGET') IN THE GUAYAS REGION OWING TO THE PROSPERITY IT BROUGHT DURING THE NINETEENTH CENTURY.

an attempt to create a designation of origin for this variety supported by an FAO study from 2007, but it did not come to fruition. There was also a Cacao Aba-jo ('lower cacao') variety on the coastal fringe, a little to the north of Guayaquil, in the vicinity of what is now the Machalilla National Park, and further north in Manabí, which was later christened with the name Bahía ('bay').

Bitricio Salazar began farming cacao in the wake of the agrarian reform of 1973 that changed the face of this part of the country, which had previously been dom-inated by large estates covering hundreds of hectares. These were broken up and came to belong to the farmers. It was a popular decision by some and disputed by others, but it had far-reaching consequences. The estates that did survive the reform shifted their crops with the banana boom, and Nacional cacao found ref-uge in the smaller holdings. It was just another stage in Ecuador's up-and-down relationship with cacao. It has taken Bitricio more than 30 years to obtain the deeds to his land. He has more than 600 cacao trees per hectare, combined with a few timber trees, including the increasingly popular bamboo, and dyers' mulberry trees, widely used for building boats, together with fruit trees such as mammee and sapote. Without them, it would be difficult to make a living.

In ideal conditions, his cacao trees produce between two and three quintals (a measure equivalent to a 50-kilogram sack) a week during the harvest, which equates to almost one tonne a year. During our visit, the going rate was 1.20 US dollars per kilogram of freshly harvested cacao beans with the external fruit flesh or baba. If everything goes according to plan and the harvest is good, the six members of the Salazar will bring in 4,200 dollars for a year of work. To this they must add the income from the fruit and deduct expenses, labourers' wages and equipment. There will be little leftover.

Ecuador exudes cacao. Its chocolate industry is by far the most advanced and developed in the region. The country's industrialised chocolate production began in Guayaquil in the late nineteenth century and has grown over time. The chocolate market today is broad and varied, with certain labels worthy of mention, such as Pakari and República del Cacao, the leaders in the sector, together with other offerings gaining in prestige, such as Hacienda and Halaku.

BITRICIO SALAZAR AND THE OTHER FARMERS OF THE AREA SUPPLEMENT THEIR INCOME BY GROWING FRUIT TREES AND BAMBOO, FOR WHICH THERE IS GROWING DEMAND.

Liquid jelly
300 g water
3 g agar-agar
50 g glucose

Chocolate²

Assembly and finishing
350 g liquid jelly
350 g chocolate²
15 g powdered egg
  white

CHOCOLATE FOAM

For the liquid jelly
Mix all the ingredients together in a saucepan and bring to the boil.

Leave to cool at room temperature. Once the jelly sets, blend in a Thermomix to a runny consistency.

For the chocolate²
See the process on page 252.

Assembly and finishing
Heat the liquid jelly to 40°C and melt the chocolate at the same temperature.

Whisk the jelly with the chocolate and incorporate the powdered egg white. Fill a siphon and insert two gas cartridges.

Shake the siphon well and leave upside down in the refrigerator for about 2 hours.

When ready to use, shake well and serve the foam.

THE PEARL OF LATIN AMERICAN CACAO

ALL ROADS LEAD TO CHUAO. There is no more highly valued single-origin cacao. Chuao and Porcelana are the two most renowned names in Venezuelan cacao, for decades the most prestigious in the Americas. These two cacaos are the stuff chocolatiers' dreams are made of around the world, and no more than dreams for many of them. They are so rare and in such high demand that their price is much higher than the average. With them are other cacaos that have also made a name for themselves: Guasare, Carenero, Ocumare, Pentagonia, Choroní and Río Caribe are a few more names on a very long list.

Chuao is a small town that is practically boxed in by the Caribbean coast and the Venezuelan Coastal Range, and it is famed for the high quality of the cacao grown on the land here. The variety is also called Chuao and is the only one to receive protected designation of origin status. María Fernanda di Giacobbe, stalwart and promoter of Venezuelan cacao, explains the mixture of varieties that have become interbred to the extent that their fruit has unique characteristics. Chocolatiers rank Chuao as the highest quality cacao. It is low in bitterness, delicate, complex, fruity, floral and spicy, and it produces chocolates that are serious, deep, elegant and exciting. It is a rare and low-yielding variety that has seen better days.

The region to the south of Lake Maracaibo is much more fertile and is home to other very prestigious varieties. Porcelana and Guasare and the best known, but in this region where cacao is in constant struggle with the oil industry, there are other varieties to consider, such as Pentagonia, another member of the Criollo family. They coexist in this region, divided between the states of Zulia and Miranda, with others that are traditionally classified as varieties of Trinitario – Choroní, Ocumare and Carenero, among others – or of Forastero, such as Amelonado, Angoleta, Calabacillo and Cundeamor.

Brazil and Bolivia are at the two extremes of Amazon cacao production. The former is the largest producer of cacao in Latin America, while the latter is ranked the lowest. Brazil accounts for 7 per cent of world production, and mainly offers ordinary or bulk cacaos. It is still suffering the consequences of the witches' broom epidemic that ravaged its plantations in the late twentieth century, followed by the arrival of hybrid strains to replace the sick trees. Production is centred on the states of Pará and Bahía, and there has been a slow recovery in the production of

CHUAO CACAO IS LOW IN BITTERNESS, DELICATE, COMPLEX, FRUITY, FLORAL AND SPICY, PRODUCING CHOCOLATES THAT ARE SERIOUS, DEEP, ELEGANT AND EXCITING.

fine cacaos in recent years.

Cacao production in Bolivia is centred on the Beni region, in the north-east of the country, where the bean is referred to as 'chocolate', and by extension, cacao plantations are known as chocolate plantations. There is growing interest in cacao in the area, but there is still a need to overcome the high cost of transport, which means it is sent to the Brazilian market, where it is mixed with local cacaos. The government of Bolivia has set out measures to protect the country's production, banning the planting of any varieties not classified as native cacaos. The Leca indigenous communities in Guaney, to the north of La Paz, are experiencing remarkable growth in their crops with the support of programmes such as those led by the Wildlife Conservation Society (WCS) and FAO.

Mexico and Central America

Mexican cacao production has kept its traditional growing areas in the states of Guerrero, Oaxaca, Veracruz and, more particularly, in Chiapas and Tabasco in the southernmost part of the country, on the border with Guatemala. Production is still suffering the consequences of the epidemics that ravaged the cacao trees at the beginning of this century, causing many of the old plantations to shift to other activities. The economic situation of the country, together with this shift and low domestic consumption – barely 700 grams per inhabitant per year, one of the lowest in Latin America – complicated things even more. Mexico today is experiencing a slow recovery in production. Production in 2017 reached 28,000 tonnes, mainly concentrated in ten of the 17 municipalities of Tabasco, where 67 per cent of Mexico's cacao is produced, and in four regions of Chiapas, led by Soconusco. The Denominacion de Origen Cacao Grijalva status given to the cacaos grown in this region of the state of Tabasco has offered protection since 2013.

Cacao production in neighbouring Guatemala barely reaches 2,000 tonnes a year, exceeded by local consumption of *chocolate de taza*, a hot chocolate drink, one of the country's national beverages. Imports are close to tripling local production, which is concentrated in the regions of Alta Verapaz, Suchitepéquez and San Marcos. Production in the rest of Central America is also low, although some countries are experiencing an awakening that shows great promise. This is the case in Nicaragua, where strong investment in the sector allows rapid growth to be predicted. Total current production is about 5,000 tonnes per year.

The scene in the Dominican Republic is completely different. It is the largest producer of organic cacao in the region, and with close to 200,000 tonnes a year, it is ranked the eighth largest cacao-producing nation in the world. It is also the second largest exporter of fine cacaos in the Americas. It is the home of Los An-cones, the first ever single-estate chocolate, which was created by the French choc-olatier Michel Cluizel. The nature of Dominican cacaos is marked by their use. A large proportion of the country's plantations grow the low-cost Sánchez variety, which is dried directly and used to produce cocoa butter and cacao paste for use in conventional confectionery. The other major variety is Hispaniola, whose beans produce chocolates with marked fruitiness and low acidity. Most of the country's production is concentrated in the north-eastern regions. More than 60 per cent of the plantations are in the regions of San Francisco de Macorís, Pimentel, Hostos, Castillo, Cotuí and La Vega.

*Sunflower seed
gianduja*
120 g 45% cacao milk
  chocolate couverture
50 g cocoa butter
30 g unsalted butter
200 g pure sunflower
  seed butter
150 g hazelnut praline
60 g caramelised
  sunflower seeds

Yuzu jelly
150 g yuzu purée
350 g mandarin purée
350 g sugar
18 g pectin NH 350 g
  isomalt
100 g glucose powder
18 g 1:1 citric acid and
  water solution

Chocolate base
500 g chocolate[2]
75 g cocoa butter

Decoration
Chopped caramelised
  sunflower seeds

CAGANER NOUGAT

For the sunflower seed gianduja

Melt the chocolate with the cocoa butter and butter in a saucepan.

Chop the caramelised sunflower seeds and mix with all the other ingredients in a bowl. Lower the temperature of the mixture to 24°C and keep at 16°C.

When the gianduja is semi-hard, fill a piping bag for use.

For the yuzu jelly

Put the yuzu purée into a saucepan and bring to the boil for 4 minutes.

Heat the mandarin purée in a pan together with a mixture made from half the sugar and the pectin and bring to the boil.

Mix the remaining sugar in a bowl with the isomalt and glucose. Incorporate the sugar mixture into the mandarin mixture and bring back to the boil. Add the yuzu purée without removing the pan from the heat and cook until the sugar content reaches a refractometer reading of 72° Brix. Remove from the heat, add the citric acid solution and leave to set in the desired container.

For the chocolate base

Temper the chocolate[2] (see the process on page 252) with the cocoa butter. Spread to a 1-mm thickness over a tray and leave to harden. Use a biscuit cutter to cut out 7-cm-diameter discs.

Assembly and finishing

Use a biscuit cutter to cut out 3-cm-diameter jelly discs. Put a jelly disc on top of each chocolate base.

Pipe the gianduja over the jelly and shape as desired. Leave to harden at 16°C for least 2 hours.

To finish, melt the chocolate leftover from making the chocolate base and dip the nougat to coat. Decorate with chopped caramelised sunflower seeds.

The *caganer* is a traditional figure of a shepherd 'doing his business' that is typically hidden among the other figures of nativity scenes in Catalonia. Children are challenged to find it. It is also a way of combining the divine with the most human, and of being aware that we all find ourselves in dire straits at some point in our lives.

4

CHOCOLATE BEGINS WITH THE PLANT

THE FAMILIES OF CACAO

FORCYPOMYIA IS TO BLAME. Everything begins with this biting midge from the Ceratopogonidae family, which is considered the main pollinator of cacao flowers, and everything ends with it. This tiny insect lies behind cacao's survival and is the reason for the soup of families, varieties and hybrids that is inherent to cacao-growing. *Forcypomyia* is not the only thing to blame. You only have to consider the thick and sticky pollen cacao produces, which is incapable of being washed away by the rain or blown by the wind to end up pollinating other flowers. The fact that the flower grows downwards to face the ground does it few favours. The result is that the plant is forced to become an entomophilous species, requiring external help in order to reproduce. Some of these resort to certain types of insects; others manage to coincide with the interests of several different species; and certain others turn to birds and mammals for this purpose.

If *Forcypomyia* existed in an environment defined exclusively by a single variety of cacao, everything would continue to be the same as it was before its arrival. It would have its job as full-time pollinator, but without further consequences other than the plant's fruiting. The cacao flower would be fertilised. It would offer its fruit and be in a position to reproduce, and all its fruits and any of the scions that might grow from its seeds would be practically identical to any other. The problem arises when the efficiency demonstrated by this tiny dipteran insect is applied to a cacao plantation or an area where several different species coexist. Interbreeding and chaos are guaranteed. The blood of each cacao tree would be mixed with that of its neighbours, and those in turn with those a little further afield, in a succession giving rise to a mass of mysterious cross-breeds, the fruit of which would be impossible to decipher at first sight.

Forcipomyia is one of the 150,000 species making up the order of dipteran insects. It includes flies, mosquitos, gnats and midges. One member is the Ceratopogonidae family, certain members of which are cacao pollinators. There are three genera that possess the morphological features required for pollination to happen: *Atrichopogon, Dasyhelea* and *Forcypomyia*. Most studies associate the last of these with the actual pollination. They proliferate among the fallen leaves, particularly when there is a thick layer, and in fallen fruit as it rots, particularly cacao.

Any doubts that might have remained as to its origin were dissipated a long

time ago: cacao originated in the Amazon rainforest. It later became itinerant and began a journey that now seems endless. Before setting out on this journey, cacao had to become domesticated in order to serve as a productive crop, as we know it today. The Amazon region is still home to many wild cacaos. They bear few flowers and fewer fruits, which are of little interest for chocolate production. The domesticated cacaos that populate the plantations of the world have traditionally been divided into three families: Criollo cacaos, Forastero cacaos, and Trinitario cacaos.

Criollo is the name given to the original cacaos and their direct descendants. Their origin has been pointed out as the northern Amazon region, from where they spread northwards into Mesoamerica. They represent racial purity and form a reduced lineage that is constantly growing in appreciation. There has been so much interbreeding and blending that they are difficult to identify and often require genetic analysis. The cacaos found in Mexico by the Spanish have also been identified by some as Criollo, in comparison with the Forastero cacaos, which according to their promoters are those discovered later in the Amazon region. A little added confusion.

There is no agreement with regard to the term Forastero cacao, because there are overlapping hypotheses. Most consider it to refer to varieties distinct from Criollo and also of Amazonian origin, and it is thought to have been discovered only 250–300 years ago. There is further speculation, but what I consider most

THE FLOWERS OF THE CACAO TREE FORM CLUSTERS ALONG THE TRUNK AND BRANCHES KNOWN AS CUSHIONS. THEY REQUIRE ASSISTANCE IN ORDER TO BE FERTILISED.

WHITE CACAO FROM JAÉN   NACIONAL CACAO FROM GUAYAS

important are the coincidences. All sources agree that it is also native to the Amazon rainforest and attribute specific characteristics, such as the higher level of bitterness and astringency of Forastero beans. Experience shows that, regardless of their origin and their nature, Forastero cacaos are neither better nor worse than Criollo cacaos. They are simply different.

Trinitario is considered the third wheel, although this status is being increasingly questioned. It identifies the first hybrids between Criollo and Forastero cacaos appearing in the cacao-growing areas of Trinidad and Tobago and other Caribbean islands, where the Spaniards established plantations. There are people who assert that the quality of Trinitario cacao is superior to that of Forastero, and those who believe the opposite.

Conventional thinking coincides in attributing precise morphological traits to each variety of cacao and sees them as grounds for their classification. According to some, Criollo cacao pods are smaller and rounded, while Forastero pods are wide and elongated, although the reality is much more complex, and includes those who describe Criollo pods as small and elongated with rough skin. I turn to a list of Criollo cacaos from Venezuela, as an example of how difficult they are to fit to a single criterion. Guasare is elongated with a short neck and rough skin; Porcelana is rounded with smooth skin; Criollo Mérida is more similar to Gua-

AWAJÚN CRIOLLO CACAO ARHUACO WHITE CACAO WHITE CACAO FROM PIURA

sare; Chuao is more or less between the two, although closer to Porcelana; while Ocumare resembles Guasare.

It is easy to see this in the production areas of Venezuela because it is the most ordered in the Americas. Work on genetic identification and the selection of varieties was carried out to bring uniformity to crops and reduce the impact of cross-breeding. We can apply this perspective to Piura, with its white cacaos, while the opposite is patent in the plantations of Temashnum, in the Alto Marañón region, where cloned strains were never introduced, and whose plantations are a jigsaw puzzle filled with all the shapes and textures, sizes and colours imaginable.

The story is even more evident in Colombia. In the Sierra Nevada de Santa Marta mountains, a region that has been isolated for centuries, we find very different cacaos that at face value could be defined as Criollo. Many of them are white and others are not, and each one has differently shaped pods. Could any Forastero cacaos have reached the area and created their own lineages? How far have the natural hybrids created by interbreeding between the ancestors of these cacaos over the last three millennia developed? What is left of the native cacaos and what proportion comes from subsequent hybrid strains? It is essential to perform genetic analysis on each variety in order to find an answer. The remainder of the Colombian cacao-growing regions are divided between apparently Criollo varie-

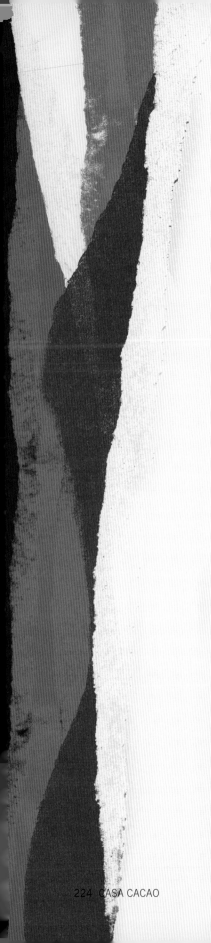

ties and many others arriving from other regions 250–300 years ago. The periods of neglect and revival of the plantations since then has led to the proliferation of hybrid strains.

The situation affecting the Colombian cacao-producing areas supports the ideas of others who propose the classification of cacao from a different perspective, with a division between old and new cacaos. It provides a few clues, although there is no definitive solution. Are they better or worse? Where do the real differences lie, aside from the time they arrived from this or that region? This takes us back to genetics; analysis is needed if we are to know. In any case, by introducing the quality of the chocolate as another differentiating feature, more questions are raised. Do all Criollo cacaos produce high-quality chocolate? Is Forastero cacao synonymous with mediocre chocolate?

Ecuador is the world's leading producer of quality cacaos, which are of the Nacional variety, which is also known as Río Arriba when it grows in the provinces of Guayas and Los Ríos. A number of experts have traditionally considered it to be a Forastero cacao, demolishing the preconceived notion of the mediocrity of this family. However, later research has identified it as a family that is different from both Criollo and Forastero cacaos, and it appears to be older than the latter.

I prefer the classification put forward by certain experts, who divide the world of cacao into two depending on the suitability of each variety to produce good or bad chocolates. On the one side would be the fine cacaos (known as 'flavour cacaos' in the United States) and on the other would be 'ordinary' cacaos, also known as 'bulk', 'basic' or 'common' cacaos. It does not bring clarity to the identity crisis affecting our cacao plantations, but it paves the way to important reflection. The first is that racial purity tends to be seen as a value, but when you combine two strains, you can obtain equally attractive results. There are cacaos that shine more brightly when a touch of make-up is applied.

The hybrid strains are not included, and here again the nomenclature is not particularly clear. For some they are hybrids, while other define them as clones. They are led by CCN-51 (Castro Naranjal 51, with the number reflecting the number of tests its creator required to achieve success), created in 1965 in Ecuador, whose presence has expanded throughout the world. It is the Frankenstein of cacaos, a monster born out of the encounter between a variety of Nacional, a Trinitario, and one more known as Oriente-1. It is a hybrid of hybrids, a cultivar designed to respond to the needs of the new cacao industry: an adaptable, disease-resistant and high-yielding fruit. It also produces considerable quantities of cocoa butter, a product that is highly prized outside of the chocolate industry by pharmaceutical and cosmetic companies. The panacea.

It is considered by some in Ecuador to be among the varieties able to produce high-quality chocolate, but in the rest of the region it is highly questioned and associated with products of less interest to the market. It has a high level of astringency and produces greater amounts of mucilaginous pulp, which means changing the fermentation technique and requiring pre-drying of the beans and changes to the stirring or rotation process. It is being replaced by other varieties in some Amazon regions. CCN-51 is the most visible and best-known face of the increasingly prolific family of laboratory cacaos.

A little light

The first scientific classification of cacao was done by Michael Morris in the nineteenth century. He divided cacao into two different groups, Criollo and Forastero. Later, Josep Cuatrecasas, a Catalan-born American, advanced this classification in 1964 in greater detail by defining the existence of two subspecies of *Theobroma cacao*: the *cacao* subspecies, to which the Criollo cacaos belong, and *sphaerocarpum*, which grouped together all the other options, including Angoleta, Cundeamor, Amelonado and Calabacillo, until that time encompassed by the generic term Forastero cacao.

Research conducted by Juan Carlos Motamayor at the Pichilingue Experimental Station of the National Institute of Agricultural Research (INIAP) in 2008 shed a little light in the midst of this maze that at times seems to have no way out. Its conclusions define areas of influence differentiated by Criollo and Forastero cacaos. It adds Nacional as a specific family, and goes further to identify ten different groups or genetic clusters: Amelonado, Contamana, Criollo, Curaray, Guyana, Iquitos, Marañón, Nacional, Nanay and Purús. It is a serious and consistent study that rules out the existence of Trinitario and Forastero cacaos as specific classifications.

When we speak of cacao, we refer to *Theobroma cacao*, one of the 22 members of the Theobroma family, which is native to the Amazon region. The group has other members which are often mistaken for cacao, and sometimes used as substitutes. The most common are *Theobroma bicolor*, known in Peru as *macambo*; *Theobroma glandiflorum*, *copoazú* for the Brazilians, and a very popular plant that provides a large amount of edible fruit pulp; and *Theobroma angustiflorum*, which is mainly found in Guatemala and used as a cacao substitute. None of them are suitable for making chocolate.

CHOCOLATE IS MADE IN THE SOIL

CHOCOLATE IS BORN ON THE PLANT; its roots are set deep in the soil that nourishes the plant; and it is brought to perfection through ingenuity. The most important steps in the life of chocolate are performed on the farm, long before the cacao is transformed. That is where its personality is defined. Without a good cacao, a good chocolate is impossible. The path that leads from the roaster to the conching machine allows for little more than disguising flaws or enhancing virtues, whichever is the case.

Cacao grows in a geographical band located along the equator, at latitudes between 18 degrees north and 16 degrees south, roughly equivalent to the Intertropical Convergence Zone, although a little narrower. These lands provide cacao with what it needs to survive: a hot and humid climate with little variation in temperature. Altitude is another factor. Cacao does not typically grow well at altitudes higher than 1,250 metres above sea level. There is a clear distribution of what are today the preferred crops to grow in tropical climes: cacao up to 1,250 metres and coffee above this altitude, to about 2,000–2,100 metres. Cacao is found both on plains or on hillsides and in ravines. It has no trouble growing on sloping land, although this does pose difficulties for plant care and harvesting.

The cacao tree needs long rainy seasons, and flourishes in deep soil. It also seeks the shade provided by other trees. When a plantation is created, the early growth stages of the tree are combined with banana trees, until it begins to bear fruit in approximately the third year of life. After this time, growers choose new travelling companions. They may be fruit trees – citrus, avocado and papaya, among others – although it is increasingly common to find a wide variety of timber trees, ranging from tornillo and tipa trees to highly sought-after varieties such as teak and mahogany. The crops grown in conjunction with cacao can be compared to an investment fund. You can pursue complementary short-term income if you focus on fruit trees, or long-term returns if you choose timber species (ranging between 15 years for tornillo trees and more than 100 years for mahogany). You need only decide who the beneficiary will be: yourself, your children or your grandchildren.

The soil of a cacao plantation benefits from the organic matter provided by fallen leaves and waste from the harvested fruit. This can help to keep in the moisture during the dry season, and is turned into food for the plant when the rains arrive.

In the meantime, it makes the perfect habitat for *Forcypomyia*.

The major factor that determines the quality and personality of a chocolate is the variety. Genetic origin will decide much of the final result. Some experts estimate it accounts for 40 per cent of the final result. This is followed, in roughly equal measure, by growing conditions (particularly soil and climate), post-harvest processing (fermentation and drying) and, finally, the way in which the chocolate is transformed.

There is an essential canon when it comes to cacao plantations: you have to choose a variety. The coexistence of different cacaos can always have consequences, which tend to be negative. With *Forcypomyia* buzzing around plantations, keeping a mixture of varieties leaves you open to constant interbreeding, and definitively foregoing the personality of the different cacaos. The process involves conducting a genetic analysis of each variety and making micro batches of chocolate with each of them before choosing the one you want. There are two

THE VARIETY OF CACAO IS THE MAJOR FACTOR THAT DETERMINES THE QUALITY OF CHOCOLATE. THIS IS FOLLOWED BY THE SOIL AND GROWING CONDITIONS.

alternatives after this: grafting the cacao trees on each plot, or replacing them with ungrafted trees raised from the seeds of the chosen variety. The shortest route tends to be grafting, although it is not typically carried out on an entire plantation at once because it affects production for at least the first year. The graft is inserted close to the base of the tree, and branches of the old tree are gradually removed, so that production can focus on the new scion.

Pods grow from the flower cushions that sprout on smooth areas of the trunk and main branches. The flower changes colour depending on the variety and the different cultivars. They are very rarely all white.

The cacao tree bears fruit almost all year round, although there is a high season that lasts between two and three months, and a low season of around the same length of time. The months change depending on the hemisphere and the features of the production area. The harvest is selective and continuous, repeated every week at peak times and every two weeks for the rest of the season. The pods are picked when they have reached peak ripeness.

The cacao pod is split open and the beans are removed with the mucilage, leaving the central thread that joins them together. Each pod contains between 20 and

WE HAVE SEEN CONTRAPTIONS IN MANY SHAPES AND SIZES. THE FERMENTING BOXES AT THE PROCESSING FACILITY IN VINCES ARE STACKED FOUR HIGH AND STAGGERED.

60 beans, depending on the variety, and the separated beans and pulp must be transferred to the fermenting boxes with the least possible delay. When the process is carried out by small-scale cacao buyers working in remote areas, part of the fermentation takes place in the sacks in which the beans are transported.

Fermentation is the key

The way in which fermentation is carried out will decide the fate of the chocolate. There are a few basic procedures, but anything is possible. There are no set rules. Depending on the aroma and flavour profiles you want for your chocolate, this process can change the personality of the cacao, for better or worse. Part of the authenticity of a chocolate is developed in the fermenting boxes.

We have seen contraptions that come in many shapes and sizes. The most modest of these was the system used by the Awajún community in Uut, on the banks of the Marañón, consisting of a single row of three boxes set a few centimetres off the floor. It is a world away from the one used at the República del Cacao processing facility in Vinces, with four rows of stacked and staggered boxes with capacity for processing 80 tonnes of cacao beans at the same time. On this journey, we saw boxes laid out over three levels, such as the system Exelino Sierra uses in the Colombian locality of Pauna, and others, such as the ones used by Cacao de Colombia in Aracataca, also laid out horizontally and with capacity for processing three tonnes. On earlier journeys, I saw systems for fermenting on Rohan trays, which can hold much less than the boxes and are used to ferment small batches, or conventional boxes set up in as many as six levels.

There are two stages to the fermentation process. The first of these is anaerobic

fermentation, which is encouraged by filling the fermentation box and covering it with sacks, mainly jute but often plastic, to provide a barrier to oxygen and keep the temperature high, which stimulates the work of natural yeasts. In some areas, a first layer of banana leaves is added, to make use of the bacteria living on the underside of the leaves and encourage fermentation. The yeasts turn the starch and sugars in the mucilage into ethanol. This stage lasts between a day and half to two days. The second stage is aerobic fermentation, which requires the mixture to be oxygenated in order to expel the carbon anhydride emitted and to activate the bacteria in the pulp, which lead the process of turning the ethanol into acetic acid, which impregnates the beans and refines their flavour and aromas. Oxygenation is induced by stirring the contents of the boxes if fermented in a single row, or moving the contents of the upper boxes to the lower ones if they are stacked and staggered. To do this, the front of the box is removed board by board, starting with the highest one, allowing the contents to be inverted as it is moved to the box below. Fermentation may take five days or longer, depending on the variety. It may take six or seven in the case of CNN-51 (the pods contain more mucilage and need longer processing, including pre-drying).

Processing triggers decisive changes in the beans. It changes the colour inside purple beans to white or brown; it eliminates the germ; it reduces the natural bitterness and astringency of the bean; it infuses them with the aromas of the mucilage, adding aromatic complexity; and it defines their acidity profile. The peak acidity achieved on the third or fourth days later diminishes. The temperature rises until the third day, before gradually falling. It should never exceed 50°C. To prevent this from occurring, the contents of the box are stirred, or the contents lessened. Observing a row of fermenting boxes with different batches and varieties is like riding in the carriage of an aromatic roller coaster through mushrooms, black olives, violets, white flowers, citrus, caramel, soil and dairy, among others. Each bean, the source of each bean, and each change in the fermentation process produces different aromatic notes. The process is stopped when the beans are 85–90 per cent fermented. To know this, the beans are split open and their state is checked. The flavour of a chocolate can be influenced by changing the pattern of fermentation, but strict and constant monitoring of the sugar content, pH level and temperature is essential.

EXELINO SIERRA HAS HIS OWN FERMENTING AND DRYING FACILITY NEAR HIS HOME IN PAUNA.

Fermentation is carried out in places sheltered from the wind and rain to promote higher temperatures inside the boxes. These tend to be made of wood, although they are being replaced with plastic ones in some places because they are easier to wash. Neutral woods are used, so as not to add flavour, predominantly laurel wood, typically from trees felled when the moon is waning in order to prolong the useful life of the wood.

The beans are sent for drying with their fermentation incomplete. There are still traces of acetic acid that need to be slowly eliminated. In more humid areas, drying is carried out on trays in enclosed and well-ventilated spaces. In drier areas, the beans can be spread directly over the floor, but this must be done carefully to prevent excessive heat from closing the pores in the beans, which would hinder completion of the fermentation process and volatilisation of the remaining acetic acid. In Piura, Iván Murrugarra spreads them out in the shade for two hours, he sees what the sun is going to be like, and then works out a series of hours of sun exposure to take place over five or six days, depending on the weather conditions. Drying is a natural process and ends when the beans have a moisture content below seven per cent. In Pauna, Exelino Sierra has a drying shed with trays set at different heights. In Vinces, República del Cacao combines retractable trays under cover with large lined surfaces that allow beans to be dried directly on the ground in the open. A fundamental part of this process is the frequent raking of the beans, allowing even drying.

Cacao beans lose a third of their original weight during fermentation and drying. Once dried and if stored well, they will keep in good conditions for about one year.

MAYUMI OGATA CHECKS THE MICRO FERMENTATION OF A BATCH OF WHITE CACAO BEANS, MAKING THE MOST OF THE FERMENTATION PROCESS FOR OTHER TYPES OF CACAOS.

CACAO QUALITY CHART

FERMENTATION	MORE THAN 85%
MOISTURE	LESS THAN 7%
EXTERNAL MOULD	LESS THAN 8%
INTERNAL MOULD	LESS THAN 1%
DEFECTIVE BEANS	2–3%
BROKEN BEANS	1%
GERMINATED BEANS	0%
SLATY BEANS	0%
COMPLETELY PURPLE BEANS	LESS THAN 2%
INSECT-DAMAGE BEANS	LESS THAN 1%

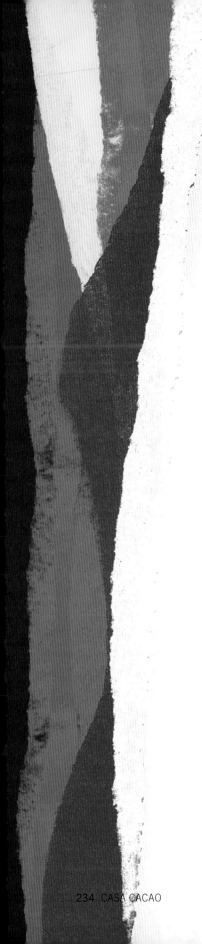

EVERYTHING IS IN CACAO

THE CACAO POD COMPRISES three parts: husk, mucilage and bean.

Husk. The thickness, shape, size and colour of the husk varies according to the variety. The husk is normally discarded or recycled as fertiliser for the soil, although there are incipient projects for its transformation, with different results. The fresh husk is sliced and soaked in an acidic medium to extract pectin, used to make jams and syrups. Experiments are being conducted to dry the husk and grind it into a fine flour for use in bread-making and granules for infusions.

Mucilage. This is the whitish and slimy pulp that coats the cacao beans. It has a fruity, sweet and sour flavour. Depending on the variety, there can be more or less mucilage in the pod. It plays an essential part in the fermentation process, and is also used to make certain by-products. Up to five per cent of the mucilage is extracted before the beans are fermented. Mucilage oxidises quickly, which is why cacao pods needs to be processed quickly. It can be frozen and is sold for use in pastries and cocktails. It is also made into syrups and jams, and is used to make fermented beverages and spirits.

Bean. The pod of each variety of cacao contains a different number of seeds. The number can range between 20 and 60. Cacao seeds are known as beans. Before use, they must undergo fermentation and drying.

In one cacao bean

A dried cacao bean contains up to 7 per cent moisture, which is removed completely during roasting. The final result will be a bean containing equal parts of two components – cocoa butter and dry cocoa solids – and a casing that encloses them, the shell.

Shell. Covering the cacao bean, the shell is removed after roasting. It is used for infusions. Casa Cacao mixes it with paper pulp to make the wrappers for single-origin chocolates.

Cocoa butter. Cocoa butter is the oil contained in the cacao bean. It has a light cacao aroma and flavour. It is separated from the dry solids by pressing, and can be refined for use in industrial chocolate manufacturing – increasing fluidity – and

in the cosmetic and pharmaceutical industries, as it melts at room temperature.

Dry cocoa solids. The solid part of the cacao bean accounts for about half its contents. It is separated from cocoa butter by pressing, and is processed into cocoa powder.

Cacao nibs. Cacao nibs, also known as cocoa nibs, are the result of cracking the cacao before shelling. Mixed with sugar, it is the base for chocolate production. It is also used without grinding or refining in certain food products.

Cacao paste. This is the result of refining and grinding the cacao nibs. It can come as a solid or a liquid, in which case it is known as cacao liquor.

Chocolate or couverture. This is the result of mixing the cacao paste with sugar and subjecting it to the conching process.

THE BEAN COMPRISES COCOA
BUTTER AND DRY COCOA SOLIDS.
THE COVERING ENCASING THE
BEANS IS KNOWN AS THE SHELL.

5

CASA
CACAO

BEYOND BEAN-TO-BAR

THE FIRST CHALLENGE was to make chocolate in the pastry kitchen at El Celler de Can Roca. Next came the test of self-supply. Now the definitive adventure begins, Casa Cacao, Jordi Roca's bean-to-bar business that is also the focal point of the Roca Brothers' latest strategy. A chocolate factory, a cacao-themed boutique hotel, chocolate bar and a shop selling chocolate and derivatives. All in one. The challenge turned out to be much more than an adventure; it was a journey beyond the concept of bean-to-bar. In fact, the overall project covered all the possible terrain associated with cacao and chocolate, including a small hotel with 15 rooms that will reflect the Roca concept of hospitality through the vision of Anna Payet.

Casa Cacao has taken over the former medical centre Clínica de l'Esperança, in *Plaça* de Catalunya, a square at the very heart of the city. Overlooking the River Ter, it enjoys a panoramic view of Girona's old town. With ringside seats for one show and the venue for another, starring chocolate. The ground floor of Casa Cacao combines a chocolate shop, bar, factory and kitchen.

The beauty that is to be found in cacao's transformation into chocolate is open to view at Casa Cacao. There are no secrets to be locked away; the entire process is shown to visitors. I sense the determination to provide an educational experience, the culmination of a joyous and, more particularly, different project. A living space is devoted to cacao and chocolate to show the ever-changing nature of the bean, translated into chocolates that seek to make a difference rather than uniformity. The flavour of Casa Cacao will be diversity. Each single origin, each batch and each creation shows one of the thousand faces that play a part in the life of cacao. The soil in which it grows, the climate that shaped its life, the work of the growers and producers on the ground and in the plant, and the difference in the pre and post-harvest processing of the crop will have their essence reflected in each product.

As I go over the Casa Cacao project, I see it as a fascinating amusement park whose theme is cacao and its consequence, chocolate, which has become a vehicle through which the cacao bean reveals its secrets. As in the other artisan chocolate factories that are flourishing around the world, here chocolate is no longer bitter or sweet, depending on the amount of sugar it contains. Instead, it showcases the acidity of the fruit and releases the thousand scintillating aromas offered by each variety. Colour is no longer a given in Casa Cacao chocolates. It is no longer black or dark, now revealing the genetic features of the species, the influence of its land of origin, and the respect or defiance that went into its transformation.

The chocolate kitchen occupies much of the ground floor of the building, which dates from the first half of the twentieth century. The façade facing Carrer Ginestra has been turned into an expanse of glass to reveal the production process to the public. The climax is Bar Cacao, a space designed to offer chocolate creations made from high-quality single-origin cacaos. They might be hot or cold beverages, chocolate bonbons or a selection of El Celler de Can Roca pastries. The architectural and interior design project was entrusted to the teams at Callís Marès Arquitectes and Tarruella Trenchs Studio.

Completing the ground floor space is the shop, stocked with chocolate bars, bonbons and other products made from all the single-origin cacaos used by Casa Cacao. Welcome to the world of *chocolatessen*. All the products here are packaged in materials made from recycling cacao fibre. Run Design is responsible for the packaging, graphic and visual design.

The two upper floors and the terrace on the roof of the building complete the Hotel Casa Cacao space. There are only 15 rooms, each about 40 m², and a terrace with one of the most spectacular views possible over the historic centre of Girona epitomises the Roca philosophy of hospitality.

CASA CACAO BRINGS TOGETHER A CHOCOLATE FACTORY, 15-ROOM HOTEL AND A CHOCOLATE BAR AND SHOP UNDER ONE ROOF.

CASA CACAO CHOCOLATE

Quality control

Each batch that arrives at the factory undergoes a strict quality control process. Checks are made to ensure that the sample corresponds to the order placed and the state of the shipment. The first inspection is visual, to ensure that there are no fungus, mould or other evident defects caused by moisture. Any mould will cause the chocolate to have a musty taste.

The second step is to choose 100 beans at random and cut them in half cleanly with a guillotine, allowing their state to be checked. We check their level of fermentation, colour (if the beans are still purplish, it means the fermentation process was incomplete) and sanitary condition. Incomplete fermentation will increase the vinegary notes in the chocolate.

Another problem with cacao is possible germination of the beans. This occurs when there is a delay in removing the beans from the fruit and the germination process begins inside the pod. The germ is destroyed in the fermentation process, leaving a gap that can be colonised by insects as the bean is dried. As a precaution against the presence of insect eggs, which can hatch in the storeroom, leading to a plague, the beans are frozen at -20°C for at least 36 hours.

AFTER THE VISUAL INSPECTION, 100 BEANS ARE CHOSEN AT RANDOM AND CUT IN HALF CLEANLY IN A GUILLOTINE TO CHECK THEIR STATE.

STORAGE   SORTING

Storage

The cacao beans are stored in sacks weighing between 50 and 60 kilograms, always below 20°C and 65 per cent humidity. Under these conditions, they can be stored for up to two years. When the level of humidity is higher, fungus can appear, with the risk that some type of mycotoxin will proliferate. An overly warm atmosphere creates conditions suited to plagues of insects such as weevils. The storeroom is an aseptic space without smells that can be absorbed by the cacao beans.

Sorting

Before their transformation, the beans undergo a sorting process. This is done by hand, one bean at a time. A sack is emptied onto one of the tables and any broken and damaged beans are removed, and any flat beans, which can add too much astringency to the chocolate. Any foreign matter (stones, fibres, twigs, etc.) is also removed. Only the round beans with good visual appearance are kept. Losses can account for 5–15 per cent of the total weight.

Roasting

This is the most important stage of the process. Roasting develops the aromas and organoleptic or sensory profile of the chocolate, defining the level of bitterness and controlling astringency, in addition to removing part of the acetic acid left-over from fermenting the beans. The high temperatures to which the beans are subjected also sterilise them. The roaster is a revolving drum into which the beans are fed, while electrical elements provide the heat to roast them. It is an exercise in

ROASTING

precision that takes place in an enclosed space in order to strictly control the temperature. The revolving motion of the drum provides uniform roasting of all the beans. It is important that the size of the beans is uniform. If not, the smallest will burn and add bitterness to the chocolate, while moisture will remain in the largest beans. We initially used a conventional oven, in which we changed the position of the trays every ten minutes, as seen in the image.

The degree of roasting depends on the astringency present in each sack, and the organoleptic profile we decide to highlight. The highest temperatures accentuate nutty notes and smooth out the flavour. If the intention is to showcase the personality of each batch, lower temperatures are used that allow this distinctive characteristic to shine through, without covering it up with aggressive roasting or the addition of vanilla flavouring, which is so common in industrial-scale processing.

The roasting formula is decided based on the tasting profile shown by the beans. The starting point also changes depending on the type of bean. Basic formulas are applied by Casa Cacao, which are subsequently modified according to the desired result.

ROASTING FORMULA

BROWN CACAO, CRIOLLO	90ºC FOR 60 MINUTES
REDDISH-BROWN CACAO	100ºC FOR 45 MINUTES
PURPLISH-BLACK CACAO	125ºC FOR 35 MINUTES

PRE-REFINING

CRACKING AND WINNOWING

Cooling

Once the roasting process is complete, the beans are quickly cooled by lowering their temperature to 45°C. The aim of this is to stop the roasting process by inertia, and to make shelling the beans easier.

Cracking and winnowing

The name of this process is quite graphic. The machine can either operate with a hammer or a set of rollers that break up the beans, causing the solid part, the nibs, to be separated from the much lighter shell fragments. The part of the bean that contains silicates, a very hard particle that can damage the refining machinery, is also removed.

Excess shell material can affect the flavour of the chocolate. It increases bitterness and affects the fluidity of the product. The type of machinery used will determine the possibility for its presence to be noted in the chocolate.

The removed shell can be used as fuel, packaged to make infusions and beverages, or delivered to an environmental management company. It is commonly used to produce industrial animal feed. At Casa Cacao it is incorporated into the paper pulp used to make packaging.

Pre-refining and refining

Pre-refining consists of reducing the nibs to cocoa mass particles the size of grains

REFINING   CONCHING

of sugar, about 40 microns thick (one micron is a thousandth of a gram). Casa Cacao uses two grinders for this process. The first is a stone roller that grinds down the nibs before the addition of sugar. The amount will depend on the character of the cacao used and the final use it will be given.

The composition of Casa Cacao chocolate is simple: cocoa and sugar, with no added cocoa butter. In order to make a 70 per cent cacao chocolate, we use 70 per cent cocoa mass and 30 per cent sugar.

The second grinding stage takes place in a grinder with three rollers, which reduces the size of the particles to 20 microns and evens out the mixture of sugar and fat particles. The aim is to allow the taste buds to perceive the flavours more clearly and for the mixture to be more fluid and smooth. Less fine grinding would produce a more floury or gritty mouthfeel. Particle size is measured using a grindometer.

Conching

Conching takes its name from the machine invented by Gustave Lindt to heat and stir the chocolate, for the purpose of aerating the mixture and improving its fluidity, which had the shape of a large conch shell. Conching machines have changed a lot since that time, and there are now many different types. The one used at Casa Cacao has flint rollers that stir and grind the chocolate while heating it.

The temperature of the chocolate during conching is about 70°C, the heat pro-

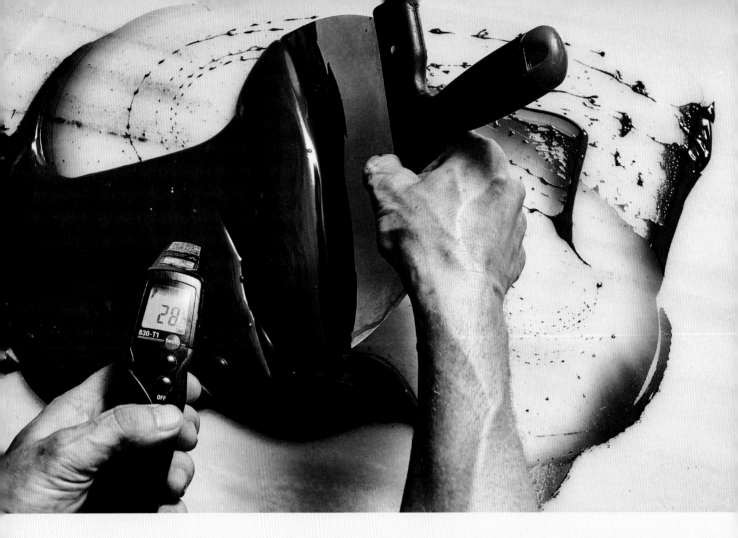

THE COCOA BUTTER IS MADE UP
OF CRYSTALS. WHEN HEATED,
THE CRYSTALS BECOME SOFT,
AND ALTHOUGH THEY CONTAIN
NO WATER, THEY GIVE THE
IMPRESSION OF BEING A LIQUID.

duced by the friction caused by the rollers. This operation completes the refining process by reducing the particles even more and homogenising the mixture. This process also allows any remaining moisture in the mixture to evaporate and eliminates the most volatile aromas, such as any remaining acetic acid that may have survived the fermenting and roasting processes. The temperature produced liquefies the fat contained in the cocoa butter and gives the mixture fluidity. It also homogenises the shape of the particles, which become round and covered with a film of cocoa butter.

The formula can change. Depending on the mixture and the type of cacao used, this can take anywhere between eight and 72 hours. Conching influences the flavour of the chocolate. The longer it takes, the less bitterness and the finer the aroma.

Tempering

Chocolate can be understood as a mixture of the oil and solid matter contained in the cacao beans with sugar. This mixture contains carbohydrates, proteins and minerals. All chocolates (dark, milk and white) can be described in this way. The difference between them lies in the solid ingredients used. This can be the actual cocoa solids, different sugars, powdered milk, powdered fruits or vegetables, or spices, among others, but the base is still the same, the cocoa butter.

Cocoa butter is made up of crystals, like any type of fat. When heated, the crystals become soft, and although they contain no water, they give the impression of being a liquid. The heating process is called decrystallisation, and it takes place at 45°C. As the temperature is lowered, the crystals harden and take on a solid consistency, known as recrystallisation.

Tempering chocolate consists of evenly controlling the recrystallisation of the cocoa butter.

Cocoa butter contains six different fat crystals that harden and soften at different temperatures and in different ways. These are classified using Roman numerals between 1 and VI.

Type V and VI crystals have a regular shape that allows a good fit. The others, however, are irregular and do not fit together.

FAT CRYSTALS IN COCOA BUTTER

TYPE I CRYSTAL	GRANULAR TEXTURE, MELTS EASILY AT 17°C
TYPE II CRYSTAL	GRANULAR TEXTURE, MELTS EASILY AT 21°C
TYPE III CRYSTAL	FIRM, FRAGILE TEXTURE, MELTS EASILY AT 26°C
TYPE IV CRYSTAL	FIRM, FRAGILE TEXTURE, MELTS EASILY AT 28°C
TYPE V CRYSTAL	LUSTROUS, FIRM TEXTURE, MELTS AT 34°C
TYPE VI CRYSTAL	HARD TEXTURE, MELTS AT 36°C

Knowing the temperature at which the different crystals form allows the presence of stable crystals to be controlled. Depending on the way tempering is performed, we can end up with a lightly crystallised chocolate – with few uniform crystals – or an over-crystallised chocolate, when there are too many crystals and the chocolate becomes thicker. The amount of crystals has to be controlled as we work. A well-tempered chocolate contains a suitable amount of desirable crystals. The temperature of the room has to be between 22 and 24 degrees Celsius.

Another important aspect is that cocoa butter is the only natural oil that melts

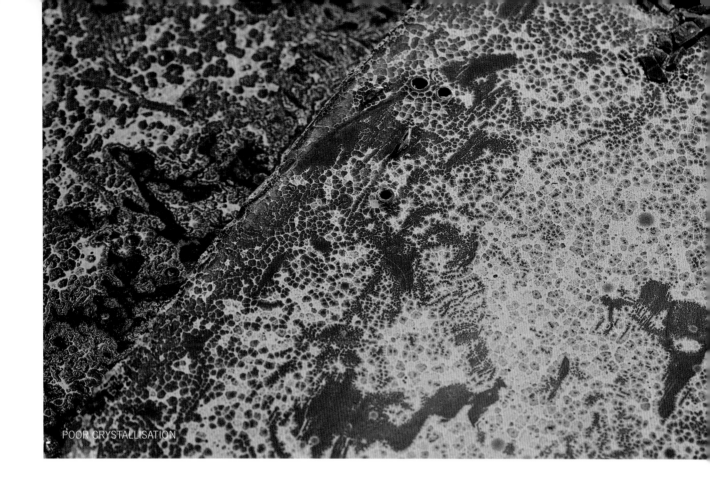

POOR CRYSTALLISATION

TEMPERATURE CURVE

WORKSPACE TEMPERATURE 22-24°C.

DECRYSTALLISATION	45°C
RECRYSTALLISATION	26–29°C
WORKING TEMPERATURE	28–34°C

THE PRESENCE OF MANY IRREGULAR CRYSTALS CAUSES A DULL FINISH, WHITE SPOTS, POOR COLOURATION AND GRITTINESS.

at body temperature, between 36 and 38 degrees Celsius.

In short, tempering chocolate involves melting cocoa butter crystals in order to recrystallise them in a controlled manner, through cooling and constant moving.

Good tempering will produce chocolate with the following characteristics:

— Glossy finish

— Hardness

— Adequate shrinkage

— Smooth mouthfeel

— Crunch when broken

— Longer life

On the contrary, the presence of a large number of irregular crystals will result in certain flaws:

— Dull finish

— White spots

— Poor shrinkage

— Grittiness

— Fat bloom formation

CORRECT CRYSTALLISATION

Crystallisation

After tempering, the chocolate is placed in a cooler environment in order to properly stabilise the crystals that have formed and to remove the latent heat it still contains. Cocoa butter crystals can continue to change in shape until the chocolate has hardened completely. The thicker the chocolate layer, the more problems there will be in removing this heat.

When the chocolate is left to harden, a lot of care has to be taken to ensure there is sufficient space and ventilation in order to remove the latent heat. An electric fan is an ideal option for circulating the air.

The temperature of the workspace is very important. When the chocolate is being tempered and worked, the temperature of the room must be between 22 and 24 degrees Celsius. When we want the crystallisation process to be completed, the temperature of the room has to be at least 18 degrees Celsius.

PROPER TEMPERING PRODUCES GLOSSY AND HARD CHOCOLATES WITH A SMOOTH MOUTHFEEL AND THAT SNAP WHEN BROKEN.

TWO-INGREDIENT CHOCOLATE OR CHOCOLATE²

When we make chocolate only using cacao beans and sugar, the result is very dense, as it only contains the oil from the seeds. The resulting product is called two-ingredient chocolate or chocolate².

It brings out the purity of the cacao flavour in the mouth. The flavour is bold, and the aroma lingers in the mouth. This technique allows an authentic product to be achieved that expresses the source of the cacao beans.

If extra cocoa butter is added, not only does it not come from the actual beans, but it also tends to be a mixture of cocoa butters sourced from different places that are first refined to remove flavours and aromas.

Preparation of this product follows the same process as that used for any chocolate, described on pages 244–251.

Owing to its texture, working with chocolate² can be challenging. During the tempering process, fat crystals are formed that thicken the chocolate. If the chocolate² is very thick, the tempering process becomes difficult. The reason artisans normally add cocoa butter is to make working the chocolate easier.

ORIGIN	CACAO NIBS	RAW CANE SUGAR
PIURA CHOCOLATE² 70%	1 kg	425 g
JAÉN CHOCOLATE² 80%	1 kg	250 g
AWAJÚN CHOCOLATE² 75%	1 kg	325 g
ECUADOR CHOCOLATE² 72%	1 kg	375 g
ARHUACO CHOCOLATE² 68%	1 kg	475 g

The large-scale producers tend to add lecithin, flavouring and vanilla, and they change the type of fat so that it can withstand higher temperatures without spoiling.

**Makes 1.5 kg
chocolate**

1 kg Ecuador cacao
   nibs
500 g The Macallan
   Double Cask 12 Years
   Old whisky
375 g raw cane sugar
135 g cocoa butter

THE MACALLAN-INFUSED CHOCOLATE BAR

Vacuum seal the cacao nibs in a bag with the whisky and leave to macerate at room temperature for 3 months.

Next, spread the mixture over a tray and dry out at 50ºC for 48 hours.

Proceed with the conventional refining, conching and tempering of the mixture to obtain XMC chocolate. Pour into a chocolate bar mould and leave at 16ºC for 30 minutes to harden.

EXTRA COCOA BUTTER CHOCOLATE
FOR CHOCOLATE BONBONS. XMC CHOCOLATE

When the tempered chocolate is very thick, it can be impossible to use it for enrobing or dipping as it will not form a thin and glossy shell. This is what tends to happen with two-ingredient chocolate.

In order to use it as a coating, cocoa butter must be added to the chocolate[2] to make it more fluid. The result is what we call *extra de manteca de cacao* (extra cocoa butter) chocolate or XMC chocolate.

The content of each variety of cacao must systematically be analysed to find its percentage of oil. This information allows us to know the oil content of each cacao and what to add.

The aim is to achieve an oil content of 36–38 per cent of the total weight, meaning that between 5 and 20 per cent cocoa butter must be added.

When the cacao beans cannot be analysed, an approximation can be worked out by testing the thickness of the chocolate with a spoon. This technique requires some practice.

If too much cocoa butter is added, the mixture will become too runny and the coating will turn out too fine and will have a very oily mouthfeel.

ORIGIN	CACAO NIBS	RAW CANE SUGAR	COCOA BUTTER
PIURA CHOCOLATE[2]	1 kg	425 g	115 g
JAÉN CHOCOLATE[2]	1 kg	250 g	100 g
AWAJÚN CHOCOLATE[2]	1 kg	325 g	130 g
ECUADOR CHOCOLATE[2]	1 kg	375 g	125 g
ARHUACO CHOCOLATE[2]	1 kg	475 g	130 g

PROCESS
Select the cocoa beans, toast, crush and husk them. Pre-refine the mass obtained and then refine it adding the sugar, conche it, add the melted cocoa butter and temper the chocolate obtained at 45°C.

EMULSION

AN EMULSION IS THE COMBINATION of two ingredients, oil and water, which are not miscible. It is a basic technique for blending the two basic ingredients into a smooth and stable mixture.

The technique can be performed mechanically, using a device such as a Thermomix, or manually. The process is the same in both cases.

The best-known emulsion is mayonnaise, and its elastic and glossy texture is exactly what we want to achieve in our chocolate emulsions. In our case, the oil is the chocolate and the aqueous base may contain sugars, fruit pulp, aromas, infusions, gelatine, etc.

Method

— Heat both the chocolate and the aqueous liquid to a temperature above 35ºC, at which all the fat crystals melt.

— Put the chocolate into a container, preferably a bowl.

— Add a third of the liquid and whisk, starting with very fast and very tight circles on one side of the bowl.

— When the mixture begins to thicken, add a little more of the liquid and continue with the same whisking motion until all the liquid is incorporated, with increasingly larger circles.

Depending on the recipe, the amount of aqueous liquid may be the same as that of the chocolate. In the case of some ganaches, it is higher, as with beverages. The process is the same: an emulsion is made first, which is extended without separating the oil from the aqueous solution.

How to fix a split emulsion

An emulsion splits or curdles when there are too many solids for the amount of aqueous liquid. In this case, the oil acts as a solid. A liquid that is too thick can also lead to a split emulsion.

In order to fix a split emulsion, the best thing is to use an implement, such as a hand mixer. Part of the split emulsion must be taken out and set aside and the whisking concentrated on one area until the consistency has been restored. Then the remaining mixture is incorporated a little at a time without stopping.

An emulsion can also split when the oil begins to solidify as it is whisked. This happens when one or two of the ingredients are too cold, or when the temperature of the room is too low. This is why it is vital to check the temperature of the ingredients and the room before making the emulsion.

WHEN THE MIXTURE BEGINS TO THICKEN, ADD A LITTLE MORE OF THE LIQUID AND CONTINUE WITH THE SAME WHISKING MOTION UNTIL ALL THE LIQUID IS INCORPORATED.

FIRM WATER GANACHE FOR HAND-CUT CHOCOLATE BONBONS

Makes 300 g ganache

65 g still mineral water
60 g atomised glucose
0.5 g salt
0.5 g citric acid
4 g glycerine
120 g 70% cacao chocolate[2]
30 g cocoa butter
30 g sunflower oil

Mix the water with the glucose, salt, citric acid and glycerine in a saucepan and bring to the boil. Leave to cool to 40°C.

Melt the chocolate at 40°C. Mix the chocolate with the water mixture and whisk to an emulsion.

Melt the cocoa butter at 40°C and whisk the oil and cocoa butter into the chocolate emulsion. Mix until smooth.

Temper the ganache to 31°C and spread on a tray over a previously made chocolate base. Leave to harden.

Follow the process for making hand-cut chocolate bonbons (see page opposite), then dip or enrobe in the same XMC chocolate (see page 256).

HAND-CUT CHOCOLATE BONBONS

Hand-cut chocolate bonbons may be made of ganache or gianduja (a nut paste similar to praline). The consistency needed for hand-cut chocolates is harder than that used for making moulded chocolates because the way of working with it is different.

To make this type of chocolate bonbon, the ganache requires a very fine chocolate base and coating that will allow it to hold its shape.

On a tray lined with acetate, spread a base of XMC chocolate (see process on page 256) at a temperature of 45°C. Before it hardens, build a frame around the tray.

Spread the tempered ganache over the chocolate and leave to crystallise to a consistency that can will allow it to be properly handled.

When the ganache is at the ideal consistency, cover with a very thin layer of tempered XMC chocolate. When the chocolate layer is about to harden, cut into the desired shape.

Separate the bonbons on a tray and leave for 24 hours at 16°C to dry the surface of the ganache.

When dry, the bonbons can be enrobed or dipped in XMC chocolate and decorated.

CASA CACAO
RECIPES

WATER-BASED HOT SINGLE-ORIGIN DARK CHOCOLATE BEVERAGE

Serves 10

1 kg water
150 g glucose
2 g salt
3 g gellan gum
200 g single-origin
  chocolate

Mix all the ingredients, except the chocolate, in a blender. Put the mixture into a saucepan and bring to the boil.

Melt the single-origin chocolate in another saucepan to 45ºC.

Whisk the chocolate to an emulsion while gradually incorporating the water base.

Serve at the desired temperature.

DAIRY-BASED HOT SINGLE-ORIGIN DARK CHOCOLATE BEVERAGE

Serves 10

500 g pasteurised milk
500 g water
150 g glucose
3 g gellan gum
200 g single-origin
  chocolate

In a saucepan, whisk all the ingredients together, except the chocolate, with a hand-held blender. Place over the heat and bring to the boil.

Melt the single-origin chocolate in a saucepan at 45ºC.

Whisk the chocolate to an emulsion while gradually incorporating the hot milk mixture.

Serve at the desired temperature.

HOT MONTEZUMA BEVERAGE

For the Montezuma beverage water base
Mix all the ingredients together in a saucepan, place on the heat and bring to the boil. Remove from the heat and leave to cool. Whisk with a hand-held blender and set aside in the refrigerator until use.

For the water-based single-origin dark chocolate beverage
Melt the single-origin chocolate in a saucepan to 45ºC.

   Heat the beverage water base in another saucepan to 40ºC. Whisk the chocolate to an emulsion while gradually incorporating the base.

   Serve at the desired temperature.

Serves 10

Montezuma beverage water base
1 kg water
150 g glucose
2 g salt
3 g gellan gum
100 g honey
4 g spiced bread
6 g cinnamon
1 g chilli

Water-based single-origin dark chocolate beverage
1 kg Montezuma beverage water base (previously prepared)
200 g single-origin chocolate

WATER-BASED COLD SINGLE-ORIGIN DARK CHOCOLATE BEVERAGE

Serves 10

1 kg water
90 g sugar
40 g glycerine
3 g salt
200 g single-origin
  chocolate

Mix all the ingredients together, except the chocolate, in a saucepan. Place over the heat and bring to the boil.

Melt the single-origin chocolate at 45°C in another saucepan, then whisk to an emulsion while gradually incorporating the hot base.

Leave to cool and chill in the refrigerator for at least 2 hours before serving.

DAIRY-BASED COLD SINGLE-ORIGIN DARK CHOCOLATE BEVERAGE (WITH JAÉN CACAO)

Mix all the ingredients together, except the chocolate, in a saucepan. Place over the heat and bring to the boil.

Melt the single-origin chocolate at 45ºC in another saucepan, then whisk to an emulsion while gradually incorporating the hot base.

Leave to cool and chill in the refrigerator for at least 2 hours before serving.

Serves 10

500 g water
500 g milk
90 g sugar
40 g glycerine
3 g salt
200 g Jaén single-
 origin chocolate

Brioche
30 g sugar
25 g milk
12 g yeast
125 g eggs
250 g flour
125 g softened butter
3 g salt

*Dark chocolate
ganache water base*
100 g still mineral
   water
90 g atomised glucose
1 g salt
0.5 g citric acid
5.5 g glycerine

*Dark chocolate
ganache*
130 g dark chocolate
   ganache water base
   (previously prepared)
120 g Jaén 72% cacao
   chocolate
60 g sunflower oil

STEAMED BRIOCHE WITH CHOCOLATE GANACHE

For the brioche

Combine the sugar, milk and yeast in a bowl and mix until the yeast dissolves. Add the eggs.

Sift the flour and incorporate half at a time. Then add the butter and salt.

Knead to a smooth and elastic dough that comes away from the sides of the bowl.

Transfer to another bowl, cover well and rest in the refrigerator for 12 hours.

Use a floured rolling pin to roll out the dough between two sheets of greaseproof paper. Chill in the refrigerator for 30 minutes, then cut into 6-g portions. Refrigerate until cold and shape the cold dough portions into balls.

Prove for 40 minutes at 40ºC. Set aside.

For the dark chocolate ganache water base

Mix all the ingredients together in a saucepan and bring to the boil.

For the dark chocolate ganache

Melt the chocolate at 40ºC and heat the water base to 40ºC.

Mix and then whisk to an emulsion.

Add the sunflower oil and mix until smooth.

Assembly and finishing

Put the brioches into a bamboo steamer basket and steam for about 20 minutes until cooked. Fill with the dark chocolate ganache.

SINGLE-ORIGIN CHOCOLATE AND HAZELNUT SPREAD

Makes 900 g

500 g hazelnuts
200 g single-origin dark
  chocolate
100 g single-origin milk
  chocolate
75 g sugar
1 g salt
40 g sunflower oil

Roast the hazelnuts in the oven at 180ºC for 15–20 minutes. Leave to cool and grind to a hazelnut butter.

Melt the two chocolates together in a saucepan at 45ºC. Mix with all the other ingredients until smooth. Temper at 24ºC and then fill glass jars with the cream. Leave to crystallise as it cools. Set aside.

CASA CACAO CHURROS

Mix the water with the milk and cream in a saucepan and bring to the boil. Add the flour while stirring constantly to a smooth cream. Add the eggs a third at a time, then add the salt and sugar, and fill piping bags fitted with small star nozzles.

Heat oil to 180°C, pipe lengths of batter into the oil and fry the churros until golden. Remove from the oil with a skimmer and drain on kitchen paper.

Dust with a mixture of the sugar and cinnamon from a height. Serve hot.

Serves 25

1.540 kg water
1.257 kg milk
300 g cream
1.761 kg flour
3.140 kg eggs
63 g salt
63 g sugar

1 kg sugar
  for dusting
60 g ground cinnamon
Oil for frying

60% CACAO MILK CHOCOLATE BAR

Makes 2 kg chocolate

395 g cocoa butter
555 g raw cane sugar
370 g powdered milk

1 kg cacao nibs

Melt the cocoa butter in a saucepan at 40°C. Add the sugar and powdered milk and mix.

Pass the nibs through the pre-refiner once. Mix all the ingredients together and pass through the pre-refiner twice in a row.

Next, pass the mixture through the refiner twice. Finish by conching for 24 hours to obtain the 60% cacao milk chocolate base. Mould into a 1–1.5-cm thick bar and leave to harden at 16°C for 30 minutes.

6

A NEW LIFE
FOR CHOCOLATE

AN EXPERIENCE THAT CHANGED CASA CACAO

JORDI ROCA AND THE JOURNEY TO THE SOURCES OF CACAO

I ONCE SAW CHOCOLATE as a product, but the journey has helped me to understand that it is the result of the work of many hands and of many variables. Now I see it as something completely different, not only from the sensory perspective, but also from that of my relationship with it. It is of great importance and merits all my respect. What lies behind it is a story of great effort, dedication, perseverance and changes. It is a mirror of passion, genetics and political action. There is much to learn through cacao, and in my opinion, it can be seen as a gauge of the world's health, a yardstick. From here on, we at Casa Cacao are going to love what we are doing much more.

We thought we could make chocolate without visiting the cacao-growing areas. After having gone and seen it for ourselves, the possibilities offered by the way in which cacao is fermented and what its cultivation entails, I see that Casa Cacao makes sense. It did before, but now it makes all the sense in the world, because we are somehow closing the cycle, in the knowledge that what we make from our chocolates will be destined more directly to the Awajún and will have a more substantial and honest impact on the life of the community. At the same time, it will breathe new life into the field of flavours on which we will attempt to fully capitalise. We are going to play and feel like children; nothing is the same as it was at the beginning. Casa Cacao is like a temple that began almost as a joke, something that would allow us to have fun making chocolate. Now it is a place where many roads meet, and we are going to continue to walk together with all those people we have encountered, and they are all going to be given a voice at Casa Cacao.

My relationship with chocolate began just like that of any pastry chef. You know a little about where it comes from, the techniques for working with it, tempering and everything that can be done with it, but in a very basic way. When I began, I saw it as just another ingredient, one more component of pastry-making, like butter, sugar and cream, even as a basic flavour – the flavour of chocolate – and I never thought to delve more deeply. I stayed at the surface. I understood it to be a process; I knew it was used as a preparation, but I never considered it to be so changeable, or that there could be such a metamorphosis in a plant or a fruit that

tastes of very little, and that its fermentation could achieve so many qualities. I already knew of them, but when you experience this transformation in the field, you see it in a completely different light.

When I created Anarkia, the aim was to make a dish that was bereft of meaning in which there were a lot of elements without a very marked flavour, although from the very first Anarkia, the focal point was chocolate. There were different single-origin chocolates, and each preparation had a hint of flavour – peppers, spices, chillies or herbs – allowing each chocolate to have an aromatic nuance that stood out and was self-explanatory. Chocolate was an important vehicle, but it was just another vehicle, understood in a way that so many other pastry chefs do, as a finished product which we receive and which is called chocolate. I thought of chocolate as a completely controlled element. There is so much information about chocolate that I believed absolutely everything had been done. It is difficult not to repeat a technique in a completely new way. You can blend flavours

AFTER HAVING GONE AND SEEN IT FOR OURSELVES, THE POSSIBILITIES OFFERED BY THE WAY IN WHICH CACAO IS FERMENTED AND GROWN, CASA CACAO MAKES ALL THE SENSE IN THE WORLD.

THE IDEA WAS TO REACH PIURA AND GET TO KNOW THE FIRST CACAO I EVER WORKED WITH. THE FIRST THING I DID WAS TO HUG A TREE.

and achieve harmony, but everything has been done on the technical side – every kind of sponge, every kind of sauce, caramels and bonbons, among others. I think everything that revolves around it has been invented. One ingredient had built up into a world of its own, but I still hadn't seen what there was before chocolate became chocolate, how it was processed or what faces the people who worked to produce it had. These are the details that open doors in a creative sense.

The idea of seeing what lay behind chocolate emerged with Damian, when we were starting out with the idea of Casa Cacao. In fact is was a little like a challenge: I bet you haven't got the guts to make your own chocolate and to do it well. When we saw that we could make chocolate from selected cacao beans, we kept talking. It became clear that neither he nor I had been to a plantation. We were intrigued to know about what happened to the beans, why we were receiving sacks with beans that were much smaller than others, with essentially poor sorting and with a 15 per cent loss from each sack due to defects. We needed to understand how cacao was sorted, how it was delivered, and why that happened. This was the spark that grew into our journey, and thanks to it, we were able to see the wide range of possibilities that exist in each pallet of beans. You realise that there are not only the three varieties we had been told about – Criollo, Trinitario and Forastero – but that each one has its own story, that there are genetics at play, that they had been interbreeding on the plantations, that the jungle is very much alive and there are hybrids that have no name, that there are very well established varieties with names, but that there are others whose names are unknown... It is fascinating.

Piura cacao was key to our starting to work with Damian, in the knowledge that by doing things our own way, but with that base, we could make a really good chocolate. It was an exceptional cacao with very fruity and acidic notes, with a balsamic acidity that would arrive very slowly and very elegantly. When we became more adept at working the machinery and the roasting process, and even when we subjected the dried beans to new fermentation processes, we saw that there was a future, that it made sense to work with those cacaos to make our chocolates. That Piura cacao was the first we used when we began to work on the Casa Cacao project. My initial idea was to arrive in Piura and become acquainted with the product we were working with, and the first thing I did was hug a tree. When I saw my first cacao tree, it was like meeting a long-lost son. I knew about it in Girona, but things had happened to it, and I wanted to know what face it had, fresh-faced and without make-up. Together with Iván Murrugarra, our host at the plantation in Piura, we split open cacao pods and ate the beans, which was the first fresh bean I tried on a plantation. It was a day to remember for the rest of my life, a day to cherish.

When I set foot on my first plantation and saw so many cacao trees, I realised there were so many possibilities, not only in terms of aroma, but owing to the amount of possible hybrids that existed. I realised how one type of bean differed from another according to where it was planted and how the character of the soil it grows in is reflected in the chocolate. For me, it was feeling the way Josep feels when he visits a vineyard. Not only does he speak of a variety of grape, but of the soil, the region and the grower; and this is what I could feel in the cradle of chocolate. I could experience the farm, the grower – whether it was well tended and clean; whether they were dedicated and liked what they were doing… We also met people who loved their work and who told us that the passion they felt was life-changing. You realise that chocolate and cacao alone affect the lives of people. For me, now it is much more than a fruit or a product; it is a good way of changing the lives of many people. Now, when we receive the cacao, we treat it with more respect. A sack arrives, and I think of what it takes to fill a sack like that, of how it is taken to the processing facility, and of how the cacao beans are moved around inside the fermentation boxes. We are very aware of what we have in our hands, and not even a bean is wasted.

THE CLIMATIC CONDITIONS
MAKE IT MORE ASTRINGENT,
WITH VERY BITTER NOTES AND A
LITTLE LESS ACIDITY THAN THAT
OF PIURA CACAO, BUT WITH
MORE FRUITINESS.

Before our journey, Piura was a prestigious single-origin cacao, given its peculiarity and the fact that a white variety of such high quality was isolated and its cultivation extended. When you arrive in Piura and get to know the farms and growers, you come to understand how they have managed to take such a particular variety so far, with great dedication, a lot of tradition and the work in the breeding of trees, an admirable labour that has involved a large number of people. Then you realise the plants are in very carefully tended rows, like a German vineyard of the sort Pitu likes – perfectly aligned and extremely well tended. That is what Piura would be like for chocolate.

Everything is different when you put a face to the product. The same thing happens with coffee, vanilla and the different varieties of pepper. They are things that arrive ready to use. We have always had them on hand with almost never a thought about who makes them. With the Awajúns I understood the reality of the people who are behind cacao, when after a long and difficult hike through the jungle, climbing through and crossing ravines, we managed to reach that magical hidden farm to meet the farmers with their faces tanned by life in the rainforest. Their joy and generosity, and their ability to give us absolutely everything, were eye-opening. I felt what there was behind chocolate. I came to understand that behind a

simple cacao bean there is a life, a community, a way of life that is so different from our own that we cannot even fathom – a community governed by spiritual rules that influence all types of relationships – and small communities that are united by cacao and chocolate. I was moved by all of this.

When we left Piura, I had the impression that cacao plantations were ordered places with evenly spaced trees. But then you reach the Awajún communities and discover that their plantations are hidden away amidst the rainforest in places that are difficult to access, sometimes growing spontaneously with trees that inter-breed, and you find different trees on every farm. You grasp the fact that Awajún cacao is wild, like life there, and completely organic, without any treatment. That is the wonder of a unique cacao. Awajún cacao has more points of flavour and is more changeable. It is difficult to find uniformity between harvests. The climatic conditions make it more astringent, with very bitter notes and a little less acidity than that of Piura cacao, but with more fruitiness, which allows us to combine it with other types of things. At the same time, it is a chocolate that expresses itself alone, needing no assistance, as it has all the possible nuances. When the next sack arrives, it is completely different and you have to start all over. Making chocolate is a challenge, especially because the cacao is always changing. It is where you notice

YOU REACH THE AWAJÚN COMMUNITIES AND REALISE THAT AWAJÚN CACAO IS WILD, LIKE LIFE THERE. THAT IS THE WONDER OF A UNIQUE CACAO.

the difference between the harvests and beans that you receive, because they depend on who has taken care of the cacao, how it has been fermented and how it has been treated. Awajún cacao changes so much that it is unmanageable, and I hope it stays that way. It is an adventure, just like going there was.

I believe the Awajúns have seen a possibility by which to change their lives. Cacao will give them the opportunity for even more profound development, without forgetting their origins and their nature. Cacao will change the Awajúns' lives for the better. When I returned to Girona, I received an exciting message from Max Drusche. He told me that the Awajúns were thrilled by my visit and that they were looking for land on which to build a processing facility for all of that scattered cacao production. We are going to support this project as far as possible because we want their cacao to have a voice and a much more promising outlook. I believe it can be given a uniformity that helps to define the character of the chocolate made from it, which in turn impacts the development of those communities, helping to strengthen a sustainable and lasting way of life. I believe we can turn chocolate into a mirror that shows the world that language, that culture and those people. We want Awajún chocolate to play a leading role and become one of our pillars; we want the Casa Cacao chocolate made from that cacao to have as much magic and future. We want to leave our mark on the fermentation process, to work side by side with them, and to receive this cacao so that it will become the pillar of Casa Cacao. Evidently, we are going to work with other varieties and other single-origin cacaos from around the world, but our flagship cacao will be Awajún cacao.

When I think of a chocolate that reflects the complexity we witnessed in the rainforest, I believe we must be as transparent as possible by allowing the chocolate to express itself on its own, by trying not to touch anything or as little as possible, so that the chocolate can reflect the climate, luxuriance and changeable nature of cacao. We are not going to touch anything. We will let the chocolates show their difference, marked by a harvest date or batch number, so people will understand that we do not want to standardise a flavour and that it will continue to change. We want to show that what we have at Casa Cacao is alive, that you can try the same variety of single-origin chocolate, but it will be completely different from one year to another, like wine.

When I arrived in Colombia and heard about Mayumi, I was captivated. Particularly by the fact that she was working with the Arhuaco communities of the Sierra Nevada de Santa Marta mountains. I discovered the dynamic and amazingly positive person that Mayumi is, and her passion when she speaks to

THE ARHUACOS ARE A VERY
SPECIAL PEOPLE. THEY
SURPRISE YOU WITH THEIR
CLOTHES, THE PRIDE WITH
WHICH THEY WEAR THEM AND
THEIR OUTLOOK ON LIFE.

you about cacao. She becomes emotional when she speaks to you about chocolate, about how it is made, the work that goes into it, and how this has helped to preserve truly interesting genetic varieties. She explains it all with a passion that you soak up, making you fall even more deeply in love with the world of chocolate. She has passion and know-how. She told me that she worked in Japan making up recipes using chocolate and had never seen a cacao tree, and that she travelled to Colombia and stayed there, with the Arhuacos, and that is like devoting yourself to the god of cacao.

The Arhuacos are a very special people. They surprise you with their clothes and the pride with which they wear them; they surprise you with their way of speaking and their outlook on life, because they are calm and unrushed, not only in the way they talk, but also in the way they walk. I imagine them being able to spend an entire day observing how a leaf moves in a tree, because when they tell you something or speak of their traditions and how they live, they do so with extraordinary serenity. Arhuacos are spiritual without being religious. Their cacao has that unexpected and wild side that I found in the cacao of the Awajúns, but Mayumi is there to provide them with stability in their work of growing and fermenting. Mayumi has the good qualities of the Japanese. She is meticulous, exacting and professional, and her character is in tune with that of the Arhuacos, who also have a very ingrained notion of order and discipline. I believe this is the reason they understand Mayumi so well. She is exceptionally focused on the post-harvest process. She controls the fermentation of the beans very cleanly, fully aware of what is happening on a scientific level every step of the way, monitoring the organoleptic levels of the cacao, and supporting the Arhuacos in everything they do, resulting in an unusually rounded cacao. It has this changeable and unexpected side, which Mayumi is polishing in an amazing way, which makes Arhuaco cacao and Mayumi synonymous.

There is a reality in Colombia that is still very apparent, which is the reality of guerrilla conflict and the drug trade. Cacao is playing an essential role as an alternative to coca crops in that region. We were lucky enough to meet several growers who have replaced coca with cacao, taking the side of the legal crop. Exelino proudly explained to us how his life had been turned around completely after shifting to cacao. You realise that cacao is a driver of social, personal and political change in those areas.

The journey has changed my way of working with chocolate. When I think about inventing a new dessert, I no longer think the way I did with Anarkia. Now I want to represent the flavour that chocolate had on this journey, to reflect the cacao as

a being, to show how it lives and what it expresses. I have created a dish I call Marabil-lao, which consists of two parts. It is a subjective expression of what fermentation and what happens during this process mean to me. There is a sequence of small gels ranging from lychee to cacao pulp, sherry vinegar and Fino sherry, by way of passion fruit and raisins, and at the end is a gel made from a dry cacao infusion. This sequence can be seen as what happens to cacao during this process, passing through the floral part and acidity of the fermentation, and the acidity of the fruit – first ripe and then dried. Then there are the chocolates made with cacaos I brought back from this journey: Arhuaco, Awajún, Piura and Jaén cacaos. In other words aromatic nuances turned into a dessert. It all makes sense to me when you can sample the original organoleptic and aromatic qualities of the cacao as it is being processed and when it is finished, plus the work I do afterwards, when it arrives here and I turn each chocolate into a gel, sponge, ice cream or caramel. It is a closed circle, an ordered and much more mature way of seeing chocolate, and one that is much more aware of what lies behind. One that tries to reflect with all due respect the work that goes into transforming cacao into chocolate.

CACAO IS PLAYING AN ESSENTIAL ROLE IN COLOMBIA AS AN ALTERNATIVE TO COCA CROPS.

Toffee cream
2 gelatine leaves
200 g sugar
500 g cream

Red fruit and Tahitian
vanilla sorbet
1 kg assorted red fruits
200 g water
20 g inverted sugar
1 Tahitian vanilla pod
200 g sugar
50 g dextrose
30 g atomised glucose
7.5 g sorbet stabiliser

Rose jelly
200 g rose water
1 g agar-agar

Bergamot sauce
50 g water
50 g sugar
2 g agar-agar
The grated zest of one
  bergamot
100 g bergamot juice

Honey jelly
1½ gelatine leaves
150 g honey
50 g water

Violet jam
100 g water
20 g fresh violets
100 g sugar
10 g pectin

Chocolate caramel
200 g fondant sugar
100 g liquid glucose
100 g isomalt
60 g 70% cacao
  chocolate

ANGEL, BY THIERRY MUGLER

For the toffee cream
Soak the gelatine leaves in cold water.

Heat the sugar in a saucepan to a temperature of 180ºC until it begins to turn golden. Stop the caramel by adding the hot cream. When the caramel has dissolved in the cream, add the softened gelatine, strain and set aside in an airtight container.

Leave to stand for at least 12 hours to stabilise the fat in the cream. Whisk in a mixer and transfer to a piping bag fitted with a star nozzle. Set aside.

For the red fruit and Tahitian vanilla sorbet
Purée the red fruits and set aside.

Combine the water in a saucepan with the inverted sugar and vanilla pod and place over the heat. Before it comes to the boil, incorporate the remaining dry ingredients and heat to 85ºC. Add the puréed berries and age the sorbet mixture in the refrigerator for 24 hours. Remove the vanilla pod.

Churn in an ice-cream maker and store in the freezer at -20ºC.

For the rose jelly
Bring a part of the rose water to the boil in a saucepan and dissolve the agar-agar. Add the remainder and pour the mixture into a tray with 5-mm sides. Leave to set and cut into 5-mm cubes.

For the bergamot sauce
Combine the water, sugar, agar-agar and bergamot zest in a saucepan and bring to the boil. Mix with the juice and leave to cool and set. Transfer to a blender and blend to a sauce-like consistency.

For the honey jelly
Soak the gelatine in cold water. Drain and set aside.

In a saucepan, bring the honey to the boil and add the water. Dissolve the softened gelatine. Pour into a tray with 5-mm sides. Leave to set in the refrigerator and cut into 5-mm cubes.

For the violet jam
Combine the water, violets and 75 g of sugar in a saucepan and bring to the boil.

Mix the remaining 25 g of sugar with the pectin in a bowl and gradually add to the pan while stirring constantly. Reduce to the consistency of jam, bearing in mind that the mixture will thicken as it cools. Set aside.

For the chocolate caramel
Mix the fondant sugar with the glucose in a saucepan and place over the heat. When

the sugar melts, add the isomalt and heat to 160ºC. Then remove from the heat and stop the cooking process by plunging the pan in a container filled with water. Wait until the temperature of the mixture falls to 140ºC and add the chocolate while stirring constantly. When the mixture is smooth, spread over a silicone mat. Cover with another mat and roll out with a rolling pin. Use a knife to mark out squares in the caramel, which will become individual portions when it cools. Vacuum seal in a bag and set aside.

Heat a caramel square on a silicone mat in the oven heated to 180ºC. Cover with a silicone mat when melted. While still hot, roll out as thinly as possible with a rolling pin and shape with your hands into very thin caramel shapes. Set aside in an airtight container with silica gel.

For the violet meringues

Mix the egg whites with the violet sugar and set aside in a bain-marie at 60ºC to melt the sugar without coagulating the whites. When the sugar has melted, beat the whites to stiff peaks and fill a piping bag. Pipe very small dots of meringue. Dry out in a hot cupboard at 50ºC for 12 hours and set aside in an airtight container with silica gel.

Assembly and finishing

Arrange two spots of bergamot sauce, two spots of violet jam, two honey jelly cubes and two rose jelly cubes over a flat plate. Pipe the red fruit and vanilla sorbet on the plate. Cover with toffee cream and arrange a few violet meringues and a chocolate caramel shape on top. Decorate with a few violets.

Serve together with a sprayed sample of Angel perfume by Thierry Mugler.

Violet meringues
100 g egg whites
100 g Azuleta violet
  sugar
Assembly and finishing
Fresh violets

Crème anglaise
420 g milk
420 g cream
84 g sugar
168 g egg yolks

Chocolate mousse
1.090 kg crème
  anglaise (previously
  prepared)
1.272 kg 64% cacao
  chocolate
1.636 kg cream (35%
  fat)

Sponge cake
237 g unsalted butter
63 g icing sugar
237 g 70% cacao dark
  chocolate
114 g egg yolks
170 g egg whites
158 g sugar
119 g plain flour

Praline crunch
492 g 35% cacao milk
  chocolate
966 g hazelnut praline
242 g feuilletine flakes
Sponge cake
  (previously prepared)

Neutral glaze
225 g water
113 g glucose
158 g sugar
7 g pectin NH
1 g citric acid

CHOCOLATISSIMO PASTEL

For the crème anglaise

Combine the liquids with the sugar in a pan and bring to the boil. Whisk into the egg yolks, ensuring that the temperature of the mixture reaches 85ºC.

For the chocolate mousse

Strain the freshly made crème anglaise over the chocolate. Wait for a minute and whisk to an emulsion. Leave to cool to 38–40ºC and add a little of the cream whipped to soft peaks. Mix a little and then add the remainder.

For the sponge cake

Mix the still slightly cold butter with the icing sugar until fluffy. Add the melted chocolate a little at a time at intervals, and continue to mix. Add the yolks a half or a third at a time without stopping the mixer.

Beat the egg whites with the sugar, and then fold into the previous mixture. Finally, sprinkle in the flour and incorporate.

Fill each 9 cm mould with 65g of batter, evenly spread, and bake for 9 minutes at 200ºC.

For the praline crunch

Melt the chocolate and mix with the praline. Incorporate the feuilletine flakes and spread 850 g of the mixture over the sponge.

For the neutral glaze

Heat the water with the glucose to 45ºC and gradually add the mixture of the sugar with pectin as the water heats up. Bring to the boil, add the citric acid and bring back to the boil. Skim off any impurities from the mixture and set aside in the refrigerator.

For the black glaze

Combine the liquids with the sugar and bring to the boil. Add the gelatine leaves softened in cold water to dissolve. Pour the mixture over the cocoa powder. Mix well. Strain and set aside in the refrigerator until use.

For the cocoa shortbread

Soften the butter, mix with all the ingredients and leave to cool. Roll out to a 2-mm thickness and bake for 12 minutes at 160ºC.

For the chocolate cream

Heat the milk and mix in the whisked egg yolks before adding the cream. Pour the mixture over the chocolate and whisk to an emulsion.

Black glaze
118 g water
504 g neutral glaze
  (previously prepared)
444 g cream (35% fat)
667 g sugar
30 g gelatine leaves
237 g cocoa powder

Cocoa shortbread
265 g unsalted butter
477 g plain flour
133 g icing sugar
5 g salt
67 g egg
53 g cocoa powder

Chocolate cream
74 g milk
74 g egg yolk
298 g cream
335 g 36 % cacao
  chocolate

*Assembly and
finishing*
Cacao nibs
Edible gold powder

Assembly and finishing

Fill the desired moulds with the freshly made mousse. Close the mould with pieces of sponge trimmed to a slightly smaller size than the opening. Chill in the freezer for a few hours. Turn out of the moulds. Heat the glaze to 40ºC and glaze the entremets. Sprinkle with a little of the crushed nibs and finish with a quenelle of cream. Decorate with a little gold powder.

Golden neutral glaze
448 g water
313 g sugar
224 g glucose
2.5 g citric acid
9 g pectin NH
2 g edible gold powder

Sponge cake
237 g unsalted butter
63 g icing sugar
237 g 70% cacao dark
  chocolate
114 g egg yolks
170 g pasteurised egg
  whites
158 g sugar
119 g plain flour

*Milk chocolate and
tea cream*
19 g Earl Grey tea
74 g milk
74 g egg yolks
298 g cream
335 g 36% cacao
  chocolate

Chocolate mousse
1.918 kg cream (35%
  fat)
346 g apricot purée
4 g gelatine leaves
1.385 kg 36% cacao
  chocolate
346 g cream (35% fat)

MILK TEA PASTEL

For the golden neutral glaze
Mix all the ingredients together in a saucepan, except the gold powder, and bring to the boil. Skim off any impurities from the mixture and then add the edible gold powder.

For the sponge cake
See recipe on the previous page (288). Mix the still slightly cold butter with the icing sugar until fluffy. Add the melted chocolate a little at a time at intervals and continue to mix. Add the yolks a half or a third at a time without stopping the mixer.

Beat the egg whites with the sugar, and then fold into the previous mixture. Sprinkle in the flour and incorporate.

Fill each mould with 1.1 kg of batter, evenly spread, and bake for 9 minutes at 200ºC.

For the milk chocolate and tea cream
Infuse the tea with the milk for 5 minutes at 85ºC and strain. Heat the infused milk and mix with the beaten egg yolks before incorporating the cream. Pour over the chocolate and whisk to an emulsion. Set aside to pour over the sponge.

For the chocolate mousse
Combine the 1.918 kg of cream with the apricot purée in a pan and bring to the boil. Add the softened gelatine leaves and mix with the melted chocolate. Cool the mixture to 35ºC and add the rest of the cream a half at a time. Fill the moulds.

Assembly and finishing
Pour the milk chocolate and tea cream over the sponge and freeze. Cut into the desired size pieces. Fill two-thirds of the pastel mould with the mousse and introduce the sponge and cream insert. Freeze. Unmould and brush with the glaze.

Neutral glaze
883 g water
618 g sugar
441 g glucose
4 g citric acid
35 g pectin NH
18 g cocoa powder

Micro sponge
166 g almond butter
249 g egg whites
166 g egg yolks
166 g icing sugar
31 g plain flour
21 g cocoa powder

Cocoa shortbread
265 g unsalted butter
477 g plain flour
133 g icing sugar
5 g salt
67 g egg
53 g cocoa powder

Sponge cake
475 g unsalted butter
127 g icing sugar
475 g 70% cacao dark
  chocolate
228 g egg yolks
342 g pasteurised egg
  whites
316 g sugar
237 g plain flour

*Passion fruit, apricot
and mandarin cream*
234 g sugar
354 g eggs
118 g apricot purée
118 g mandarin purée
118 g passion fruit
  purée
7 g gelatine leaves

DULCE DE LECHE CAKE

For the neutral glaze
Mix all the ingredients together in a saucepan and bring to the boil. Skim off any impurities.

For the micro sponge
Mix all the ingredients together and strain. Fill a siphon and set aside in the refrigerator for a few hours. Heat in a bain-marie to 50ºC before use.

For the cocoa shortbread
Soften the butter, mix with all the ingredients and leave to cool. Roll out to a 2-mm thickness and bake for 12 minutes at 160ºC.

For the sponge cake
Mix the still slightly cold butter with the icing sugar until fluffy.
Add the melted chocolate a little at a time at intervals, and continue to mix. Add the yolks a half or a third at a time without stopping the mixer.

Beat the egg whites with the sugar, and then fold into the previous mixture. Sprinkle in the flour and incorporate.

Fill each mould with 1.1 kg of batter, evenly spread, and bake for 9 minutes at 200ºC.

For the passion fruit, apricot and mandarin cream
Mix the sugar with the eggs and add the purées. Transfer to a pan and heat gently until the mixture is about to come to the boil. Add the softened gelatine and cool.

For the dulce de leche gel base
Mix all the ingredients together in a pan, bring to the boil and reduce to the desired consistency. Vacuum seal in a bag and freeze.

For the dulce de leche gel
Heat the dulce de leche base to 45ºC and add the softened gelatine and leave to cool.

For the dulce de leche mousse base
Mix all the ingredients together in a pan, bring to the boil and reduce to the desired consistency.

For the dulce de leche mousse
Heat the dulce de leche mousse base to 45ºC and add the softened gelatine and mix well. Cool the mixture to 30ºC and add the cream whipped to soft peaks a half or a third at a time.

Dulce de leche gel base
298 g milk
149 g sugar
0.4 cloves
0.4 g bicarbonate of
  soda
45 g glucose

Dulce de leche gel
493 g dulce de leche
  gel base (previously
  prepared)
7 g gelatine leaves

Dulce de leche mousse base
1.200 kg milk
600 g sugar
1.8 pieces cloves
1.8 g baking soda
180 g glucose

Dulce de leche mousse
1.984 kg dulce de
  leche mousse base
  (previously prepared)

32 g gelatine leaves
1.984 kg cream (35%
  fat)

Assembly and finishing

Pipe the micro sponge batter into a 33-ml container and cook in the microwave for 30 seconds and leave to cool. Set aside. Press stainless steel ring moulds into the sponge cake, cover with the passion fruit, apricot and mandarin cream, and leave to set. Freeze. Pour the dulce de leche gel into the 7-cm x 4-cm moulds and return to the freezer. Cut the sponge and cream inserts into the desired size. Fill three-quarters of the moulds with the mousse and close with the sponge and cream insert. Freeze, un-mould, brush with the glaze and arrange each cake over a piece of cocoa shortbread. Decorate with a piece of micro sponge.

Patchouli ice cream
500 g milk
200 g cream
200 g dextrose
50 g powdered milk
100 g sugar
6 g ice-cream stabiliser
20 g dried patchouli
  roots
35% cacao milk
  chocolate

*Milk chocolate
mousse*
120 g cream
80 g egg yolks
20 g sugar
500 g cream
260 g 44% cacao milk
  chocolate

Cocoa biscuit
200 g unsalted butter
50 g icing sugar
20 g egg yolks
275 g flour
40 g cocoa powder

Earth distillate
300 g soil
500 g water

*Thickened earth
distillate*
1 g xanthan gum per
  430 g distillate

Jasmine tea air
500 g skimmed milk
10 g jasmine tea

Decoration
Orange segments
Beetroot leaves
Shisho leaves

TERRE D'HERMÈS

For the patchouli ice cream

Mix the milk and cream with the dextrose and powdered milk in a saucepan and heat to 70°C. Incorporate the sugar and stabiliser and heat to 85°C while stirring constantly. Next, add the patchouli and leave to infuse as the mixture cools. Set aside.

Wait for 6 hours before churning in the ice-cream maker. Set aside at -18°C.

When the ice cream has firmed, shape into small balls and freeze again, before dipping in the melted chocolate. Set aside in the freezer.

For the milk chocolate mousse

Make a pâte à bombe by mixing the 120 g of cream, egg yolks and sugar in a saucepan and heat to 85°C. Whisk the hot mixture and sugar until it triples in volume and cools. Set aside.

Whip the 500 g of cream in a separate container and set aside.

Gradually mix the pâte à bombe with the chocolate couverture and then fold in the whipped cream. Set aside in an airtight container in the refrigerator.

For the cocoa biscuit

Mix the softened butter, icing sugar and egg yolks in a bowl. Sift the flour and cocoa together and incorporate. Set aside.

Spread the mixture to a 5-mm thickness over a baking tray lined with a silicone mat. Bake at 180°C for 5 minutes. Set aside in an airtight container.

For the earth distillate

Mix the soil with the water, cover the container and leave the mixture to infuse for 12 hours in the refrigerator.

Transfer the infusion to an evaporation flask and position a 0.22 µm membrane filter between the flask and the outlet towards the condenser. Distil at 30–35°C (bath temperature) for 1–2 hours and finish at 40–45°C for 30 minutes.

Vacuum seal the distillate to prevent loss of aroma. If it is to be stored for several days or weeks, it should be frozen.

For the thickened earth distillate

Use a hand-held blender to mix together the earth distillate and xanthan gum (1 g xanthan gum per 430 g distillate) in a container and set aside in the refrigerator.

For the jasmine tea air

Heat the milk to 80°C in a saucepan and infuse with the jasmine tea for 4 minutes. Strain and refrigerate. Whisk with a hand-held blender before use.

Assembly and finishing

Make a quenelle of milk chocolate mousse and arrange in a deep dessert plate. Cover it with three patchouli ice-cream balls, a few orange segments, crumbled cocoa biscuit, a few drops of thickened earth distillate, a few beetroot and purple shiso leaves and a pinch of grapefruit zest. Finish with jasmine tea air to one side.

Serve together with a sprayed sample of Terre d'Hermès perfume.

CHOCOLATES, CUPS AND GLASSES
STORIES OF LOVE BY JOSEP ROCA

PART OF THE SUCCESS of contemporary cuisine is a result of the constant investigation into why culinary processes are possible for each food product. The thirst for knowledge has brought chefs closer to the source of the ingredients they use. The observation of dietary habits and migratory movements help us to better understand life styles, the mixture of races and interculturality. The writer Josep Pla once said 'we are what we eat'; to these wise words I would add an important question, are we what we drink? There is no doubt that knowing how to drink is a part of knowing how to live.

In a world marked by globalisation, the combination of dishes with wines opens up a world of possibilities, which is appropriate for a society which absorbs trends and customs from distant places, as it reinvents itself and evolves.

Throughout the centuries, humans have been adapting in a complex but complementary way the combination of solid food and liquid creations. Endemic wisdom is always reflected in local customs and manners. Wine is deeply rooted in European society as a result of the habits of the Greeks and Romans. So, when it comes to speaking about the way of accompanying cacao and its chocolate derivatives, it is necessary to reflect on the knowledge we have of wine that goes beyond the Western perspective. The dietary habits of the different civilisations allow us to understand the reality of other ancient cultures, like those of tea, coffee, beer, spirits, liqueurs and xocolatl, which includes the mixture of ground cacao beans and toasted cornmeal with water known as pinolillo and others made from cacao.

Our approach to the world of possible cacao combinations can come with varieties and different states of fermentation, maturing and roasting, or from the perspective of harmony, contrast, versatility and complementarity. We know that the connections between dishes and beverages can arise through physical associations and molecular correspondence, connecting cacao aromas with the aromas of coffee and other beverages, through associations with local customs, seasons or emotions. It is true that cacao is not easy to combine, but we can use our astuteness for each taboo food, which allows us to modulate, temper, adapt and cook as best suits us, seeking points in common with coffee and the other beverages they evoke. When chocolate desserts contain air, cream or cocoa butter, they are brought closer to the world of wine. Contrasts in the temperatures at which drinks are served can also be taken to extremes. The other option is to weaken the extreme acidity or bitterness of chocolate with changes in texture and flavour intensity. Giving consideration to its elasticity, adhesiveness, chewiness, cohesiveness and rubberiness, paving the way to modifying the texture and producing more or less salivation, will provide better understanding of choice when combining the solid texture with liquid elements. It is no easy task to find wines and other beverages of sufficient personality and character which emerge unscathed from their encounter with cacao nibs.

The great challenge is to find wines that structurally hold their own against the acidity and sharply bitter notes of the roasted cacao bean. Perhaps a suitable way of countering that strength is the more subtle line of smoked and spiced flavours found in the fine black teas of Fujian, such as lapsang souchong. Tea counteracts the acidity and develops its character of fermented leaf in perfect combination, setting up an encounter between noble versions of bitterness.

We had initially assumed that cacao belonged to the empyreumatic family of roasted aromas, such as those of caramel, toasted bread, leather, coffee, tobacco and smoked foods. Greater knowledge of cacao and chocolate, and better traceability have allowed us to receive fresh cacao and delve more deeply into the aromatic and gustatory aspects of the raw bean, expressed through fruity, exotic, floral and fermented aromas, filled with marvellous volatile substances. The aromatic spectrum of cacao is opened up. We might dare to combine fresh cacao pulp with an aged Alsatian Gewürztraminer wine or a sour beer made with spontaneous fermentation, or a lightly roasted cacao with a Peruvian mistela (a mixture of pisco – Peruvian brandy – and grape juice) supplied by Antiguas Familias Wines and Spirits.

Perhaps I could pair a Piura white cacao with a *pisco acholado* (blended pisco) or a *pisco de falca* (distilled using a traditional falca still), made from aromatic grape varieties such as Torontel or Italia, among others.

If there is a product with matching DNA and organoleptic potential, it is coffee. The result of environmental conditions, soil, ageing, fermentation and roasting. The aromas of the Gesha variety, with notes of flowers and peach, or coffee produced from the IAPAR cultivar, with subtle hints of cacao and artichoke, are examples of a parallel world that embraces the harmony of flavour, local customs and landscapes found in cacao's native lands.

Coffees with floral and citrus notes, combined with lightly roasted cacaos served as infusions, offer a range of possibilities that is open to exploration. To-

gether with dark chocolate, they can hold their own against ales and also aged sugar cane or grape brandies of different origins.

The different possibilities for combining chocolate depend on its physical and chemical properties, the variety of cacao and the fat content or addition of cocoa butter. Dark chocolate with a proportion of cacao between 45 and 70 per cent, the result of mixing cacao paste with cocoa butter and sugar, can be paired with fortified wines, wines with a lingering finish, and dessert wines. Depending on the ingredients used with the chocolate, the decision changes.

The ideal wines for chocolate desserts containing red fruits (cherries, raspberries, blackberries, blueberries, etc.) can be young fortified wines made from red grapes such as Maury and Monastrell, young vintage or ruby ports, and Spanish mistela wines. In the case of chocolate desserts with orange, peach and mandarin, among others, we choose triple sec or, depending on the level of acidity in chocolate and its texture, aged botrytised wines with high levels of acidity, such as Tokaji and German Trockenbeerenauslese (TBA) wines. When the chocolate desserts contain toffee, mocha or spices, they could be paired with aged Peruvian mistelas, a direct connection with the geographical association with Peruvian cacao. But the great fortified wines are those that are best able to withstand the intensity and complexity of the different aromatic modifiers. This is where the great wines produced by oxidative ageing come into their own, such as the legendary Fondillón wines of Alicante, the Commandaria wines of Cyprus, Sicilian Marsala wines, aged Moldovan wines, aged tawny ports, rancio ('rancid') wines of Roussillon, solera-aged Banyul wines, Oloroso sherries from Andalusia and very old Pedro Ximénez and muscatels aged in hundred-year-old soleras. White chocolate could be called 'sugared milk paste' given that it bears no relation to dark chocolate, among other reasons because it contains no cacao paste. The ingredients of white chocolate are cocoa butter, powdered milk, soya lecithin and a lot of sugar. However, a good match for white chocolate could be white rum, pisco or triple sec.

THE GREAT CHALLENGE IS TO FIND WINES THAT STRUCTURALLY HOLD THEIR OWN AGAINST THE ACIDITY AND SHARPLY BITTER NOTES OF THE ROASTED CACAO BEAN.

NEW
CONFECTIONERY

100 g caramelised
   chopped almonds
400 g milk chocolate
   couverture
5 g metallic green food
   colouring

ALMOND BAMBOLESCAS

Put the caramelised almonds into a Comfit chocolate panning machine, gradually adding layers of milk chocolate couverture and leaving enough time for each layer to harden. Once all the couverture has hardened, add the metallic green colouring and leave the nuts revolving in the machine for 20 more minutes.

100 g caramelised
   hazelnuts
300 g milk chocolate
   couverture
20 g cocoa butter
10 g metallic gold food
   colouring

HAZELNUT BAMBOLESCAS

Put the chopped caramelised hazelnuts into a Comfit chocolate panning machine, gradually adding layers of milk chocolate couverture and leaving enough time for each layer to harden. Once all the couverture has hardened, add the cocoa butter and gold colouring and leave the nuts revolving in the machine for 5 more minutes.

RASPBERRY BAMBOLESCAS

Makes 1.655 kg

400 g freeze-dried
raspberries
1.2 kg milk chocolate
couverture
30 g cocoa butter
25 g freeze-dried
raspberry powder

Put the freeze-dried raspberries into a Comfit chocolate panning machine, gradually adding layers of milk chocolate couverture and leaving enough time for each layer to harden. Once all the couverture has hardened, add the melted cocoa butter and freeze-dried raspberry powder and leave the raspberries revolving in the machine for 2 more minutes.

MACADAMIA BAMBOLESCAS

Makes 450 g

150 g caramelised
macadamia nuts
300 g milk chocolate
couverture
37 g cocoa butter
15 g metallic red food
colouring

Put the caramelised macadamia nuts into a Comfit chocolate panning machine, gradually adding layers of milk chocolate couverture and leaving enough time for each layer to harden. Once all the couverture has hardened, add the melted cocoa butter and metallic red colouring and leave the nuts revolving in the machine for 20 more minutes.

Caramelised pecans
50 g water
200 g sugar
2 g salt
400 g pecan nuts

50% cacao milk chocolate
425 g cacao nibs
400 g cocoa butter
250 g non-fat
  powdered milk
500 g raw cane sugar

Banana powder
100 g freeze-dried
  bananas
100 g dextrose powder

Assembly and finishing
100 g 50 % cacao milk
  chocolate
35 g freeze-dried
  passion fruit powder
100 g cocoa butter

PECAN, PASSION FRUIT AND BANANA BAMBOLESCAS

For the caramelised pecans
Mix the water with the sugar and salt in a saucepan and heat to 118ºC. Remove from the heat and immediately add the nuts. Stir until the sugar crystallises and turns white and gritty.

Return the saucepan to the heat and cook until the sugar caramelises. Spread the caramelised nuts over baking parchment to cool, stirring from time to time to prevent from sticking. Cover and chill for 30 minutes in the refrigerator before chocolate panning.

For the 50% cacao milk chocolate
See the process on page 318.

For the banana powder
Grind the bananas with the dextrose in a Thermomix to a fine powder. Set aside in an airtight container.

Assembly and finishing
Mix the milk chocolate with the passion fruit powder and temper at 45ºC.

Add a little of the mixture to the nuts in the chocolate panning machine while revolving until the chocolate hardens and the nuts become loose. Repeat the operation one layer at a time until the chocolate is used up.

Melt the cocoa butter in a saucepan at 40ºC. Add a little cocoa butter and a little banana powder to the nuts in the machine while revolving. Continue until the cocoa butter and banana powder are used up.

Store in an airtight container at 16ºC.

*Caramelised
pistachios*
12 g water
35 g raw cane sugar
5 g inverted sugar
2 drops 1:1 citric acid
  and water solution
2 g salt
150 g peeled pistachio
  nuts
Mint crunch
100 g mint leaves
100 g sugar
5 g glucose

PISTACHIO, PEA AND MINT BAMBOLESCAS

For the caramelised pistachios

Mix the water with the sugar, inverted sugar and citric acid in a saucepan and bring to the boil. Leave to cool and refrigerate for 24 hours.

Mix the syrup with the salt and coarsely chopped pistachios, and spread out over a tray lined with baking parchment.

Bake for 12 minutes at 160°C until completely caramelised. Leave to cool for 30 minutes in an airtight container in the refrigerator before chocolate panning.

For the pea chocolate

See the process on page 320 to make 300 g.

For the mint crunch

Blend all ingredients in a Thermomix to a smooth paste. Spread over a sheet of silicone paper and dry out for 24 hours in the oven or in a dehydrator at 40°C.

Break the crunch into very small pieces. Set aside in an airtight container.

Assembly and finishing

Melt the pea chocolate in a saucepan at 45°C.

Put the pistachios into a bowl and add a little of the chocolate, stirring constantly until the chocolate hardens and the nuts are loose. Repeat the operation one layer at a time until practically all the chocolate is used up. When adding the last chocolate layer, incorporate the mint crunch.

Polish in a chocolate panning drum for a glossy surface, revolving without stopping at low speed and 15°C. Polish for 45 minutes.

Pecan gianduja
12 g water
35 g sugar
5 g inverted sugar
2 drops citric acid
  solution
150 g pecan nut halves
90 g 60% cacao milk
  chocolate
18 g cocoa butter
1 g salt

*Chocolate² and char-
grilled cinnamon
ganache*
2 cinnamon sticks
60 g water
60 g glucose powder
5 g glycerine
1 g salt
120 g chocolate²
15 g cocoa butter
35 g sunflower oil

*White paint and carrot
chocolate decoration*
Milk chocolate
60 g white chocolate
40 g cocoa butter
3 g fat-soluble white
  food colouring
2 g metallic silver food
  colouring
Carrot chocolate (see
  process on page 321)

CARROT CAKE BONBON

For the pecan gianduja
Make a syrup by combining the water, sugar, inverted sugar and critic acid in a sauce-pan and bringing to the boil. Cool and then leave to rest for 24 hours in the refrigerator.

Mix the syrup with the pecans and spread over a baking tray lined with baking parchment. Bake for 12–14 minutes at 160°C until completely caramelised. Leave to cool, then blend to a smooth paste.

Mix the pecan paste with the chocolate, cocoa butter and salt to make the gianduja and temper at 24°C. In the meantime, line a tray with a sheet of acetate and spread a fine layer of milk chocolate at 45°C. Position 5-mm thick acrylic confectionery bars around the edges of the tray to create a frame in which to pour the gianduja.

Pour the gianduja over the hardened chocolate. Leave to set at 16°C for 24 hours.

For the chocolate² and char-grilled cinnamon ganache
Char-grill the cinnamon sticks for 2 minutes to aromatise.

Combine the glucose, glycerine, salt and cinnamon in a saucepan and bring to the boil. Cover with cling film and leave to infuse in the refrigerator for 24 hours. Strain and heat the mixture to 40°C.

Melt the chocolate and cocoa butter separately at 40°C. Whisk the cinnamon infusion with the chocolate to an emulsion. Incorporate the cocoa butter and sunflower oil.

Temper the ganache to 29°C. In the meantime, remove the 5-mm bars from the gianduja and replace with 10-mm bars.

Pour the ganache over the gianduja. Leave to set for 24 hours, until the surface is dry.

For the white paint and carrot chocolate decoration
Melt the chocolate with the cocoa butter at 40°C. Add the food colourings and temper between 29° and 31°C. Use a paint sprayer to apply a very fine layer of the white paint over a tray lined with an acetate sheet. Wait until the paint begins to set before etching a design into it with a sharp point. Pour the carrot chocolate on top and spread out to create a fine layer.

Leave to harden in the refrigerator and cut into small squares. Set aside at a temperature below 18°C.

Assembly and finishing
Spread a fine layer of tempered milk chocolate over the bonbon base. When the chocolate starts to harden, use a guitar cutter to cut into individual bonbons.

Separate the bonbons on a tray and leave to stand for 24 hours to dry the surface.

Enrobe with the tempered milk chocolate.

Decorate the top of each bonbon with a carrot chocolate square.

SOLID LIQUEUR SHOT CHOCOLATE BONBON

*50° carob liqueur
ganache*
40 g water
50 g glucose powder
10 g glycerine
30 g 50° carob liqueur
110 g XMC chocolate
65 g sunflower oil

Bronze paint
25 g cocoa butter
1.5 g fat-soluble bronze
food colouring

For the XMC chocolate
See the process on page 256.

For the 50° carob liqueur ganache
Combine the water, glucose and glycerine in a saucepan and bring to the boil. Cool to 40°C and incorporate the liqueur with the melted chocolate. Whisk to an emulsion with the sunflower oil to make the ganache.

For the bronze paint
Melt the cocoa butter at 40°C and add the bronze food colouring. Temper the ganache at 29–31°C.

Apply a fine layer over a sheet of acetate.

Assembly and finishing
Coat polycarbonate chocolate moulds with a thin layer of XMC chocolate and pipe the liqueur ganache into the cavities. Leave to set and dry overnight.

Close each cavity of the filled moulds with chocolate, and then apply the bronze paint by pressing the acetate sheet against the freshly applied chocolate.

Lemon verbena ganache
60 g water
60 g glucose powder
5 g glycerine
1 g salt
20 g fresh lemon
  verbena
35 g sunflower oil
120 g pea chocolate
15 g cocoa butter

Caramelised pistachios
See ingredients on
  page 305

Dark green paint
30 g white chocolate
20 g cocoa butter
3 g fat-soluble green
  food colouring

Light green paint
30 g white chocolate
20 g cocoa butter
1 g fat-soluble green
  food colouring

Silver paint
30 g white chocolate
20 g cocoa butter
2 g metallic silver food
  colouring

150 g pea chocolate,
  for assembly

PEA, LEMON VERBENA AND PISTACHIO CHOCOLATE BONBON

For the pea chocolate

See the process on page 320.

For the lemon verbena ganache

Mix the water with the glucose, glycerine and salt in a saucepan. Bring to the boil and leave to cool to 60ºC. Blend in 10 g of lemon verbena. Strain and leave to cool, setting aside both the liquid and solids.

When cold, combine the liquid with the solids and leave to infuse for 2 days in the refrigerator.

Heat the sunflower oil, add the remaining 10 g of lemon verbena and leave to infuse in the refrigerator for 2 hours.

Melt the pea chocolate with the cocoa butter at 40ºC in a saucepan.

Strain the lemon verbena-infused syrup and heat to 40ºC. Whisk to an emulsion with the chocolate, and finish by whisking in the infused oil. Temper the ganache at 31ºC.

For the caramelised pistachios

Mix the water with the sugar, inverted sugar and citric acid in a saucepan and bring to the boil. Cool and then leave to rest for at least 24 hours in the refrigerator.

Mix the syrup with the salt and coarsely chopped pistachios, and spread out over a tray lined with baking parchment.

Bake for 12 minutes at 160ºC until completely caramelised. Leave to cool.

For the dark green paint

For the light green paint

For the silver paint

For each colour of paint, melt the cocoa butter with the chocolate couverture at 40ºC. Add the food colouring and temper between 29º and 31ºC.

Assembly and finishing

Prepare polycarbonate moulds, attaching a thin tape inside the cavities to protect from the first layers of paint.

Warm the three paints to 29ºC. Apply dots of dark green with a paint brush and leave for 5 minutes to set. Apply a layer of silver paint over them. Leave to set again. Remove the tape and apply a layer of light green paint in the space that was previously protected.

Temper the pea chocolate and apply a thin layer with a paint brush. Fill the cavities with the lemon verbena ganache and leave to set for 15 minutes. Then leave to dry for 12 hours.

Close each cavity of the filled moulds with a thin layer of pea chocolate and arrange a few caramelised pistachios over the chocolate before it hardens.

Bread chocolate
130 g toasted bread,
  ground to a powder
45 g raw cane sugar
125 g cocoa butter
1 g salt

Tomato jelly
40 g tomato passata
15 g raspberry purée
1 g pectin NH
20 g sugar
50 g isomalt
2 g 1:1 citric acid and
  water solution

*Assembly and
finishing*
Freeze-dried tomato
  powder

BREAD AND TOMATO CHOCOLATE BONBON

For the bread chocolate
Mix the ingredients in a conching machine and refine for 24 hours.

For the tomato jelly
Mix the tomato passata with the raspberry purée in a saucepan and bring to the boil.

Mix the pectin with the sugar and gradually fold into the tomato and raspberry mixture.

Add the isomalt and cook until the sugar content reaches a refractometer reading of 75° Brix.

Remove from the heat, add the citric acid solution and immediately pour into a greased polycarbonate mould. Leave to cool.

Assembly and finishing
Temper the bread chocolate and spread a thin layer inside a tray. Use a knife to cut into 2-cm squares. Arrange a cold jelly dome over each square, enrobe in tempered dark XMC chocolate (see page 256) and decorate by sprinkling with freeze-dried tomato powder.

CACAO PULP CHOCOLATE BONBON

Serves 30
Type: moulded
chocolate bonbons

XMC chocolate
(see page 256)

Cacao pulp ganache
50 g cacao pulp
45 g glucose powder
15 g glycerine
135 g white chocolate
15 g cocoa butter
30 g sunflower oil

Red paint
30 g white chocolate
20 g cocoa butter
3 g fat-soluble red food
  colouring
2 g metallic red food
  colouring

Yellow paint
30 g white chocolate
20 g cocoa butter
3 g fat-soluble yellow
  food colouring
2 g metallic yellow food
  colouring

For the XMC chocolate
See the process on page 256.

For the cacao pulp ganache
Combine the cacao pulp with the glucose and glycerine in a saucepan and bring to the boil. Cool quickly to 40°C.

Mix the white chocolate with the cocoa butter and sunflower oil and melt. Whisk the pulp mixture with the chocolate, cocoa butter and oil mixture to an emulsion and temper at 28°C.

For the red paint
For the yellow paint
For each colour of paint, melt the cocoa butter with the chocolate couverture in a saucepan at 40°C. Add the food colouring and temper between 29° and 31°C.

Assembly and finishing
Temper the red paint and apply it inside the cavities of a cacao bean-shaped polycarbonate mould with a paint sprayer. Leave to set and then apply a layer of yellow paint over the red.

Apply a layer of tempered XMC chocolate and leave to harden.

Fill the mould with the tempered cacao pulp ganache at 28°C and leave to set for 24 hours to dry the surface.

Close each cavity of the filled mould with a thin layer of tempered XMC chocolate.

Serves 50
Type: moulded
chocolate bonbons

Chai tea ganache
165 g water
105 g glucose powder
30 g glycerine
18 g black tea
3 g cardamom
9 g fresh ginger
6 g fresh fennel
6 g liquorice root
390 g 60% cacao milk
  chocolate
90 g sunflower oil
45 g cocoa butter

CHAI TEA CHOCOLATE BONBON

For the chai tea ganache

Mix the water with the glucose and glycerine in a saucepan and heat to 60°C.

Add the tea and spices, cover with cling film and leave to infuse in the refrigerator for 20 minutes.

Strain the liquid and incorporate into the melted chocolate. Whisk with the sunflower oil and cocoa butter to a smooth emulsion.

For a more intensely flavoured ganache, the oil can be infused with the same spices as those used for the water.

For the XMC chocolate

See the process on page 256 to make 2.5 kg.

Assembly and finishing

Temper 500 g of ganache and spread over a tray lined with acetate using 8-mm thick acrylic confectionery bars for a smooth and even surface. Use a 3-cm-diameter ring mould to cut out discs and enrobe in XMC dark chocolate.

Decorate with an *R*.

Serves 30

Corn nut chocolate

Coconut, lime and chilli jelly
15 g lime juice
40 g coconut milk
1.5 g pectin
30 g sugar
40 g muscovado sugar
1 g chipotle chilli
2 g 1:1 citric acid and
  water solution

Mezcal ganache
40 g water
50 g glucose powder
10 g glycerine
30 g 45° mezcal
110 g chocolate[2] (see
  page 252)
65 g sunflower oil

Green paint
25 g white chocolate
25 g cocoa butter
3 g fat-soluble green
  food colouring

Red paint
25 g white chocolate
25 g cocoa butter
3 g fat-soluble red food
  colouring

White paint
25 g white chocolate
25 g cocoa butter
3 g fat-soluble white
  food colouring

Assembly and finishing
Tempered corn nut
  chocolate

MEXICO BONBON

For the corn nut chocolate
See the process on page 320.

For the coconut, lime and chilli jelly
Combine the lime juice and coconut milk in a saucepan and bring to the boil. Add the pectin mixed with the sugar and bring back to the boil. Add the muscovado sugar and chipotle chilli, and continue to cook until the sugar content reaches a refractometer reading of 75° Brix. Remove from the heat, add the citric acid solution and cool.

When the jelly has set, blend to a smooth paste in a Thermomix. Fill a piping bag and set aside.

For the mezcal ganache
Combine the water, glucose and glycerine in a saucepan and bring to the boil. Cool to 40°C and add the mezcal. Incorporate the melted chocolate and whisk in the sunflower oil to a smooth emulsion.

For the green paint
For the red paint
For the white paint
For each colour of paint, melt the couverture with the cocoa butter and mix. Add the food colouring when the temperature of the mixture reaches 40°C. Strain and fill a paint sprayer.

Assembly and finishing
Paint the cavities of a polycarbonate mould with the three paints tempered at 29°C to resemble the Mexican flag. For this, use a paint sprayer to apply the three paints in the same operation. Leave to set for a few hours.

Temper the corn nut chocolate and line the mould. Leave to harden overnight.

Fill the cavities with a little of the coconut, lime and chilli jelly and finish filling with the mezcal ganache tempered at 29°C. Leave to set for 24 hours and close each cavity of the filled moulds with a thin layer of tempered corn nut chocolate.

Milk chocolate
250 g Awajún cacao
  beans
150 g raw cane sugar
100 g non-fat
  powdered milk
100 g cocoa butter

Beetroot crunch
250 g beetroot juice
65 g raw cane sugar
65 g isomalt
4 g agar-agar

BEETROOT CRISP AND MILK CHOCOLATE BAR

For the milk chocolate

Select the beans, roast for 30 minutes at 120ºC, changing the position of the trays every 10 minutes. Leave to cool and then crack and winnow. Refine with the sugar and powdered milk. Incorporate the cocoa butter, add the dry ingredients and refine.

For the beetroot crunch

Juice the beetroots and mix the juice with the sugar, isomalt and agar-agar in a pan. Bring to the boil and cool quickly to make a jelly. Blend to a paste, spread over a silicone mat and dry out at 40ºC for 48 hours. Crush into granules.

Assembly and finishing

Melt the chocolate at 45ºC, add the beetroot crisp granules and temper together. Fill a 5-g bar mould and leave to harden. Unmould and serve.

CHOCOLATE AERO

Serves 20

500 g 70% cacao
chocolate[2] (see page
252)
75 g cocoa butter

Melt the chocolate and cocoa butter at 45ºC and fill a siphon with the mixture. Insert three gas cartridges, shaking well after each insertion.

Put the siphon into a temperature-controlled water bath at 29ºC and leave for 20 minutes, shaking after 10 minutes. Raise the water temperature to 32ºC and leave for 20 minutes, shaking after 10 minutes.

Pipe the mixture into a plastic container and place inside a chamber vacuum sealer at an ambient temperature of 15ºC. Turn on the vacuum, causing the foam to rise, and keep the vacuum on for 15 minutes so the chocolate can harden. If the machine is unable to stay on for this length of time, turn it off. The vacuum will be maintained within the chamber. Then turn it back on after 15 minutes.

PEA CHOCOLATE

Makes 1.5 kg chocolate

2 kg peas
250 g raw cane sugar
275 g isomalt
2 g ascorbic acid
500 g puffed rice
700 g cocoa butter

Blend the peas with the sugar and isomalt to a smooth paste.

Spread the paste thinly over a sheet of silicone paper and dry out overnight at 50°C to make a pea crunch.

Crush the pea crunch in a bowl with the ascorbic acid and puffed rice. Refine the mixture in a chocolate refiner, adding the melted cocoa butter at 40°C.

Finish by tempering as for a normal chocolate. Pour into moulds or reserve for other uses.

CORN NUT CHOCOLATE

Makes 1.5 kg chocolate

800 g corn nuts
400 g raw cane sugar
400 g cocoa butter

Grind the corn nuts with the sugar to a uniform powder.

Refine the mixture in a chocolate refiner, adding the melted cocoa butter at 40°C.

Finish by tempering as for a normal chocolate. Pour into moulds or reserve for other uses.

BEETROOT CHOCOLATE

Makes 1.5 kg chocolate

2 kg beetroot
100 g raw cane sugar
275 g isomalt
2 g ascorbic acid
500 g puffed rice
700 g cocoa butter

Clean the beetroots and pass through a juicer. Combine the beetroot juice and pulp with the sugar and isomalt in a Thermomix and mix to a smooth paste.

Spread the paste thinly over a sheet of silicone paper and dry out overnight at 50°C to make beetroot crunch.

Crush the beetroot crunch in a bowl with the ascorbic acid and puffed rice. Refine the mixture in a chocolate refiner, adding the melted cocoa butter at 40°C.

Finish by tempering as for a normal chocolate. Pour into moulds or reserve for other uses.

CARROT CHOCOLATE

Clean the carrots and pass through a juicer. Combine the carrot juice and pulp with the sugar and isomalt in a Thermomix and mix to a smooth paste.

Spread the paste thinly over a sheet of silicone paper and dry out overnight at 50°C to make carrot crunch.

Crush the carrot crunch in a bowl with the ascorbic acid and puffed rice. Refine the mixture in a chocolate refiner, adding the melted cocoa butter at 40°C.

Finish by tempering as for a normal chocolate. Pour into moulds or reserve for other uses.

*Makes 1.5 kg
chocolate*

2 kg carrots
100 g raw cane sugar
275 g isomalt
2 g ascorbic acid
500 g puffed rice
700 g cocoa butter

Rocher centres
170 g 50% hazelnut
  praline
130 g 100% hazelnut
  butter
1.5 g salt
100 g milk chocolate
40 g cocoa butter

50 g feuilletine flakes
50 g corn nut powder

Rocher coating
170 g white chocolate
35 g cocoa butter
20 g silver food
  colouring powder

CORN NUT ROCHERS

For the rocher centres

Combine the praline, hazelnut butter and salt in a container and blend with a hand-held blender to a very smooth paste.

Transfer to a large bowl, add the milk chocolate and cocoa butter and melt in a bain-marie. Incorporate the feuilletine flakes and ground corn nuts and mix until smooth.

Temper at 25°C and fill moulds. Leave to set and unmould.

For the rocher coating

Melt the chocolate in a bowl in a bain-marie. Temper at 27°C and dip the rocher centres twice.

Melt the cocoa butter in a saucepan. Temper at 31°C, add the silver colouring and mix until smooth. Dip the bonbons twice before serving.

ROCAMBOLESC, FROZEN CHOCOLATE

THE ROCAMBOLESC CHOCOLATE ICE CREAM is no longer the same, despite its appearance. Like the other ice creams that are made and served to be enjoyed here in this establishment, this is the frozen version of one of the desserts created by Jordi Roca for El Celler de Can Roca. It is assembled over a chocolate ice-cream base and is completed with chocolate couverture, cacao nibs, a chocolate biscuit and a few pieces of Peta Zeta popping candy scattered over the dish. Everything is like it was a few months ago, but it does not taste the same. The recipe for the couverture that is used as the base for the ice cream is new, and this detail transforms the combination. The current product comes from the Casa Cacao chocolate factory and bears little resemblance to what was previously used. The source of the cacao beans is divided between Peru and Ecuador, and the formulation seeks to emphasise the fruity character and aromatic notes of these two cacaos. The amount of sugar has been reduced and the vanilla aroma added to conventional chocolate has disappeared. The new cacaos that are arriving after the journey are giving life to different chocolate, taking the flavour of the combinations in a whole new direction. The current chocolates are built up over more prominent acidic notes and offer greater aromatic complexity, but the defining feature is naturalness. They are less sweet and more authentic. The new Rocambolesc chocolate ice cream reflects the source of the cacao that gives life to it.

Alejandra Rivas, jointly responsible for the direction taken by the ice-cream parlour together with Jordi Roca, confirms that other novelties will be coming. The journey they shared through the cacao plantations of Colombia and those made by Jordi to Peru and Ecuador have altered the perspective taken by the work at the Rocambolesc factory, and major changes are in the pipeline.

The idea is clear. Jordi had already given me an outline, but Alejandra is much more direct. 'Casa Cacao, Rocambolesc and El Celler are siblings, and after this journey we coincided with the same idea: selecting different types of cacaos; and when they run out, we'll move on to others and offer different things with each one and at each moment. What we want is to make chocolate ice cream using new single-origin cacaos, so as to be able to say, "the chocolate this week is from Peru", or "the chocolate ice cream this week is from Colombia", so that people can sample them and compare. It provides an opportunity to speak about the different

ROCAMBOLESC AIMS TO OFFER A RANGE OF DIFFERENT SINGLE-ORIGIN CHOCOLATE ICE CREAMS AND TO DEMONSTRATE THE DIFFERENCES.

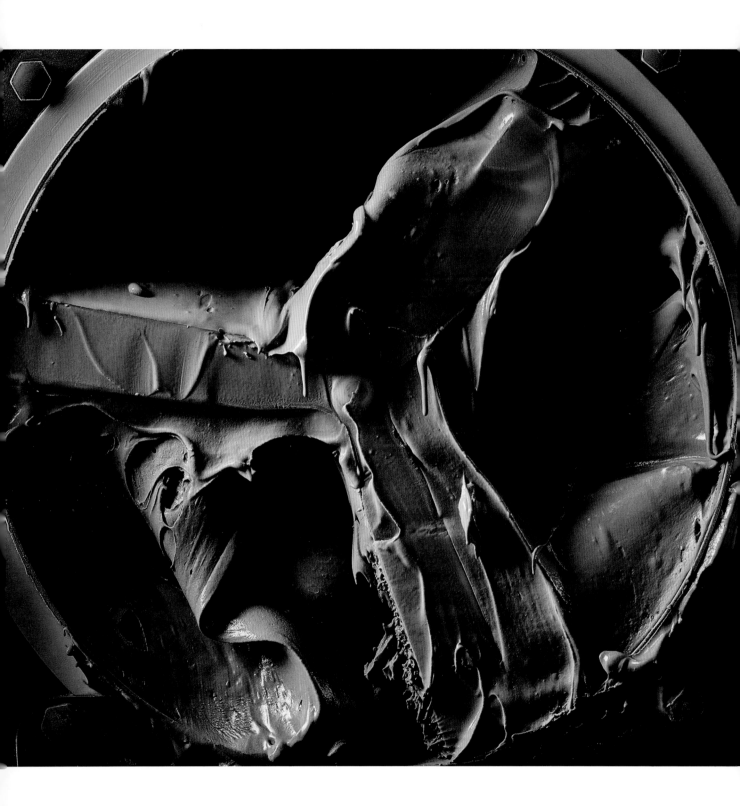

origins and to tell a little more of the story of each cacao. It's difficult to say "I like this one" or "I like the other one", when you haven't been able to compare them. I'd like to end up having a range of different single-origin chocolate ice creams, to give customers the chance to try them and decide which region they like more and why. By comparing them, they'll notice the level of acidity, if it's fruitier, if it's more or less aromatic, if it tastes of honey, if it's more intense...'

The kitchen at El Celler de Can Roca is working on new desserts with the cacaos discovered on the journeys to the Amazon region, and some of them will end up as adaptations and be made available to Rocambolesc customers. Ice creams to eat on the go are one of the three lines of work at the ice-cream parlour. Unlike the ice creams that are meant to be taken home, these are complete offerings that are assembled on the spot as frozen representations of El Celler de Can Roca creations. Làctic is one of them. At its base is a ricotta-style cheese made from Ripollesa breed ewe's milk, and finishing flourishes include guava jam, dulce de leche milk caramel and a candy floss cloud. The coconut sorbet is topped with strawberry pieces, honey caviar and a violet marshmallow. The uplifting Madagascar (Bourbon) vanilla ice cream – ten pods per litre are used to achieve its distinct aromatic intensity – has also seen changes since the journey to the sources of cacao. It now includes a chocolate sponge and continues to feature the caramel crunch and cocoa sauce from the previous version.

Alejandra's journey to the Colombian cacao plantations of the Sierra Nevada de Santa Marta mountains has led to a few changes being made in this establishment. 'I am as excited as I was when I started learning to cook and everything was new to me. I've discovered chocolate from another perspective. We'd receive the beans, work them and make chocolate, but having them sent to the restaurant and going to where they're grown are two completely different things. There I experienced it in the tree; I've put a face to each variety of cacao; I've seen how it's fermented; and I've felt a very special vibe. I've also become aware of the efforts made by the growers before it reaches me. It was very important for me to see all that, and to meet the people I have in order to have a real, very different perspective from the one I had before the trip.'

Chocolate has a very special place in life at Rocambolesc. While it is not the star, it has been given a leading role, just as it has in the pastry kitchen at El Celler de Can Roca. It is a product that features repeatedly in many of their desserts, which end up inspiring Rocambolesc ice creams, although they never share the same story. The ice-cream parlour has none of the spontaneity that defines the relationship with customers at the restaurant, allowing combinations of textures

EACH CACAO VARIETY AND EACH NEW SINGLE-ORIGIN CACAO OFFER DIFFERENT PERSPECTIVES AND OPEN DOORS NEVER BEFORE KNOWN TO DAMIAN OR JORDI.

and temperatures that are impossible to replicate on the counter at Rocambolesc, a business that offers its ice creams at five different locations in four cities: Girona, Barcelona, Madrid and Alicante. The creative work must take into consideration logistics and the restricted space and means, but it is there, in all the offerings at the ice-cream parlour. The take-away ice-cream menu changes with the seasons, but there are always between 15 and 18 varieties. The flavours are by no means run of the mill, or in the least ambiguous, including Parmesan, junket, baked apple, asparagus and truffle, milk chocolate and flowering tea, roses, and toast with olive oil. The world of ice cream is overlapping with savoury cuisine to offer everything from a traditional breakfast to a restaurant starter. By reviewing the evolution of El Celler de Can Roca's cuisine and some of the trials conducted for Rocambolesc, I find names of creations that follow very similar paths, such as ice creams with the flavours of mustard, roast chicken, and grilled mushrooms.

Some did not live up to expectations. Asparagus and truffle did not work in a soft version to be eaten there and then. It was tried out in the first Madrid shop and was unsuccessful, but it found a home among the take-away ice creams. 'The key is that it tastes good,' Alejandra tells me. 'I don't think there are any limits, but that's the basic rule; it has to taste good. We'll keep on trying a bit of everything, but before it makes it to the ice-cream parlour, it has to taste good and people have to like it.' Rocambolesc opened in April 2012, with the first shop in Girona, little more than 150 metres away from the building that will house Casa Cacao, in the centre of town. The business is structured with two principles: Alejandra Rivas's management and Jordi Roca's creative input.

Dedo de Colón ('Columbus' finger') is one of the two chocolate ice lollies on the current menu at Rocambolesc. The base is a sorbet made from chocolate, olive oil and salt, made into the shape of a finger (a replica of the pointing finger on the Columbus Monument in Barcelona) on a traditional ice lolly stick. Polo Feliz ('Happy Ice Lolly'), on the other hand, is shaped like a birthday cake and is made from milk chocolate and chai tea ice cream adorned with cacao nibs and banana bambolescas, and topped with a candle. It is a birthday ice cream. They are two of the ten ice lollies on the menu that exemplify the Rocambolesc. They are not exactly conventional, either for their flavour or their whimsical shapes. Others include the gold hand from *Game of Thrones* in La Mano ('The Hand'); the head of Darth Vader from *Star Wars* in Helado Oscuro ('Dark Ice Cream', a play on the Spanish words *el lado oscuro*, 'the dark side'); Jordi Roca's nose in Rocanas (Catalan for 'Roca nose'); and the body of model Andrés Velencoso in Velencoco (coco being the Spanish word for coconut, one of its ingredients). I have seen how they are made at their artisan production facility and it amazes me how they can make enough to supply five shops. There is only one mould, which is filled one at a time. Each piece is then finished off individually.

Rocambolesc is a constant hive of activity. Dynamism is the hallmark of their ice-cream offering. There are six varieties of ice creams to be enjoyed on the spot, because this is the number of dispensers available to serve them, but this number is multiplied throughout the year. The story is the same with the take-away ice creams. There used to be more. At first, it was believed that customers would like this. 'We'd change our flavours every 10 or 15 days, and people would get upset because they couldn't find the ice cream they liked. So we left three or four basic flavours and changed the rest. Now people ask us about the new flavours for each season or for Christmas. They still go for the basics, but they watch out for the new ice creams.' There are always novelties in the pipeline when Jordi Roca and Alejandra Rivas are around. Madness may be Jordi Roca's thing, but when it comes to creativity, both have their weapons of choice, and Alejandra's are nothing to sniff at. The experience of her year at the helm of the pastry kitchen at El Celler de Can Roca and a whole year spent in charge of the one at Enrique Olivera's Pujol restaurant in Mexico City drives her work, allows her to keep up creative debate and returns her to the kitchen, which continues to be her space. When she worked with Jordi Roca at El Celler de Can Roca, she learnt the basics. 'With him it's always "why not?". He questions everything the others reject, and his creative work often begins from his unwillingness to conform.' There is freedom to create at Rocambolesc, and the path to creation tends to be unpredictable.

What about after the trip to Colombia? 'The trip left me with the desire to know more, because chocolate is increasingly gaining in value, but we still have so much to learn and a long way to go. For now, I'll stick with Mayumi Ogata's words, that there is no bad cacao, only that we don't know how to treat it, because we can transform it with suitable fermentation, drying or roasting. Depending on how we do it, we'll manage to discover completely different nuances.'

Makes 5 litres

Flower tea infusion
1.5 kg water
150 g flower tea

Milk chocolate
395 g cocoa butter
555 g raw cane sugar
370 g powdered milk
1 kg Arhuaco cacao
  nibs

Flower tea ice cream
85 g water
1.420 g whole milk
1.5 kg strained flower
  tea infusion (1.5 kg
  water and 150 g
  flower tea)
260 g skimmed milk
  powder
555 g dextrose
150 g sugar
30 g neutral ice-cream
  stabiliser
150 g inverted sugar
850 g milk chocolate
  couverture (previously
  prepared)

MILK CHOCOLATE AND FLOWER TEA ICE CREAM

For the flower tea infusion
Steep the flower tea in the cold water for 12 hours and strain.

For the milk chocolate
Melt the cocoa butter in a saucepan at 40ºC. Add the sugar and powdered milk and mix.

Pass the nibs through the pre-refiner once. Mix all the ingredients together and pass through the pre-refiner twice in a row.

Pass the mixture through the refiner twice. Finish by conching for 24 hours to obtain the milk chocolate base.

For the flower tea ice cream
Mix the water, whole milk, tea infusion, powdered milk and dextrose in the pasteuriser. When the pasteurisation temperature reaches 40ºC, add the sugar, stabiliser and inverted sugar. When the temperature reaches 70ºC, add the Arhuaco milk chocolate couverture. When the temperature of the mixture reaches 85ºC, remove from the pasteuriser and cool to 4ºC. Then age the mixture for 12 hours in the refrigerator.

Churn and store in the freezer at -18ºC.

Makes 5 litres

980 g water
1.705 kg whole milk
195 g fresh cream
900 g dextrose
200 g cocoa powder
150 g sugar
35 g neutral ice-cream
  stabiliser
185 g skimmed milk
  powder
150 g inverted sugar
500 g Madagascar
  dark chocolate
  couverture

MADAGASCAR CHOCOLATE ICE CREAM

Combine the water, whole milk, cream, dextrose and cocoa powder in the pasteuriser. When the pasteurisation temperature reaches 40°C, add the sugar, stabiliser, powdered milk and inverted sugar. When it reaches 70°C, add the Madagascar dark chocolate couverture. When the temperature of the mixture reaches 85°C, remove from the pasteuriser and cool to 4°C. Then age the mixture for 12 hours in the refrigerator.

Churn and store in the freezer at -18°C.

PIURA CHOCOLATE ICE CREAM

Makes 5 litres

85 g water
2.920 kg whole milk
260 g skimmed milk
  powder
555 g dextrose
150 g sugar
30 g neutral ice-cream
  stabiliser
150 g inverted sugar
850 g Piura dark
  chocolate couverture

Mix the water, whole milk, powdered milk and dextrose in the pasteuriser. When the pasteurisation temperature reaches 40ºC, add the sugar, stabiliser and inverted sugar. When it reaches 70ºC, add the Piura dark chocolate couverture. When the temperature of the mixture reaches 85ºC, remove from the pasteuriser and cool to 4ºC. Then age the mixture for 12 hours in the refrigerator.

Churn and store in the freezer at -18ºC.

COLUMBUS' FINGER

Make a ganache with the dark chocolate couverture and water. Add the olive oil, syrup, salt and stabiliser to the cold ganache and mix until smooth. Blend, strain and set aside in the refrigerator until use. Then fill 60-g moulds in the desired shape.

For the simple sugar syrup
Combine the water and sugar in a pan, mix well and bring to the boil. Remove from the heat and leave to cool. Set aside in the refrigerator.

Makes 1 litre or 16 servings

120 g dark chocolate couverture
270 g water
300 g extra virgin olive oil
180 g simple sugar syrup
1 g salt
4 g ice-cream stabiliser
Simple sugar syrup
150 g water
150 g sugar

290 g fresh cream
4 g chai tea
20 g dextrose
10 g sugar
2.4 g neutral ice-cream
  stabiliser
80 g milk chocolate
  couverture

Milk chocolate coating
160 g milk chocolate
  couverture
20 g cocoa butter
20 g sunflower oil

Assembly and finishing
80 g banana *bámbolas*
50 g cacao nibs
10 white candles

HAPPY ICE LOLLY

For the milk chocolate and chai tea ice lolly
Mix the cream with the chai tea in a saucepan and heat to 40°C. Add the dextrose, sugar and stabiliser, and continue to heat to 85°C. Finally, blend in the chocolate couverture. Strain, cool to 4°C and age for 12 hours in the refrigerator.

Transfer the mixture to a mixer and beat to the consistency of whipped cream. Pipe into the cake ice-lolly mould and freeze in a blast chiller for 2 hours at -30°C. Unmould and set aside in the freezer until ready to dip in chocolate.

For the milk chocolate coating
Melt the milk chocolate couverture with the cocoa butter at 30°C. Mix in the sunflower oil.

Assembly and finishing
Dip the ice lollies in the chocolate. Quickly decorate with banana *bámbolas* and cacao nibs and insert a candle into the tip of each ice lolly.

THE END OF THE JOURNEY

I return to Girona two months after completing the last journey with Jordi through the cacao plantations of Colombia and Ecuador. The last takes for the documentary and the second last interviews with Jordi and Alejandra, who came with us to Colombia, are still pending. There have been no tables available in the dining room at El Celler de Can Roca for months, but the Rocas generously offer me a space at the pass, the counter from where they can keep an eye on the plates being sent out to the tables. The main kitchen is to my right and the pastry kitchen lies ahead of me, and in between is the constant coming and going of trays and plates from and to the dining room. A fascinating spectacle. From time to time, Joan brings me samples of some of the ideas he is working on, still halfway to becoming a dish, or not, such as baby eels cooked in the same bowl in which they are served or spit-roasted squab on which they are starting to work. They are accompanied by peas with baby octopus, the surprise cannelloni from Can Roca to make up for missing out on the Rocas' family meal at their parents' eatery (having lunch on a Friday at El Celler de Can Roca typically implies missing out on Montse's cannelloni), Parmesan couscous, artichoke and truffle, a dish of Galician Rubia beef marrow foam with sea urchin, followed by another foam in the sequence – this time T-bone steak with oyster, rhubarb and black pepper – and pickled rabbit with langoustines and snails. Everything runs according to plan in a kitchen that has turned brilliance and surprise into routine, and yet continues to leave room for the unexpected.

And at the end, after the woodcock with gentian, liquorice and eucalyptus, it is time for chocolate. It appears before the desserts, in a mole accompanying the hare, and in the cacao used to flavour it. It is also the exclusive feature of two of the three desserts that round off the tasting menu. The first is a version of Chocolate Anarkia topped with a coin, also made of chocolate and wrapped in gold foil. I count 40 different ways of doing chocolate arranged over the plate and I have a feeling of déjà vu when I see the coin, which reminds me a little of the treasure troves in pirate films, and a lot of the chocolates that I would be given from time to time in my childhood, although I have no clear recollection of it ever arriving on a plate. At times, the memories of what you eat are mixed with things you see on social media or in certain publications, and become blurred. Have I eaten it or

have I only seen it? Jordi explains it to me after lunch. It is an exact replica of a gold medal exhibited in a museum in Colombia which they reproduced for the dinners they served in Bogotá, during the first BBVA Roca Tour. Some of those coins must have made it to Lima because – now it comes to me – I remember it from the demonstration that Jordi shared with the inmates from the Virgen de Fátima women's prison in Chorrillos on the tour's following stop. At the same time, it is a nod to the previous journey we made with Casa Cacao, a representation of that journey with the cacao picked up on our latest one.

The second dessert is called Grated Coconut, and it is one of those jokes that so intrigue Jordi. Fun, startling and delicious, it is a way of interrupting the sequence and cleansing mouth and mind a little after all the intensity of the chocolate. I see it as a way of breaking with the discourse of the menu, which is that of flavours, and hitting the reset button for customers and bringing them back to their world. After 21 dishes followed by an entire chocolate menu, coconut ice cream helps to keep you functioning. What comes next will make it all worth your while. It is called Marabillao, recalling *Cacao Maravillao*, a cocoa product made famous in a song by the Mama Chicho dancers on a Spanish television show that we never got to see in the shops. One joke inside another, although it is no longer a bit of mischief or a joke turned into a flavour, like the coconut ice cream, but something much more substantial that gives a nod to and references our journey through the cacao plantations of the Amazon region, while showing some of the keys that allow the path chocolate is starting to take in Jordi Roca's new perspective to be understood.

Marabillao is presented in a way somewhat resembling a chessboard, with 21 small cubes arranged in three rows that go to form a sequence of colours and flavours. They have been graded for aesthetic reasons, and together with them are some creations made out of chocolate. An ice cream, a sponge, a caramel... What really matters is on this chessboard that starts from the left, with the softer and more transparent colours, and finishes on the opposite side, with visual references that take you straight to the chocolate.

Jordi has given flavour to the synthesis of what we have seen and shared on the journey that ends with this book, because, above all, Marabillao is an account of an experience. I close my eyes as I eat and I find myself surrounded by the acrid, harsh and pungent aroma of the fermenting boxes in Iván Murrugarra's processing facility in Piura, and those of the indigenous community of Uut, on the banks of the River Marañón. I picture myself elbow-deep in the fermenting beans of the Arhuaco community of Catanzama, in the Sierra Nevada de Santa Marta mountains, and immersed in the aromas and sensations created by the immense processing facility in Vinces, surrounded by Ecuadorian cacao plantations. The first jelly cubes provide acidic flavours and notes we came to discover in the fermenting boxes, or references drawn from them. The presence of the acetic acid that is turned into vinegar, the yeasts that bring on the fermentation process, the aromatic notes of such fragrant fruit as lychees and other tropical fruits, the gentle sweetness of the dried pods... After them comes the result of everything we have looked for, seen and done: cacao, or cacaos to be precise, representing the beans that arrived in Girona in Jordi's suitcase at the end of each trip. Six of the cubes capture the flavour of those cacaos and are a starting point for the diversity Casa Cacao pursues. It is cacao with just the right amount of fermenting, drying and transformation to showcase its primal nature. Chocolate is relegated to one side of the plate. There is ice cream, cake, jelly and caramel that embody the personality of the chocolates made at Casa Cacao from the beans brought back from that journey. Each mouthful is like finding a light in the midst of a labyrinth, or the complete opposite.

Many readings can be made of this dish, but the main one is emotional. I am led to relive some of the most emotional experiences of our journeys to the land of cacao, turning them into a personal and private landscape, a reference written in symbols that only we can decipher. Or not. I sit and think for a while, and when I manage to subdue my emotions, I discover the key to this dish, which is revealed as a sequence telling the story of cacao, from the moment the pod is split open to remove the beans to when they are turned into chocolate, and when the chocolate changes to take on the character of the creations to which it gives rise. Jordi has summarised three exhausting journeys in a sequence of 21 cubes of jelly and half a dozen creations.

I leave El Celler de Can Roca thinking about Marabillao. I suspect it is the end of a cycle that began with Anarkia, and as always happens when one cycle comes to a close, it is the sign that another one is beginning. It is my last morning in Girona and I speak to Jordi about the dish.

'Marabillao is no longer Anarkia,' he tells me. 'Because Anarkia is the meaninglessness we've spoken about so often, where the fun is in the madness. Here, I set the rules. There are two things here. They're what I've perceived on an aromatic level as regards the processing of the cacao, how it's fermented, the aromas given off by the fermenting boxes, and what we've made with the cacao beans that have come to me from Peru and Colombia. There are two elements on the plate. There is no freedom to choose products, which are evidently there, but it's designed to be understood that way, and therefore there's an argument that makes sense. It's the dessert that somehow represents that journey.'

Is it the beginning of order? The transition from Anarkia towards a more regulated and ordered world? 'Let's just say that Anarkia was a collection of techniques and possibilities I had in my head. Now I ask myself, what is chocolate? For me, in aromatic terms, it's this, this process, which is no longer just cacao as we used to see it. It's the starting point for a series of dishes that have to come from this chocolate which is more than old-school cocoa – cocoa, butter, cocoa and sugar to make it flow better – now it's been turned into a completely new vision.'

He is right. Chocolate is changing, the way Marabillao has changed, turned a few months later into 'From Cacao to Chocolate', the recipe which marks the end of this journey, for now. We will most certainly see more before you come to hold

this book in your hands. The first cacaos picked on the different trips are only just beginning to arrive. At the end of June, a 200-kilogram sack of Awajún cacao beans arrived at Casa Cacao. It is only a sample prior to the starting up of the processing facility, which will not be in operation until some time after the main harvest, but it is paving the way. At home, next to my table, there is a box with two sacks made of white cloth. Each contains three kilograms of cacao beans. Óscar Velásquez has sent them to me from Jaén. One is a Criollo cacao, from the area for which he has high expectations, and the other is from a few white cacao trees that have flourished on a farm with which he works. They will soon be at Casa Cacao. White cacao from Piura is already a regular tenant in the chocolate factory storeroom, as are the cacaos that have been arriving from Colombia. Both have their place in the chocolate kitchen together with the Venezuelan beans from Chuao, the Mexican beans from Tabasco, and the Ecuadorian and Bolivian beans that are joined by others from India and Madagascar. The chocolate kitchen at Casa Cacao is beginning to seem like a melting pot of cacao, and the party has not even started yet. A few months are still required before the opening of the new factory, the new chocolate kitchen, and the beginning of real life at Casa Cacao, at its permanent home in the centre of Girona.

This marks the end of our journey and opens the door to a new part of the story that is still to come. Both shared a common starting point, with the creation of Anarkia, and have endured one of the most important moments experienced by sweet cuisine at El Celler de Can Roca, and with a shared ending in Marabillao. After this, a new chapter will commence in the story that is beginning to weave itself around the new Casa Cacao and all the lives and hopes that its chocolates will reflect.

Cacao pulp gel
400 g cocoa pulp
2 g iota carrageenan

Lychee gel
400 g lychee purée
2 g iota carrageenan

Almond milk
200 g peeled almonds
1 kg water

Almond milk gel
400 g almond milk
    (previously prepared)
2 g iota carrageenan

Raisin and prune gel
100 g raisins
100 g prunes
100 g water
3 g iota carrageenan

Sherry jelly
100 g Pedro Ximénez
    sherry
100 g water
2 g iota carrageenan

FROM CACAO TO CHOCOLATE

For the cacao pulp gel

Mix the iota carrageenan with the cacao pulp in a saucepan and bring to the boil. Remove from the heat, strain and leave to set in the refrigerator. Set aside.

For the lychee gel

Mix the iota carrageenan with the purée in a saucepan and bring to the boil. Remove from the heat, strain and leave to set in the refrigerator. Set aside.

Almond milk

Mix the raw peeled almonds with the water and blend. Strain through a fine-mesh sieve. Set aside.

For the almond milk gel

Mix the iota carrageenan with the almond milk in a saucepan and bring to the boil. Remove from the heat, strain and leave to set in the refrigerator. Set aside.

For the raisin and prune gel

Use a hand-held blender to purée the raisins and prunes with the water in a bowl. Transfer to a saucepan, add the iota carrageenan and bring to the boil. Remove from the heat, strain and leave to set in the refrigerator. Set aside.

For the sherry jelly

Mix the sherry and water in a saucepan, add the iota carrageenan and bring to the boil. Remove from the heat, strain and leave to set in the refrigerator. Set aside.

For the brownie

Beat the eggs with the sugar while melting the chocolate with the oil. Sift the flour.

Fold the chocolate mixture and flour into the beaten eggs in the bowl used to beat them, alternating a little at a time so as to deflate as little as possible. Pour into a 20-cm x 8-cm cake tin and bake at 180°C for 15 minutes.

For the Piura chocolate cream

Mix the sugar and dextrose with the stabiliser in a bowl. Heat the water with the sugar and stabiliser mixture in a saucepan. Heat while stirring constantly until the temperature reaches 90°C. Remove from the heat and add the chocolate. Whisk with a hand-held blender and set aside in the refrigerator.

For the chocolate caramel

Mix the sugar, water and glucose in a saucepan over a low heat. Add the isomalt and wait until it melts, then raise the heat to 160°C. Allow the temperature to fall to 140°C and add the chopped chocolate couverture. Mix and spread out into very thin sheets. Set aside in an airtight container with silica gel.

Brownie
320 g eggs
400 g sugar
150 g sunflower oil
230 g Piura chocolate[2]
  (see page 252)
160 g flour

Piura chocolate cream
100 g sugar
50 g dextrose
50 g glycerine
7.5 g ice-cream
  stabiliser
1 kg water
400 g Piura chocolate

Chocolate caramel
180 g sugar
40 g water
100 g glucose
100 g isomalt
80 g Piura chocolate

Chocolate shavings

*Assembly and
finishing*
Lychees
Almonds
Dried apricots
Raisins
Roasted cacao beans

For the chocolate shavings

The aim is to use the shavings that are formed during the refining process as they come out of the grinder. If this is not possible, the chocolate can be tempered, spread over a marble slab and scratched with a spatula to make shavings.

Assembly and finishing

Pipe a line of each type of gel over a guitar sheet, starting with the cacao pulp gel and continuing with the lychee gel, almond milk gel and raisin and prune gel.

Freeze until just before serving. Cut an 8-cm-long strip of each gel and arrange together in the middle of a plate. Arrange a piece of fresh lychee, some grated almond, a cube of sherry jelly, a piece of dried apricot and a raisin in this order from bottom to top over the strips.

Place three brownie cubes at one end, and arrange the chocolate cream, roasted cacao bean and chocolate shavings over them.

ACKNOWLEDGEMENTS

My thanks to you, Ignacio, naturally! To Óscar Moya at BBVA for having faith in fine food and being the driving force behind this book. To Anna Payet, who has been and continues to be a major partner on the Casa Cacao project. To Héloïse Vilaseca and Gemma Barceló from La Masía, for their help in organising the recipes. To Damià, Abraham, Marta, Judith, Rosetta, Angélica, Ilhia, Tai and Luca, my pastry team, who have helped me to make them. To my brothers Josep and Joan for their unconditional support; to my beloved Alejandra, who plays a leading role in one part of the book and in so many other things. To the team at Planeta for their impeccable work on this book, and in particular to you the readers.

Jordi Roca

Thanks go to Jordi, of course, and to Óscar Moya for his commitment, trust and collaboration. To the team at La Masía for their patience and perseverance, ability to keep me sane, and tenacity to find ways out of the maze we often created for them. To Iván Murrugarra, Max Druschke, Mayumi Ogata and José Merlo, for their incredible generosity and for showing us the secrets of Amazonian cacao, one grower at a time, and often one tree at a time. To Astrid Gutsche, who led me to find the reality experienced by cacao growers. To Christophe Henry and Antonio Tolsada, for opening the doors to knowledge about chocolate, and to Damian Allsop, for showing me the new face of this exciting story that we have turned into a book.

Ignacio Medina

To BBVA for the great faith they have shown in fine foods on both sides of the ocean and their ability to understand everything that lies behind a product, a dish and a restaurant.

INDEX OF RECIPES IN ALPHABETICAL ORDER

BIBLIOGRAPHY

Arosamena, Guillermo: *El fruto de los dioses*. Editorial Graba, 1991.

Bau, Frédéric: *Chocolate fusión*. Montagud Editores, 2006

Bau, Frédéric *et al.*: *Encyclopedia of Chocolate*. Flammarion, 2018.

Beailleux, Nathalie *et al.*: *The Book of Chocolate*. Flammarion, 2004.

Bernachon, Maurice, and Bernachon, Jean Jacques: *A Passion for Chocolate*. William Morrow & Co, 1989

Bertrand, Philippe, and Marand, Philippe: *Chocolat, l'envers du décor : Chocolate, behind the scenes*. Les éditions de l'if, 2000.

Brack Egg, Antonio: *Diccionario enciclopédico de plantas útiles del Perú*. Centro de Estudios Regionales Andinos Bartolomé de las Casas, 1999.

Coady, Chantal: *Chocolate. Manual para sibaritas*. Evergreen, 1998.

Coe, Sophie and Michael: *The True History of Chocolate*. Thames and Hudson, 2007.

Doutre-Russel, Chloé: *The Chocolate Connoisseur*. Tarcher, 2005.

Duytsche, Yann: *Sweet Diversions*. Montagud Editores, 2007

Flores Paytan, Salvador: *Cultivo de frutales nativos amazónicos*. Tratado de Cooperación Amazónica, 1997.

Giller, Megan: *Bean to Bar Chocolate*. Storey Publishing, 2017.

Goldstein, Dara *et al.*: *Sugar and Sweets*. Oxford University Press, 2015.

Grivetti, Louis Evan, and Howard-Yana Saphiro: *Chocolate History, Culture Heritage*. Willey Interscience, 2009.

Gutsche, Astrid: *Los guardianes del cacao*. Editorial Planeta, 2015.

Jolly, Martine: *El libro del amante del chocolate*. Ediciones José Juan de Olañeta, 1985.

Marcolini, Pierre: *Cacao*. Librooks, 2016.

—: *Chocolat: From the Cocoa Bean to the Chocolate Bar*. Rizzoli, 2017.

Martí Escayol, Maria Antònia: *El plaer de la xocolata. La Història i la cultura de la xocolata a Catalunya*. Editorial Cossetània, 2004.

Martín de Acuña, Carmen, and Arias de Guerrero, Ana María: *Bibliografía sobre cacao*. Centro Agronómico Tropical de Investigación y Enseñanza, 1984.

Masonis, Todd *et al.*: *Making Chocolate: From Bean to Bar to S'More*. Clarkson Potter Publishers, 2017.

Métenier Beatrice: *Aux sources du grand chocolat, Valrhona*. Glénat, 2016.

Morató, Ramón; Ribé, Josep Maria; Bernal, Raúl, and Guarro, Miquel: *Four in One*. Grupo Vilbo, 2016.

Olivera Núñez, Quirino: *Arqueología altoamazónica. Los orígenes de la civilización en el Perú*. Apus Graph Editores, 2014.

Páez Paredes, Lourdes: *Ecuador, tierra del cacao*. Trama Ediciones, 2017.

Persoone, Dominique: *Shock-o-latier*. Njam!, 2012.

—: *Cacao - Expedition in Mexico: The Roots of chocolate*. Françoise Blouard Editions, 2008.

Roca, Jordi: *Anarkia*. Montagud Editores, 2016

Ramsey, Dom: *Chocolate*. H. Blume, 2017.

Shuterland Smith, Beverley: *Chocolate & Petit Fours*. Ediciones Elfos, 1993.

Tovar Pinzón, Hermes: *El cacao en la sociedad colonial*. Revista Credencial Historia, 2000.

Various authors: *Chocolate*. Artes de México 103, 2011.

Various authors: *Chocolate II*. Artes de México 105, 2012.

Various authors: *Chocolate III*. Artes de México 110, 2013